REPRESSED SPACES

repressed
THE POETICS OF AGORAPHOBIA
spaces

PAUL CARTER

REAKTION BOOKS

Reaktion Books Ltd
79 Farringdon Road
London EC1M 3JU

www.reaktionbooks.co.uk

First published 2002

Printed and bound in Great Britain by
Bookcraft, Midsomer Norton

British Library Cataloguing in Publication Data

Carter, Paul
Repressed Spaces : the poetics of agoraphobia
1. Agoraphobia – History 2. Agoraphobia – Social aspects
3. Space (Architecture) – Psychological aspects
I. Title
616.8'5225

ISBN 1 86189 128 8

CONTENTS

Looking for something else, I came across an anecdote in Theodor Reik's *The Search Within*. One evening, in the Kaertnerstrasse in Vienna, Reik met his master, Sigmund Freud, and accompanied him home:

> We talked mostly about analytic cases during the walk. When we crossed a street that had heavy traffic, Freud hesitated as if he did not want to cross. I attributed the hesitancy to the caution of the old man, but to my astonishment he took my arm and said, 'You see, there is a survival of my old agoraphobia, which troubled me much in younger years'.[1]

I didn't recall Freud attributing a significant role to agoraphobia in his intellectual biography. And a quick scan through some of the many biographies and memoirs of the great man reinforced this impression: if mentioned at all, Freud's 'slight phobia' was dismissed as of little importance. Reik, by contrast, took an entirely different view. Far from passing over Freud's fear of open spaces as a personal quirk without further significance, he attributed to it a central role in the history of psychoanalytic theory.

According to Reik, in Freud's 'confession of a lingering fear of crossing open places' can be found 'the hidden missing link between his primarily psychological interests and his later occupation with the neuroses'.[2] Freud recognized that, 'in addition to the wish to help nervous patients, there was the demand: Physician, heal yourself'. To heal himself, he had to 'move beyond psychology's distinction between the mind of the sick patient and the mind of the normal person'. This was the appeal of the dream – as 'an abnormal mental product created by normal people', it supplied 'the common ground of normal and abnormal mental activities'. Dreams 'secured the bridge from one shore to the other, from the limited island of his own neurosis to the larger continent of general pathology and psychology'.[3] However, the personal *motivation* of Freud's ingenious bridge-building was, if Reik is to be believed, his own agoraphobia, or fear of crossing open places.

Was it possible, I wondered, that, at the origin of psychoanalysis an *environmental neurosis* had been repressed? Interpreting his agoraphobia as a neurotic symptom concealing something else, Freud turned away from the possibility that his hesitation at the roadside was an entirely *reasonable* response to the sickness of the urban scene. The 'heavy traffic' of which he was afraid was not, in the first instance, his own unruly instinctual drives. It was due to a more mundane and measurable form of driving: the immensely increased volume and accelerated pace of traffic in Vienna's newly enlarged roads and squares. This speculation suggested two further questions: Why did Freud repress the unconscious drives shaping his environment? And what would be the consequence of attending to these and therapeutically *unrepressing* them?

Repressed Spaces is the meditation produced by these questions. The book's four parts can be thought of as successive moments in a journey towards the centre of a city. 'Turning Out' is a short modern history of the term *agoraphobia*. The clinical literature on agoraphobia is immense, highly repetitive and inconclusive. The non-clinical literature is the opposite: sparse, ambiguous and highly creative. The efforts of scholars such as Esther da Costa Meyer and Anthony Vidler mean that the cultural history of agoraphobia is relatively well-trodden ground. Since its first clinical description in the late 1860s, cultural critics and clinical psychologists have disputed its nature. For critics of modernity, it is a symptom of urban estrangement. The soul doctors, on the other hand, have treated it as a symptom of psychic displacement. Neither orthodoxy, it seems to me, grasps the point that, whatever else it may be, agoraphobia is a *movement inhibition*. Teasing out the implications of this, the condition can be relocated within a neglected history of urban mobility and its discontents. When this is done, the immobile elements of the urban scene are also freed up, and a different relation between the pedestrian and the city square comes into focus.

The next part of the book, 'Driving', takes up the first questions I posed after reading Reik's anecdote about Freud. Psychoanalysis, of course, wanted to locate the drives, or instincts, in a realm of the psyche known as the unconscious. But a traffic that was more easily accessible, and whose chaotic violence matched anything the Oedipus complex could conjure up, existed outside every late nineteenth-century Viennese doorway. Freud had compelling psychological and professional reasons for internalizing the anxieties he experienced every day in negotiating the wide-open places of Vienna. His space fear was, in fact, widely shared. What is interesting is that, although Freud repressed his own movement inhibition, the repressed returned. The dream territory he set out to map surprisingly resembled the *environmental* unconscious of the modern city.

When the term *agora* is regarded as a synonym for space, there is a temptation to treat agoraphobia pathologically. This changes, though, if it is recognized that it defines a particular kind of space, or place, with a distinctive physical form and political history. This also applies to the equivalent terms in German (*Platzangst*) and French (*crainte des places*). The third part of *Repressed Spaces*, 'Alighting', is a road-map to the history of a term which, in ancient Greece, meant not only the place of political assembly, but the assembly gathered there. Something else emerges from this day-tour into the remote past. The democratic space of the agora turns out to be twinned with the wilderness. The traffic between these opposite environments suggests why agoraphobes feel anxiously torn between exposure and suffocation, solitude and the crowd, and why, either way, they fear being hunted.

The section entitled 'Meeting' tries to make good the promise of the subtitle. Many modern artists and writers have devoted their talents to exploring and depicting the modern faces of agoraphobia. One thinks of Munch, Beckett, Giacometti, Breton, Joe May, Rilke, Douanier Rousseau, di Chirico or Canetti. But an agoraphobic poetics is not a poetics of agoraphobia. It is one thing to characterize the smoothly imprisoning wastes of modern estrangement, quite another to track them. A different design on place-making is required to transform places of gathering into meeting places. Such a design can, perhaps, only emerge when the repressed spaces (of which agoraphobia is the symptom) are recognized as relations, as movement-multiples, as cloud-like formations and deformations of groupings, and their well-being as dependent on arrangements made uniquely for this occasion.

Agoraphobia can be temporal as well as spatial. Perhaps under the influence of another kind of marketplace-induced anxiety, most writers blithely pretend to address the living (the reader). But most writing is addressed to the dead. It is from the dead that the ideas come, and the echoes of their thoughts, from which a book like *Repressed Spaces* is composed, return to them. It is this other conversation that gives books their liveliness. How horrible it is when a writer perpetuates the fiction that all arose Minerva-like from the brow of genius. A double debt of gratitude is owed to those who have passed away and who, besides their own writings, gathered together the writings of others and bequeathed them to posterity. *Repressed Spaces* would not have been written but for a serendipitous coincidence: the Australian Centre's acquisition of the Alan Davies library. Davies, for many years Professor of Political Science at the University of Melbourne, died in 1986. His forethought in securing the rich and curious history of his reading for posterity created a meeting place where, otherwise, there must have been a void.

It seems strange to exculpate a shade, but I hasten to say what will be obvious to all who, unlike me, had the privilege of knowing Davies: the labyrinth I have found in his library is entirely my own. I am indebted in this regard to the Australian Centre, University of Melbourne and to the Australian Research Council, whose joint and generous support gave me the means to spin my thread, and let it out. Sign-pointers along the way included Gregory Burgess, Horst Trossbach, Donald Bates and Peter Davidson. My thanks to them all.

Lastly, the signs in the labyrinth deserve a word. As *Repressed Spaces* is loosely conceived as a drive from the periphery of a city towards its centre, the use of road signs as section breaks is logical enough. Collecting them for this purpose, though, I couldn't help but begin to read them differently. Their verbal formulae, previously so familiar that their meaning was absorbed unconsciously, now came into focus – and grew correspondingly strange. Having compared the instinctual traffic of Freud's unconscious to the 'moving chaos' of the modern city's wheeled and pedestrian traffic, I found the comparison working in the opposite direction. Instead of regulating my movement through physical streets and squares, the signs pointed in the direction of another city, one archaeologically buried beneath the present structure.

This other city is the one travellers make for. Signs are interpreters. The divinity of interpretation is Hermes, who is also the patron saint of travellers. Residents don't need signs, only foreigners do. Only the homeless have to have home pointed out to them. In this sense, all signs are signs of not belonging, of coming from somewhere else. Then, logically, a city in whose streets signs cluster like bees is designed for strangers. It is constitutionally home for the other. Seeing signs in this way I became, again, a foreigner. I might have been entering Vienna, not Melbourne. Travelling again, I could inhabit Kierkegaard's dictum, 'Becoming is a movement *from* some place, but becoming oneself is a movement *at* that place.'[4]

1 turningout

The history of mankind is the instant between two strides taken by a traveller.

FRANZ KAFKA[1]

T JUNCTION

Modern definitions of agoraphobia are legion. Clinical characterizations of the condition differ from sociological ones. The term means one thing when applied in the realm of aesthetics, quite another when a philosopher like Emmanuel Levinas invokes it. Feminists persuasively argue that it is a logical extension of the cultural sex-role stereotype for women. Radical economists, interpreting the term radically, take it as literally a fear of the marketplace, reflecting the plight of the individual in an age of commodification. Within the no less competitive psychiatric domain, the symptom-lumpers gather under its name a bewildering variety of physiological, behavioural and attitudinal phenomena. Symptom-splitters, on the other hand, seem confident that it is an illness in its own right. The vertigo, or dizziness, associated with it is really a different neurosis, with a different cause. As for *acrophobia*, the mere existence of so imposing a name is halfway to proving its separate existence.

For our purposes, though, characterizations of agoraphobia fall roughly into two groups. One group, best represented by Freud and psychoanalytic orthodoxy, understands the illness as, primarily, a self-fear displaced onto a fear of the street. I'll come to their explanation of this later. The salient point here is that the focus of the agoraphobe's anxiety is not so much the street, but the opportunities for encounter offered by it. It is the crowd incubated by the street which alarms him, because it tempts him to plunge into its anonymous mass and lose himself. Our other group is more urbanistically inclined. In Carl Otto Westphal's often-cited paper of 1871, no mention is made of crowds. On the contrary, the experience of panic can be quite solitary, brought on merely by 'the sight of a large room, a long street, or a wide square'.[2] In this version, agoraphobia remains primarily an environmental uneasiness. No doubt the patient is predisposed to it, but his illness remains proof of something rotten in the state of modern urban design.

These two descriptions are not mutually exclusive or contradictory. As I've already mentioned, the ancient Greek term *agora* can refer both to an assembly of people and to the place of assembly, and its meaning will depend on the context in which it is used. The same is true of the modern term *agoraphobia*. If the psychiatric tradition emphasizes the crowd, the phenomenologically inclined urbanists stress the places where crowds gather. The value of the distinction is that it enables us to identify the experience common to both, and about whose interpretation the psychiatrists and urbanists differ. Whether manifested as a reluctance to cross wide, empty spaces or as a fear of being caught up in the crowd, the universal symptom of agoraphobia is a *movement inhibition*. In effect, the two theories are a kind of T-junction so far as this idea is concerned: they turn it into something else when in fact it would be useful to follow up the inhibition itself.

First, a brief road-map of the T-junction's two branches.

ONE WAY

In 1889, Camillo Sitte published *Der Städte-Bau nach Seinen Kunstlerischen Grundsätzen* (City Building according to its Artistic Fundamentals), 'a critique of the modern city from the point of view of the ancients, using the Ringstrasse as a negative model'.[3] At first sight, Sitte's angry dismissal of Vienna's new urbanism is remarkably *static*. The effect of opening up vast, symmetrically designed squares and immense, monotonous boulevards was to reduce pedestrians to immobility. Instead of moving about freely, they did not know which way to go.

Panic rooted them to the spot. They might almost have been statues. Even statues were frightened of the new spaces. As he writes:

> . . . recently a unique nervous disorder has been diagnosed – 'agoraphobia.' Numerous people are said to suffer from it, always experiencing a certain anxiety or discomfort when-ever they have to walk across a vast empty place. We might supplement this observation on psychology with an artistic one: that also people formed out of stone and metal, on their monu-mental pedestals, are attacked by this malady and thus always prefer . . . to choose a little old plaza rather than a large empty one for their permanent location.[4]

This static conception of agoraphobia derived directly from the Berlin psychologist Carl Otto Westphal, who described three cases of this 'singular affection' in Berlin:

> They all felt a peculiar uneasiness or anguish in crossing over wide squares or free, unenclosed spaces. One of the patients compared it to the feeling of a swimmer crossing a lake, uncertain whether he will be able to reach the other side . . . The feeling of distress was sometimes overpowering, and prevented them crossing many of the wide streets and squares.[5]

If one didn't know how Westphal's unfortunate young men overcame their anxiety, one would guess that it was a pretty solitary experience. The remedies prove otherwise: '. . . [they] often felt quite at ease when accompanied by a companion. One of them used to follow someone going the same way, or a coach crossing the square.'[6] Immobility is produced not by a lack of directions, but by an excess of them. Public spaces filled with coaches, tradespeople and pedestrians present the onlooker with a giddiness-making urban Brownian motion. The friendly companion or agreeably oriented coach was an Ariadne's thread through the new kinetic labyrinth.

In a characteristically vigorous passage, Marshall Berman gives this new experience a Marxian inflection. The urbanism of Napoleon III and Haussmann produced Parisian streets in which streams of traffic overwhelmed their older function as centres of shopping, entertainment and business. It was the new urbanism, Berman points out, which was

> the setting for Baudelaire's primal modern scene. 'I was crossing the boulevard, in a great hurry, in the midst of a moving chaos, with death galloping at me from every side.' The archetypal modern man, as we see him here, is a pedestrian thrown into the maelstrom of modern city traffic, a man alone contending against an agglomeration of mass and energy that is heavy, fast and lethal. The burgeoning street and boulevard traffic knows no spatial or temporal bounds, spills over into every urban space, imposes its tempo on everybody's time, transforms the whole modern environment into a 'moving chaos'.

Berman continues,

> The chaos here lies not in the movers themselves – the individual walkers or drivers, each of whom may be pursuing the most efficient route for himself – but in their interaction, in the totality of their movements in a common space. This makes the boulevard a perfect symbol of capitalism's inner contradictions: rationality in each individual capitalist unit, leading to anarchic irrationality in the social system that brings these units together.[7]

This may be systemically valid, but what was the human experience of plunging into that moving chaos? Traffic signals, Berman tells us, were invented in 1905:[8] if the problem of the streets was purely organizational, then agoraphobia should have withered away shortly after the signals' installation. But, if anything, digitizing traffic movements made things worse. The new mobile jigsaw, composed of oscillating movement/non-movement states, might have produced an illusion of freer traffic movement. But it also inculcated a sort of neo-Zenonian anxiety, a hare-and-tortoise paradox, in which the faster you went, the slower you moved (and vice versa). Stricter traffic regulations created a contrapuntal traffic movement, in which ever greater acceleration alternated with ever more pronounced deceleration. The one state this new system ruled out was an easy, evenly paced, flexibly oriented locomotion. When, today, joggers run on the spot, waiting for the lights to change, they tell you it's to keep the circulation going, but really it's a magical movement charm against catatonia and keeps at bay the ever-present nightmare that all this running, after all, delivers you nowhere.

In any case, at the scale of the late nineteenth- and early twentieth-century walker in the street, the sensation of being rushed off one's feet naturally produced a reaction, a desire to slow things down. The first chapter of Robert Musil's book *The Man Without Qualities* – the chapter is presciently called 'Which, remarkably enough, does not get anyone anywhere' – opens with a road accident. Half a century on, the urban scene closely recalls Baudelaire's, with the difference that it has developed its own rhythm, pace or organic metre:

> Motor-cars came shooting out of deep, narrow streets into the shallows of bright squares. Dark patches of pedestrian bustle formed into cloudy streams. Where stronger lines of speed transected their loose-woven hurrying, they clotted up – only to trickle on all the faster then and after a few ripples regain their regular pulse-beat.[9]

Then there is the accident, from which the Man, after examining the accident victim in a detached sort of way for a minute, hastily escapes.

The acceleration of events in the street produces a reaction in Musil's mathematically-minded Man. He wants to render its chaos calculable:

> For the last ten minutes, watch in hand, he had been counting the cars, carriages, and trams, and the pedestrians' faces, blurred by distance, all of which filled the network of his gaze with a whirl of hurrying forms. He was estimating the speed, the angle, the dynamic forces of masses being propelled past,

which drew the eye after them swift as lightning, holding it, letting it go, forcing the attention – for an infinitesimal instant of time – to resist them, to snap off, and then to jump to the next and rush after that.[10]

By blinking rapidly, one can make a spinning wheel appear to slow down. At a certain frequency of blinks, the spokes of the turning wheel suddenly come momentarily into view, and one glimpses the stationary parts out of which the moving image is built. This is the same technique that Musil's anti-hero used to analyze the traffic into its component parts.

One of the strongest arguments agoraphobes use to avoid going out is a statistical one. If the psychiatric literature is to be believed, they are as a group remarkable for their knowledge of train derailments and the incidence of air crashes: 'Often these patients offer statistical proof of the dangers of the street; some take careful note of every traffic accident, of every collision between streetcars or automobiles.'[11] As well they might, to judge from Musil's symptomatic opening scene. In this case, the novelist's hero is obviously agoraphobic: 'According to American statistics,' he observes, 'there are over a hundred and ninety thousand people killed on the roads annually over there, and four hundred and fifty thousand injured.'[12] Be that as it may, Musil's man without qualities intuitively grasps that agoraphobia is not so much a fear of wide-open spaces as a fear of their slipperiness, their tendency to incubate uncontrolled, unco-ordinated movement, both in individuals and in the mass. The subjective locus of this anxiety-forming 'moving chaos' is not Berman's 'system'. It occurs where the individual becomes aware of his own movement. He suddenly senses that he is walking out of step with his time and, unlike Charlie Chaplin, cannot impose his different pace on his surroundings. When he slows down and comes to a standstill, his immobility is the expression of his fear of walking differently.

So much for environmental theories of agoraphobia. They don't merely root the sufferer to the spot. They would, if possible, cure him by *removing his legs*. In his essay 'Abstraction and Empathy', Wilhelm Worringer explains the urge to abstraction in art and architecture by presupposing a primary agoraphobia, one which, far from being invented in 1871, was a universal condition. According to Worringer, sufferers of agoraphobia were psychological throwbacks. They recapitulated a condition perhaps constitutional amongst primitive peoples:

> The physical dread of open places, a pathological condition to which certain people are prone . . . may be explained as a residue from a normal phase of man's development, at which he was not yet able to trust entirely to visual impression as a means of becoming familiar with a space extended before him, but was still dependent upon the assurances of his sense of touch. As soon as man became a biped, and as such solely dependent upon his eyes, a slight feeling of insecurity was inevitably left behind. In the further course of his evolution, however, man freed himself from this primitive fear of extended space by habituation and intellectual reflection.[13]

What a grotesque image of the Cartesian ego slowly climbing to its feet and, at first tottering, then stumbling, learning to stand upright and make its way in the world! But it underlines the point that, in characterizing agoraphobia as an environmental ailment, no thought is given to the changing *kinetic* qualities of the urban scene. If the moving chaos is noted, it is only in order to insist that the modern man in the street must learn to deal with it, even if 'the expenditure of muscular energy made by a citizen quietly going about his business all day long is considerably greater than that of the athlete who lifts a huge weight once a day'.[14]

Or, as the turn-of-the-century sociologist Georg Simmel put it,

In buildings and educational institutions, in the wonders and comforts of space-conquering technology, in the formations of community life, and in the visible institutions of the state, is offered such an overwhelming fullness of crystallised and impersonalised spirit that the personality, so to speak, cannot maintain itself under its impact . . . This results in the individual's summoning the utmost in uniqueness and particu-larisation, in order to preserve his most personal core. He has to exaggerate this personal element in order to remain audible even to himself.[15]

In other words, and this was true of Westphal's original clinical description, the environmentalists ultimately regarded agoraphobia as a *pathological* condition. The same, of course, applied to the soul doctors. Freud's explanation of agoraphobia goes back at least to the time he spent observing Jean-Martin Charcot's work on hysteria at the Salpêtrière in Paris (late 1885–early 1886). What he learned there, and how he departed from it, is captured in a note he made on one of Charcot's Tuesday lectures. Charcot had declared that heredity was the 'true cause' of a patient's hysterical attacks, his vertigo and his agora-phobia. Freud ventured to contradict him: 'The more frequent cause of agoraphobia as well as of most other phobias lies not in heredity but in abnormalities of sexual life. It is even possible to specify the form of abuse of the sexual function involved.'[16]

And so on. The point is that, while urban critics might not have agreed with psychiatrists as to the causes of agoraphobia, they shared the view that it was a symptom of something else. Indeed, Freud, who, in this regard, was decidedly a lumper, was blasé on the topic, implying, in more than one place, that agoraphobia was a ragbag of symptoms with little identity of its own: 'One patient avoids only narrow streets and another only wide ones; one can go out only if there are few people in the street, another only if there are many.'[17] (And so on.)

In this regard, Camillo Sitte was really a kind of environmental Freud. He would have agreed with the cartoonist who, some time later,

„Los von der Architektur."
(Aus der Silvesterzeitschrift des Oesterreichischen Ingenieur- und Architektenvereines.)

— Kunstbrütend ging der Modernste durch die Straßen. Plötzlich blieb er erstarrt stehen; er hatte gefunden, was er solange vergeblich gesucht:

(Bitte wenden!)

1 'Freed from Architecture': 'Reflecting on Art, the most modern man walked the streets. Suddenly he stopped abruptly: he had found what he had looked for in vain for such a long time.' A caricature from *Illustrirtes Wiener Extrablatt*, 1911.

depicted a façade designed by the Viennese Modernist architect Adolf Loos as a sewer grate. To tear aside the picturesque veils of the urban scene was to find an instinctual abyss of destructive drives gaping in one's path (illus. 1). The thrust of Sitte's *Der Städte-Bau* is to encourage a return to traditional forms of urban design. But, anticipating Worringer, his proposal presupposes a primary agoraphobia, which earlier architects consciously sought to diminish by their skilful arrangement of closed and open spaces. It was the hypothesis of a primary alienation – one rather similar to Freud's 'realistic anxiety' coeval with 'separation from the mother'[18] – that enabled Sitte to attribute such an important role to architects in securing the mental and emotional wellbeing of a nation. In his view, 'the right kind of square could lift from the soul of modern man the curse of urban loneliness and the fear of the vast and bustling void. Anonymous space is transmuted by the containing sides of a square into a human scene, infinite urban riches in a little room.'[19]

The rival discourses of agoraphobia are twinned in another way. Worringer's pre-bipedal primitive has his counterpart in psychoanalysis' preconscious walker. Freudians recognized that it was characteristic of agoraphobia 'that the locomotion of which the patient is otherwise incapable can always be easily performed when [the patient] is accompanied by some specially selected person'.[20]

But the proprioceptive mechanisms governing stopping and starting – the bodily self-awareness evident in our senses of balance, distance-judgement and relations with other mobile bodies – did not interest them. Under the influence of Charcot, Freud presented to the Viennese Physicians' Society a male patient suffering from hysteria. He exhibited 'many of Charcot's "hysterical stigmata" . . . including the hysterogenic regions'.[21] His symptoms included a tremor in the left arm and leg, and pains in the back and groin, left knee and sole of the left foot. If he walked for long times, he experienced a strange sensation in his throat; his tongue was immobilized.

This patient's loss of feeling in his left side was dramatically shown when he and Freud walked together:

Today the patient walked briskly beside me for a good hour on the streets, without looking at his feet: I could notice only that he flung out his left leg slightly, placed it somewhat to the outside, and frequently dragged his left foot on the ground. But when I ask him to walk, his eyes follow all movements of the anaesthetic leg, which are slow and uncertain and tire him easily. Finally, his gait is completely uncertain when his eyes are shut; then he pushes himself forward, both feet feeling the ground, as we would do in the dark if we were unfamiliar with a place. It is also very difficult for him to remain standing on his left leg; if he shuts his eyes in this posture he falls down immediately.[22]

It seems extraordinary that Freud felt no empathy for the man's gait, that the obvious body wandering before him was dismissed in favour of another, entirely mythical one, the wandering womb of the hysteric. But locomotion, as such, did not concern the Freudians. What concerned them were drives. Copying the traffic-signal classification of street traffic, they might focus on speeding up – the patient 'could not walk across a bridge, but was compelled to run, as if she were being chased or persecuted. But running proved peculiarly difficult'[23] – or on slowing down and toppling over – the patient 'felt forced to walk very slowly, and in a rather stiff manner'.[24]

True heirs to an intellectual suspicion of movement that goes back, via Descartes, to both Aristotle and Plato, the Freudians understand movement instrumentally, as a wilful overcoming of inertia in order to gratify needs. The possibility that the bipedal tracking of the environment and its others, and the complex primary relationships evolving through this, have their own history and grammar, was not seriously considered.

DEAD END

One way or another, agoraphobia as a definable illness seems to be on the decline. Vidler, who treats it as a historical symptom of environmental change, one of a constellation of anxieties associated with urban modernization, has dated its demise to early in the last century. If the 'inexorable logic of modern spatialisation: from claustrophobia to agoraphobia'[25] climaxed in the triumph of transparency and openness, and in the substitution (courtesy of Le Corbusier) of the void for the home, then it is only logical that the disappearance of *Platzangst* should be coeval with the birth of architectural Modernism. Where the walls, doors and windows separating the open from the closed have been destroyed, how can one be afraid of going out? Where the distinction between the homely and the unhomely has been rendered meaningless, how can one even think of such things, let alone worry about them?

On this reading, agoraphobia is really an *aesthetic* stance. Sitte, Worringer and, before them (according to Vidler), a tradition of anti-modernizing aesthetic criticism running from the brothers Goncourt to Ruskin, liked standing still. Others, though, took the plunge: Le Corbusier himself, for example. One day shortly after the end of the First World War, he was standing on the Champs-Elysées:

> It was as though the world had suddenly gone mad. After the emptiness of the summer, the traffic was more furious than ever. Day by day the fury of the traffic grew. To leave your house meant that once you had crossed your threshold you were a possible sacrifice to death in the shape of innumerable motors. I think back twenty years, when I was a student; the road belonged to us then; we sang in it and argued in it, while the horse-'bus swept calmly along.[26]

So far so good: Le Corbusier's sentiments echo those of Baudelaire or Musil. Then something happens, a kind of modern road-to-Damascus conversion:

> Motors in all directions, going at all speeds. I was over-whelmed, an enthusiastic rapture filled me. Not the rapture of the shining coachwork under the gleaming lights, but rapture of power. The simple and ingenuous pleasure of being in the centre of so much power, so much speed. We are a part of it. We are part of that race whose dawn is just awakening. We have

2 'Heartrending farewells of the father of a family about to cross the street in front of the Gare de L'Est.' A 1911 cartoon by 'Capy', as reproduced by Le Corbusier in *The City of Tomorrow*, 1926.

confidence in this new society, which will in the end arrive at a magnificent expression of its power. We believe in it.[27]

Le Corbusier was writing with the zeal of a fundamentalist convert. Even allowing for the stylistic conventions proper to a polemic, his tone might be described as hysterical. Had a cure been effected? Or had he merely displaced his agoraphobia onto another object – the city itself? Identifying himself with the traffic, Le Corbusier took precisely this step:

> Its power is like a torrent swollen by storms; a destructive fury. The city is crumbling, it cannot last much longer; its time is past. It is too old. The torrent can no longer keep to its bed. It is a kind of cataclysm. It is something utterly abnormal, and the disequilibrium grows day by day.[28]

A cartoon Le Corbusier reproduced in *The City of Tomorrow* ironically illustrates the point (illus. 2).

Whatever the psychological roots of Le Corbusier's conversion, its expression is, of course, aesthetic. Henceforth a champion of the straight line and an advocate of roads for traffic, Le Corbusier missed no opportunity to attack Sitte and his nostalgia for the old wimbling-wambling ways:

> Man walks in a straight line because he has a goal and knows where he is going; he has made up his mind to reach some particular place and he goes straight to it. The pack-donkey meanders along, meditates a little in his scatter-brained and distracted fashion, he zigzags in order to avoid the larger stones, or to ease the climb, or to gain a little shade; he takes the line of least resistance.[29]

(And so on.)

In the clinic, agoraphobia has survived longer. But here, too, over the last 30 years, it has been under a growing attack. The Foucauldian argument is increasingly advanced that the condition is an ideological construction of a patriarchal culture, one whose interests the largely White, middle-class, male medical profession mirrors in its patrol of the shifting boundary between health and illness. Hence, feminist psychologists argue that agoraphobia should be viewed not in terms of individual pathology but in relation to women's experiences in general. The contributing causes are societal:

> The batterer goes on to beat another woman; the dominating husband continues to dominate the agoraphobe or dominates someone else. Anxiety and fearfulness are still engendered in girls and women. Public streets and other settings remain dangerous or inhospitable for women who must have a 'safe' companion to escort them. It remains customary to isolate young married women from their family and friends.[30]

Or, more graphically:

> When one woman out of every four in the United States is raped (or one every ten minutes), agoraphobia – the fear of

public spaces – takes on a different colouration . . . In the case of rape victims, public space as such does not exist except as part of a topology of fear.[31]

In this regard, Maureen McHugh's figures are striking:

> Agoraphobia is the most common of phobias. Over 50 percent of the individuals who report phobic distress are diagnosed as agoraphobic. Moreover, clinicians have described agoraphobia as the most distressing, and all-consuming of the phobias. Agoraphobes represent about 5 percent of the [United States] population.[32]

If these figures, or indeed the term itself, mean anything, we should revise our earlier statement: it's not agoraphobia that is dying out, but the utility of the discourses applied to it. The discourse-makers have not stood by idly. There is no twentieth-century psychological theory or psychiatric practice that has not attempted to make agoraphobia its own. In consequence, its definition and proposed cure have closely tracked clinical fashion. In the 1930s and '40s, the psychoanalysts held the field. They discovered chronophobia[33] and cremnophobia[34], not to mention agoraphilia.[35] There were the physiologists, who attributed the condition to 'functional disorders of a vasculo-vegetative character'.[36] There were also the behaviourists, with remedial arcana including contingency management, systematic desensitization, assertiveness training, septal stimulation, contingency contracting, aversion therapy and reciprocal inhibition.[37]

They all met at the drugs counter, which, by the beginning of the 1970s, was doing a thriving trade. Imipramine was popular ('prevents panic attacks deriving from separation anxiety'[38]), then propranolol,[39] diazepam,[40] MAOIs[41] and sodium D2 lactate or glucose saline infusions.[42]

The clinic is our modern Byzantium. Thus it comes as no surprise that its language is byzantine. But nothing in the golden horn of its pharmocopoeia is a simple for agoraphobia. It would be disrespectful, in the light of the figures just quoted, to deny the reality of agoraphobia. Yet the condition, whether regarded as a sensibility or a neurosis, is either too vague to present a stable clinical picture or too history-bound to be of more than historical interest. Unless it can be identified differently, it is likely to go the way of other 'idols of the marketplace'[43] – Francis Bacon's prophetically apt phrase for the names of things which do not exist – that is, things that remain in the language purely as metaphors.

In her recent collection, *Evictions*, for example, Rosalind Deutsche refers to the agoraphobic woman who rationalizes her need to walk in the gutter by saying that she is looking for something she has lost. Assuming the correctness of the feminist critique, Deutsche feels free to treat the woman metaphorically. She is, Deutsche writes, like those critics whose anxieties about the disappearance of public space are, in reality, 'panicked reactions to the openness and indeterminacy of the democratic public as a phantom', representing 'a kind of agoraphobic behaviour adopted in the face of a public space that has a loss at its beginning'.[44]

A kind of *terminus ad quem* is surely represented by philosopher Emmanuel Levinas's appropriation of the term:

> Ethical agoraphobia is not an anxiety provoked by just any open space. It is an emphasis of the dread Pascal felt before the eternal silence of infinite space . . . The open space before which I suffer ethical agoraphobia is a space without walls and without place, a u-topic exteriority in which I feel the presence of responsibility for the others to whom I find that I have already responded, though always too late. A pressure that makes an unmeetable demand on the lungs from the first intake of breath to the last. A hyperventilation, as of the cry with which one comes naked into the world or the last choke of Nietzschean laughter that sticks in the throat at the approach of the other – 'tragic and grave and on the verge of madness'.[45]

Back at the T-junction, let's try another exit.

So far, our day-tour of agoraphobia has focused on a topographical interpretation of the term *agora*. Our spokesperson for the anti-Modernist urban designers, Camillo Sitte, associated the new illness – he called it *Platzcheu* – with 'the rage for open spaces'.[46] The psychologists of the unconscious agree with this characterization. They describe agoraphobia as a fear of the street. In both cases, a phantom agora is being invoked. Sitte's open space is the antithesis of his 'human scene', with its 'infinite urban riches in a little room'.[47]

As for the soul doctors, the street is an alibi for a repressed desire whose true origin is Oedipal. Whether as open space, or as street, or as both, this agora signifies in inverse proportion to the clarity of its definition. Is every open space, including the sea and the wilderness, an agora in this sense? Is every phobia a fear associated with transgression and, poised between the closed and the open, constitutionally agoraphobic?

But the topographical definition of agora may be secondary. In fourth-century-BC Athens at least, it co-existed with another definition – *assembly of the people*. Here, the word could also refer to the business of the agora – *agoreusis* means a speech, oration or proclamation.[48] Another definition of agoraphobia, then, might make no particular reference to the 'bland, neutralising spaces' of the contemporary urban realm, whose origin, Richard Sennett suggests, 'can be traced back to the belief that the outside world of things is unreal'.[49] Instead, it would associate the illness primarily with the idea of the crowd. It is not the street or open square that causes panic, but the crowd. The 'moving chaos' of wheeled and pedestrian traffic signifies the modern city's depersonalization. It is the prospect of plunging into its uncontrollable and instinctual flow that fills individuals with dread and that makes them feel that, like Westphal's patient, they are at risk from drowning.

The agora as crowd helps to explain a linkage between agoraphobia and claustrophobia. If going out implies plunging in, if isolation risks engulfment, then the association is logical. Vidler has noted that, shortly after Westphal's paper, the French psychologist Legrand du Saulle rejected the term *agoraphobia* because 'it limited the disturbance to one specific kind of public space. He preferred the vaguer term "peur des espaces" as comprising all spatial fears.'[50] Legrand added to the fear of empty and open spaces 'the fear of spaces . . . produced among certain patients in a very frequented place, or among crowds'.[51] Then, in 1879, agoraphobia's 'apparent opposite', claustrophobia, emerged – Benjamin Ball described a patient who combined a fear of contact with 'a panic fear of being alone in a closed space, a sensation of being able to go nether forward nor back, an intolerable terror that was generally followed by a flight into the fields'.[52]

Whether regarded as linked neuroses or as separate conditions, both claustro- and agora-phobia were seen as characteristically urban neurasthenias, symptoms of the anxieties produced by life in the modern city. But the relationship between the two conditions is much stronger than this: it is no accident that in everyday German, Sitte's *Platzangst* means 'claustrophobia', not 'agoraphobia'. The two states seem to be phases of one anxiety, which expresses itself in an oscillation between the desire for contact with the other and a fear of it, between the desire to enter a relationship and panic at the thought of it. Believing this to be the case, Emanuel Miller, writing in 1930, even invented a new term, *agora-claustrophobia*.[53] In his often-quoted 'Friendly Expanses – Horrid Open Spaces' (1955), another psycho-analytic writer, Michael Balint, also yokes the two conditions. He also coins new words. His *philobat* (a claustrophobic type) encounters a world crowded with 'dangerous and unpredictable objects' and strives to inhabit 'the friendly expanses'. His *ocnophil*, on the other hand, is agoraphobic, afraid of horrid, empty spaces. Like a drowning man clutching at a straw, he clings to whatever will give him immediate emotional and physical support.[54]

But the best account of this double condition doesn't come from the psychoanalysts – who, having linked them, devote their theoretical ingenuity to unyoking them again and locating them on different rungs of the ego's ladder of development. It comes from that refreshing denouncer of the Freudian unconscious, R. D. Laing. In *The Divided Self* (1959), Laing circles nearer the orbit of Levinas. Drawing on his reading of Heidegger and Sartre, he interprets space phobias as symptoms of a profounder ontological insecurity. A person who lacks a strong sense of his being in the world may, Laing says, fear *engulfment* – a 'dread lest in any relationship he will lose his autonomy and identity'[55] – or *implosion* – a similar dread extended to external reality in general. Feeling empty, such a person is terrified that the world may at any moment 'crash in and obliterate all identity'.[56] He may even fear *petrification*, the dread of being immobilized, turned from a live person into a dead thing, a stone or robot.[57]

On this reading, there is both a failure to sustain the sense of oneself as a person with the other and a failure to sustain it alone. A sense of dependency is substituted for a sense of relatedness, and 'utter detachment and isolation are regarded as the only alternative to a clam- or vampire-like attachment'.[58] Agoraphobia, a sense of complete isolation, and claustrophobia, a complete merging of identity, are, then, two poles of a single existential dilemma, and 'the individual oscillates perpetually, between the two extremes, each equally unfeasible'.[59] The psychoanalytic appeal to the unconscious, and its supposed Oedipal fixation, is an unnecessary hypothesis: the central issue for the agoraphobe 'is not to be discovered in [his] "unconscious"; it is lying quite open for [him] to see, as well as for us'.[60]

The agoraphobe's dread of being in the street is a dread of the lonely crowd. So long as he feels that the people there notice him, he can be alone because he is not really alone. When he becomes aware of their indifference, he succumbs to agoraphobic dread. At home, though, the same dread might manifest itself oppositely, as a claustrophobic panic of *being alone with his lover*. Then, once again, his longing is to make space for others.

Laing's scepticism about what Freud (in 1933) called a 'cauldron of seething excitations'[61] isn't exceptional. Behaviourists have always been hostile, wondering how one can be conscious of what is unconscious. Cognitive psychologists, in principle more sympathetic to the notion of a dynamic unconscious, have taken a different tack. Suppose, they say, that the unconscious is inhabited, not so much by instinctual wishes and impulses, but by 'pathogenic beliefs'. For example, an agoraphobic woman can be shown to operate according to the rule 'If I separate [from my mother] I will not survive.' This belief does not arise from a castration anxiety, but is 'based on implicit and early parental messages communicated to the child'. Such unconscious beliefs, and the rules they impose, originate in the family environment, not in the libidinal predispositions of the id.[62]

Yet these kinds of variation on a theme only underline Laing's distinctiveness in linking the well-being of the individual's subjective world to her objective being in the world. In the formulation of ourselves, Laing gives agency to space and space-making. The woman who discerns the lack of relatedness of the people on the street is not mistaken. She may be wrong to take their indifference personally, but her observation is, after all, sociologically accurate. She notices the same phenomenon identified by Karl Popper. The open society – whose emergence Popper detected in Periclean Athens – confronts two challenges. One comes from a regression to the closed, 'magical, tribal or collectivist' society. The other comes from the pseudo-progress (already apparent in 1930s Vienna) towards an abstract society, in which the character of a concrete group of men and women is lost, and where, 'although we do not always drive alone in closed motor cars (but meet face to face thousands of men walking past us in the street) the result is very nearly the same as if we did – we do not establish as a rule any personal relation with our fellow-pedestrians'.[63]

Georg Simmel had anticipated this observation. He attributed to the late nineteenth-century city-dweller a feeling of alienation that closely anticipated Laing's description of ontological insecurity. The cultivation of distance in modern life was, Simmel thought, a reaction to sensory overload: 'The psychological basis of the metropolitan type of individuality consists in the *intensification of nervous stimulation* which results from the swift and uninterrupted change of outer and inner stimuli.'[64] This produced a fear of touching, a desire for spatial isolation. Like Laing's patients, Simmel's metropolitan types experienced their anxiety as a 'rapid oscillation': the over-close identification with things and, alternatively, too great a distance from them. For Simmel, as Vidler noted, agoraphobia was only a specific instance of a generalized 'estrangement'.[65]

Mention of Popper suggests the missing term in this analysis. Agoraphobia can turn inside out, becoming claustrophobia: the estranged individual in the street can find his emotional magnetic field reversed – instead of seeking isolation, he is seized by an overwhelming desire to join up, to plunge into the moving chaos of the crowd and be swept away. In this way, Elias Canetti's crowd is born. According to this organic analogy, the modern crowd, with its endless traffic, experiences a collective ontological insecurity: what, then, is the mass or collectivity which is *confident* of its being in the world? Popper's answer is clear: it is the *public* whose coming into being is historically linked with the growth of democracy in Pericles' Athens. When the American sociologist Robert Park wrote of two alternatives to traditional society, 'not only the crowd, swayed by the emotion of the moment, but also the public, emancipated from customary beliefs but not from the capacity of rational discussion of means and ends',[66] he identified the latter with democracy. It is the public that as a mass possesses sufficient surface tension to absorb change without either imploding or exploding.

It is the rationally grounded public whose influence holds in check those *unconscious seething excitations* that so easily fuse individuals into an uncontrollable crowd. It was in just these terms that the French pioneer of mass psychology, Gustav LeBon, who, like Freud, found the empirical basis of his theory in the phenomenon of hypnotism, attempted to explain collective behaviour. In 1871–2, LeBon had

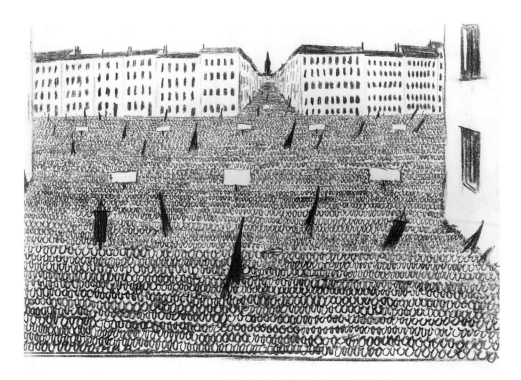

3 Werner Heldt, *Parade of Nobodies (Meeting)*, 1933–4, charcoal drawing.

witnessed Baudelaire's moving chaos in human form in the collective behaviour of the masses in the Paris Commune. Observing the capriciousness of the crowd, its unpredictable destructiveness, its capacity to act irrationally as one, LeBon hypothesized a 'collective hallucination'.[67] The crowd thinks in images, and, having lost its ability to distinguish a real (perceived) from an unreal (internal) image owing to its dream-like torpor, its mental functioning is reduced to hallucination. 'These hallucinations are the unifying foci of any crowd, and spread from individual to individual by "imitation" or "mental contagion" until they universalise themselves'[68] – a sensation captured by Werner Heldt. In his drawing *Parade of Nobodies* (illus. 3), the 'foci' are black banners seemingly transformed into vortices, goading the crowd into a single, united mass, driven now this way, now that. In short, social action was a kind of 'somnambulism' and depended upon 'suggestibility'.[69]

If the members of a crowd behave like the contents of a dream, freely associating and dynamically metamorphosing, according to rules of which the individual is unaware and is powerless to control, then the moral is obvious. It is not only the analysand but society that has to wake up to itself. Otherwise, how can it ever feel at home? But here is the rub: suppose that the public is a *phantom*. Suppose, more disturbingly, that public *space* is a phantom. In her essay on this theme alluded to earlier, Rosalind Deutsche reminds us that, in 1925, Walter Lippmann had declared the public to be a phantom, 'because the democratic ideal of a responsible, unified electorate capable of partici-pating in the machinery of government and able to supervise the state is unattainable'.[70] Deutsche argues that public space is constitutionally a site of conflict because, to quote Claude Lefort, 'democracy is insti-tuted and sustained by *the dissolution of the markers of certainty*.'[71]

On this logic, Deutsche claims, to pine for certainty, to cling to a nostalgic vision of a democratic citizenry formerly representing a coherent body of public opinion, is to fail to stand up to the challenge that democratically constituted spaces (and their publics) represent. It is to be afraid of the intellectual invitation they embody to go on constituting ourselves as a social body. Shrinking from this privilege and responsibility is to succumb to a form of ideological agoraphobia in the name of a phantom democracy (and public).

There seems to be a corollary to this. Laing's lonely patient is not only an acute observer of a collective estrangement that renders the public a phantom. She is also presumably aware of a concomitant fact: that the public space is also phantasmatic. On Deutsche's logic, this insight should be uplifting: the first step towards both psychic and political emancipation is to rid the spaces of our lives of disabling phantoms. Unfortunately, though – and Deutsche doesn't consider this point – the public space she might wish to claim is not neutral. Its design has already rendered it phantasmatic. Its expanses, especially if they are American or, in Europe, if they have been modernized after Haussmann, Speer or Sitte's *bête noir*, Otto Wagner, are already fashioned to maximize the amplitude of that oscillation both Simmel and Laing describe.

Here is Le Corbusier again: 'The street is a traffic machine; it is in reality a sort of factory for producing speed traffic. The modern street is a new "organ".'[72] And: 'Today traffic . . . is like dynamite flung at hazard into the street, killing pedestrians. Even so, *traffic does not fulfill its function*. This sacrifice of the pedestrian leads nowhere.'[73] Le Corbusier fantasized the petrification of the crowd because he wanted to optimize the moving chaos of traffic. He needed loneliness in order to create a mechanical crowd. You could say that he fantasized a universal petrification, cities where, in true Zenonian fashion, a continuous semblance of movement gave the impression of a people profoundly cocooned in an endless slumber. 'One of the most profound shocks of migrating to Brasilia,' James Holston wrote of the city that comes closest to incarnating Le Corbusier's theory of urban design, 'is the discovery that it is a city without crowds.'[74] Holston was not referring here to the Kristallnacht mob or the mass behaviour associated with the Paris Commune. His crowd is the public as it socially inhabits the streets.

Unlike the Viennese, the residents of Brasilia cannot even pretend to invoke a lost community formerly animating the place. In any case, they have no need to conjure up such phantoms. They attribute the absence of people to the city's design. Brasilia 'lacks street corners'.[75] A civil engineer has described his 'allergy to Brasilia' as being due to 'the absence of the kinds of "traditional public places of encounter" . . . especially the neighbourhood street corner'.[76] Socializing is 'interiorised, and diminished', and the result is 'a profound sense of isolation'.[77] In these crowdless public spaces, a negative agoraphobia is experienced. The danger and allure of streets and squares are not feared. It is their *anomie*, their lack of desire, that appals. In this situation, we can no longer hide behind the rhetoric of inside and outside, near and far, closed and open. The question, in an environment where differences wrap round themselves and collapse, is: What difference does it make to go anywhere?

NO WAITING

I must be six or seven years old. I am standing with my mother on a busy pavement edge. Next to me is a signpost: proud of my new skill in reading, I look up at it. I spell out: NO WAITING. How can I doubt that the words are addressed to me? Their accusation is plain: standing there, I am breaking the law. Ever obedient, I step off the kerb and, slipping from my mother's grip, run without hesitation towards my self-sacrifice in the path of the oncoming traffic . . .

This recollection seems to me to capture the true anxiety produced by the modern street. In the modern street, there is nowhere to wait. But there is also nowhere to go. There is no relationship between the different components of the contemporary urban space. An absolute speed and an absolute, statue-like immobility rule out the kinds of movement associated with meeting and parting. The individual feels most exposed where there is least room to move.

It's time, then, to return to the road less travelled. To come a little closer to our object, it is necessary to recognize that, however fertile its environmental or psychological applications may be, agoraphobia manifests itself as a movement inhibition.

More exactly, it is a resistance to the ideology of the straight line. To walk in a straight line, Le Corbusier assumed, is to think ahead. It is to have a goal. In the straight line, reason and the will fuse perfectly. Their fusion is powerful: instead of responding to the lie of the land, taking the line of least resistance, the intellectually upright and forward-looking logical walker can push aside all resistances. Suppose you are lost in a forest, Descartes wrote. Your best way out is to walk in a straight line: even if you do not know where you are going, at least you are bound to arrive *somewhere*. The Modernist counterpart of the Cartesian ego, mentally reducing the earth's surface to a grid, is Walter Benjamin's 'destructive character' (said to have been modelled on the Viennese architect Adolf Loos): 'Where others encounter walls or mountains, there, too, he sees a way.' The result of his vision was the production of those immense voids Sitte deplored: 'Because he sees a way everywhere, he has to clear things from it everywhere.' His vision inevitably led to 'empty space'.[78]

If society's sense of historical purpose and social cohesion depends on thinking and acting in straight lines, the corollary is obvious: whoever declines to walk in the orthodox manner displays their evolutionary unfitness, their primitive state of moral and emotional development. Vidler has linked Benjamin's interest in the slow-walking urban *flâneur*, and his darker, more subversive double, the vagabond, to Jean-Martin Charcot's studies of 'ambulatory automatism', an urban disorder that, in contrast with the largely middle-class phenomenon of agoraphobia, seemed far more prevalent among the working classes. It was especially found among those 'without avowed profession, without fixed domicile, in a word vagabonds, those who often sleep under bridges, in quarries or lime kilns and who are exposed at any instant to the blows of the police' – in a word, among those associated with the 'criminal activity of vagabondage'.[79]

Exposing the cultural construction of agoraphobia as a 'quintessential women's issue', McHugh cited a study that shows that 'agoraphobic women may be deficient in map-reading and way-finding skills', adding that this suggests 'that skill-building in these areas could be part of the solution'.[80] Historically, though, McHugh's feminist critique can equally be applied to men. If the patients Westphal described in his 1871 paper were all young men, it was presumably because they, rather than young women, mostly ventured out into the city's public spaces; they, in consequence, felt most exposed to the coercive patriarchal gaze and its implicit injunction to stand upright like a man. Perhaps little had changed 60 years later, when Benjamin attributed the 'impotence' he felt before Berlin, firstly, to 'a very poor sense of direction' – 'it was thirty years before the distinction between left and right had become visceral to me, and before I had acquired the art of reading a map'[81] – and, secondly, to his mother.

Benjamin's mother's habit of pointing out his practical short-comings did not spur him to rectify matters. It made him cling more resolutely to his dreamy ways. In particular, it made him translate his lack of map-reading skills into a resistant mode of locomotion. To her earnest efforts to make him *catch up*,

> I owe the dreamy recalcitrance with which I accompanied her as we walked through the streets, rarely frequented by me, of the city centre . . . nothing was more intolerable to my mother than the pedantic care with which, on these walks, I always kept half a step behind her. My habit of seeming slower, more maladroit, more stupid than I am, had its origins in such walks.[82]

Later, this refusal to keep in step with his own class expressed itself in another normal transgression: the accosting of prostitutes.

But the temptation of the street Benjamin felt was not Freud's sexual one. Under the 'auspices of prostitution', it was another *space* that opened up, one whose thrill and terror is uniquely revealed to the agoraphobe: '. . . is it really a crossing, is it not, rather, an obstinate and voluptuous hovering on the brink, a hesitation that has its most cogent motive in the circumstance that beyond this frontier lies nothing-ness?'[83] In this moment of hesitation before stepping off the kerb, in between waiting and not waiting, a different kind of space is disclosed, and a prospect of ceasing to walk over the ground, unconnected to it. Then, pushing himself forward, 'both feet feeling the ground, as we would do in the dark if we were unfamiliar with the place',[84] the subject might for the first time *touch down*.

MIND THE GAP

Why did Musil say that a citizen quietly going about his business expends more energy than an athlete lifting a huge weight? The straight line of progress is a product of the will. It is also the expression of the ideology, going back to Plato, that identifies being with stasis. According to this view, movement involves overcoming an initial inertia. The strongest, most wilful individual is also the one who has to expend the greatest energy to get going. By contrast, those who lack the gravitas of a fully developed and self-sufficient ego – the wanderers and vagabonds of this world – are light as thistledown and, blown down the pathways of least resistance, follow the drift-lanes of their desires.

The paradox of the straight line is that its universal grid is both everywhere and nowhere. Cancelling out difference, it cancels out the history of movement. It erases the history of the will that brought it into being. It embodies the paradox of imperialism, whose opportunistic expansionism poses as the imposition of a hitherto unimagined stability. Kafka understood this when he imagined that Alexander the Great 'might have remained standing on the bank of the Hellespont, and never have crossed it, and not out of fear, not out of indecision, not out of infirmity of will, but because of the mere weight of his body'. As Paul Goodman has commented, 'Alexander the Great is the imperial ego; to the ego, shut off from the energy of time and the world, there is no action and power in the life of the body, but the body is a dead weight.'[85]

The immobility, the sense of petrification, that assailed Westphal's patients occurred when they felt the hand of the father pushing them to start moving. It was telling that one of them could only overcome his movement inhibition when on horseback. The father's hand also forced them to stand erect and affect tallness. But that which is perfectly erect is perfectly balanced and, except under the impact of an external force, cannot move. Here is the sensitive young man's dilemma: how, bowing to the father's will and standing tall – an erectness that disguises servitude – can he ever move under his own volition? How, under the imperious pressure his culture exerts to march purposefully, can he ever experience walking as anything other than tottering? Not allowed an inclination of his own – any personal leaning is interpreted as transgressive - no direction presents itself as preferable to another. Even to decide which foot to place in front of the other presents an insurmountable logical conundrum.

Or so a philosopher might feel – Arthur Schopenhauer, say,

whose steadily progressive prose style 'does not flow – it strides, with a firm step, clear, positive, but with little wooing appeal. It keeps its distance'.[86] Why, a generation in advance of Simmel's metropolitan type, did Schopenhauer act, stylistically at least, from a great distance? Rudiger Safranski has offered a psychological explanation. Neither father nor mother provided the boy with that primary love without which 'the confident belief that something other than himself is aware of him just as he is'[87] can develop; hence a premature detachment, the reinforcement of a predisposition 'to casting at all living things that alienating glance from which philosophy springs'.[88] Or, again:

> Life's pulsating reality – was to him, simultaneously, the most distant and the most strange, so distant and so strange that it became a mystery to him, the philosophical mystery. He would subsequently make this corporeal reality, which he called the 'will', *the* core of his philosophy.[89]

The will, *qua* father, drives forward mercilessly, perpetuating itself via the sexual instinct: it has no care for its progeny, no interest in them.

No doubt, Schopenhauer's theory of the will sprang from what Laing would have called his ontological security. The point, though, is that it also sprang from a movement inhibition, and from the viewpoint this inhibition produced. Safranski relates that when Arthur worked in his father's office, his father lectured him:

> . . . make sure that you do not acquire a round back, which looks ghastly. Good posture at the writing desk is equally necessary as in ordinary life; for if, in the dining rooms, one catches sight of someone stooping, one takes him for a disguised cobbler or tailor.[90]

Was it this onerous sense of the father's hand and eye on his back that later led Arthur to write, 'As we all know, our walking is a continuously prevented falling; and in the same way the life of our body is a continuously prevented dying.'[91]

Schopenhauer overcame his fear of falling not by lying down, but by climbing aloft and staring down into the abyss: 'He had a well-developed sense of the vertical: it catapulted him upwards. Only thus could the horizontal be tolerated, from the bird's-eye view . . .'[92] Three times on his 1804 walking tour, Arthur climbed a mountain. Each time, he advanced closer to achieving a bird's-eye view, disembodied, re-embodied as an all-seeing vision. There was the Chapeau near Chamonix ('In striking contrast to this sublime grand view was the laughing valley far below'[93]); then Mount Pilatus, where 'one is no longer tied to "separate objects", one is now only an "eye" resting on a "colourful radiant picture"' ('I felt dizzy as I cast a glance at the crowded space before me'[94]); and, finally, the Schneekoppe ('One sees the world in chaos below one'[95]).

Schopenhauer's momentary sense of vertigo as he looked down into the chaos was a moment of identification with his father, who committed suicide by throwing himself from the attic or warehouse section of his house in Hamburg into the Fleet. Then Arthur pulled back. By an act of will, he took hold of the vision born of the detachment of distance and asserted his independence. But it was a most curious vision, immobile, even monocular. It was as if the anxiety of being tied to separate objects had been overcome by a wilful shrivelling up of the mobile body. The view Schopenhauer cultivated was without feet or gait: he stood aloft the mountain like a funerary monopod from Egypt. His eye would be his walking stick: he would advance mentally along the straight line of vision.

Extending the abyss around him, Schopenhauer turned the world into an object of aesthetic contemplation. Elation replaced depression. 'If I climb up to the platforms of the Eiffel Tower,' Le Corbusier explained,

> the very act of mounting gives me a feeling of gladness; the moment is a joyful one, and also a solemn one. And in proportion as the horizon widens more and more, one's thought seems to take on a larger and more comprehensive cast: similarly, if everything in the physical sphere widens out, if the lungs

expand more fully and the eye takes in vast distances, so too the spirit is roused to vital activity. Optimism fills the mind. For a wide horizontal perspective can deeply influence us at the expense of little actual trouble. Remember that up till now our horizons have never been more than those revealed to eyes quite close to the earth's surface; Alpine climbers alone enjoyed the intoxication of great heights.[96]

But what does he see from that great height?

A modern city lives by the straight line, inevitably; for the construction of buildings, sewers and tunnels, highways, pavements. The circulation of traffic demands the straight line; it is the proper thing for the heart of the city. The curve is ruinous, difficult and dangerous.[97]

To overcome the fear of surroundings, topography must be flattened out and the resulting sightlines extended to infinity. The vision of Leibniz's angel, balanced on a pinnacle far above the earth's surface, collapses into another kind of flat-earthism. When an absolute agoraphobia is normalized, particular agoraphobias can be redefined as pathological. In this way, the inner contradictions of imperial space are once again repressed.

SLIPPERY SURFACE

No wonder acknowledgment of the movement inhibition must itself be inhibited. Much more depends on slipping than a momentary loss of face or a muscle twinge. An entire cultural teleology is bound up with an illusion of movement so smooth as to appear stationary. Between the extremes of autonomy and speed, and their linking concept, distance, any sign of hesitation amounts to a kind of treachery. The walker who stumbles invalidates the modern city. It would be no wonder if the outraged crowd turned on him and kicked him to death.

Le Corbusier grasped this. It explains why his road-to-

Damascus conversion had to be instantaneous. The modernization of the city, and the supremacy of the traffic that circulates there, renders walking a criminal activity, and the walker a hunted animal. Benjamin may have found hovering on the brink a voluptuous experience; Le Corbusier found it a terrifying one: with the advent of motorized traffic, 'we have all forgotten the joy of being alive, the everyday happiness of walking peacefully on one's legs.' Yet, he seems to imply, that old pleasure was sinful, an excessive indulgence of the senses. In any case, it rendered us vulnerable to punishment: '. . . all our being is now absorbed in living like hunted animals a daily *sauve qui peut*.'[98] In a footnote, Le Corbusier added, 'This is perfectly true; one risks one's life at every step. If you happened to slip, if sudden giddiness made you fall . . .'[99]

In this situation, it would not be surprising if you began to avoid the middle of the pavement, where the greatest density of pedestrian traffic is concentrated. It has been suggested that Camillo Sitte's attack on modern urban design was motivated by his own agoraphobia – noting that 'his description of promenaders, "craving for protection from the flank," calls to mind the figures in contemporary street scenes painted by Edvard Munch', his American editors commented that he was 'apparently not comfortable himself when "on axis" or "in the centre", and he knew that many people felt skittery in large open squares.'[100] Yet here I am reminded of French-Jewish philosopher Vladimir Jankelevitch's remark made when, fleeing from the Nazis, he found himself in internal exile in Toulouse: 'J'ai un peu perdu l'usage de la liberté. Je ne sais plus marcher au milieu du trottoir. J'ai perdu l'habitude de mon propre nom.'[101]

As for Munch, what is pathological about *Der Schrei*, *Angst* or *Die Mädchen auf der Brücke* except that they are composed of 'ruinous, difficult and dangerous' curves? The orthodoxy that Munch was agoraphobic is contradicted by the biographical evidence. To say that 'he feared the countryside as he feared a woman'[102] is to ignore the fact that he happily lived there. It is as absurd as identifying Kafka with Alexander the Great, or any of his other petrified figures, when we know from Max Brod that, in other circumstances, the writer was quite capable of plunging in, spending 'countless happy hours on the boards of the bathing establishments of Prague, in rowing boats on the Vltava, in doing climbing stunts on the mill weirs'.[103] Francis Macnab was closer when he argued that the anguish of Munch's paintings reflects civilization's discontents.[104] But can't we be more precise? They anatomize the effects of distance, showing the strain they place on relationships. The 'lines' are not simply wilful gestures. They indicate tense lines of communication. They are also telephone wires, telegraph wires, whether suspended between poles or running under the asphalt. Of his *Separation* images (1896), Munch wrote, 'I symbolised the connection between the separated ones through the long undulating hair . . . the long hair is a kind of telephone line.'[105]

His editors nicely point out that Sitte's taste for semi-enclosed urban prospects, in which more was concealed than revealed, recalled the characteristic urban 'shots' of the Impressionist painter Camille Pissarro, which, by displacing the axis to the side of the observer, close off the vista. But it is this unmanly sliding aside from the central viewpoint, and the symmetrical scene it subtends, this slippage towards cultivating the voluptuous, sidelong glance, that has to be resisted and corrected. Hence, like Sitte, the progressive Otto Wagner might have acknowledged that 'metropolitan man suffered from only one pathological lack: the need for direction. In his fast-moving world of time and motion, what Wagner called "painful uncertainty" was all too easily felt.' But his solution was radically different: to overcome it 'by providing defined lines of movement'.[106]

It is not by chance that the poet Hugo von Hofmannsthal coined the term '*das Gleitende*, the slipping away of the world,'[107] to describe the collective neurasthenia said to have characterized fin-de-siècle Vienna. Nor is it perhaps mere chance that between 1894 and 1901, Otto Wagner was in charge of the construction of the Vienna city railway system. In discerning a world in which concepts slid apart to disclose a 'wholly irrational mass of the non-homogeneous',

Hofmannsthal was describing the vision of the new literary impressionist, or feuilletonist, who

> . . . tended to transform objective analysis of the world into subjective cultivation of personal feelings. He conceived of the world as a random succession of stimuli to the sensibilities, not as a scene of action . . . his characteristics were narcissism and introversion, passive receptivity towards outer reality, and, above all, sensitivity to psychic states.[108]

In this dangerously decadent context, what could better serve the artist's task of knitting together disparate elements to build 'the world of relations [*Bezuge*]'[109] than the railway train (*der Zug*). The train *could* be a form of automatic writing, threading into a seamless continuity the most disconnected of scenes. Yet its progressive credentials were impeccable. Running on iron tracks, it subjugated the chaotic world of appearances to the linear logic of a higher vision. It is true that, climbing aboard, one felt the cares of the world slipping from one's shoulders, but in indulging this voluptuous sensation, one had an alibi, the assurance that, as the walls of the city receded and the countryside began to slide by outside the window, one was purposefully directed. By train, what's more, even the curvilinear behaved as if it were straight.

PEDESTRIAN CROSSING

One begins to see that walking in the city implies a *resistance* to the straightnesses everywhere threatening to engulf the walker. The agoraphobic stroller has to keep faith with a lost, curvilinear topography. To lose contact with its ground is to risk falling into the crowd. He affects a carefreeness, but it is melancholic: his lightfootedness refers to intervals that have long been swept away. There is in his step a nostalgia for heights and depths. Cultivating obstacles that are not there, he asserts the possibility of other arrangements. The remaining dimples in the macadamized surface attract him like whirlpools. His railway line is the gutter, or the line of the kerbstone. His study of the cracks between paving flags is not necessarily a symptom of anxiety. It might signify his refusal to slide away, to be swept off his feet by the new urban planner's rectilinear traffic: the evidence of paces are footholds to the urban mountaineer.

Carl Schorske underlines the kind of progress Otto Wagner intended to promote:

> The natural placement of houses in a row created 'long, even surfaces framing the street.' Regulated as to height and stripped of disturbing surface ornament, the houses made the street a monument in itself. The smooth, linear façade of the housing block offered a psychological advantage too. It reinforced the trajectory of the street, so important . . . to providing direction and orientation to the pursuit of business.

He adds:

> The vehicular perspective dominated Wagner's urban concepts as the pedestrian's governed Sitte's. Wherever Wagner affirmed the pedestrian urban experience, it was in the spirit either of a man of business or of the shopper. Like a Baudelaire of consumerism, Wagner gloried in the bright 'unbroken chain of beautiful stores glittering with the artistic products of town and country'.[110]

In an environment characterized by the provision of 'defined lines of movement',[111] the walker's determination to define lines of his own inevitably appeared subversive. Here was one who inverted the dominant ideology, who remained detached from business because attached to the street, who made an eddy in the steady flow of human traffic, like a branch or rock causing a disturbing irregularity in the bed of the stream. It would hardly be surprising if the walker became self-conscious, or if he felt the need of certain props to give him confidence. Westphal found that one of his agoraphobic patients was relieved of his dread of crossing open places 'when he used a walking stick'.[112] A hat might be helpful, lending the human figure a loftier port. But most therapeutic was a double, another like him walking a few paces ahead. Perhaps even for non-agoraphobic pedestrians, the desire the street propagates depends on imagining it filled with like-minded others. In the agoraphobe, self-consciously acting out the death of the street, the discovery and tracking of these revenants is an item of faith.

Yet the pressure of adopting such a pose was enormous. If the citizen going about his ordinary business felt weighed down by a burden far greater than a weight-lifter could raise, what of the walker who confronted his city's agoraphobia? He not only accepted that burden, but determined to move it, to dance with it and make it his partner. An episode in *The Notebooks of Malte Laurids Brigge* recounts his fate. It is the poet Rilke's autobiographical narrator who, suffering from a neurasthenia characterized by agoraphobia, pays a visit to Charcot's clinic at Salpetrière, but it is his double, encountered in the street a few days later, who suffers the consequences. 'I went out so bravely, doing, as I thought, the simplest and most natural thing,' the narrator begins. 'And yet, something came again, which took me like paper, crumpled me up and threw me away; something unprecedented.'[113] Feeling 'the twinge of an incipient fear' in the Boulevard Saint-Michel,[114] he becomes aware that the people in the street are staring at someone – not at him, but at a man a few paces ahead.

Just then, the man stumbles:

As I was following close behind him I was on my guard, but when I came to the place there was nothing there, absolutely nothing. We both walked on, he and I, the distance between us remaining the same. Then there came a street-crossing, and there the man ahead of me hopped down from the pavement to the street, one foot held high, somewhat as children walking now and again hop and skip, when they are happy. On the other side of the crossing he simply made one long step up. But no sooner was he up than he raised one leg a little, and jumped high into the air with the other, immediately repeating this action again and again.[115]

The man behaves as if avoiding something on the ground, 'some small object, a pip, or slippery fruit-peel'.[116] He is annoyed that passers-by seem unable to see it.

The two proceed, whereupon the hopping impulse transfers itself to the man's nervously agitated hands. It 'was wandering about his body, trying to break out at different points'.[117] The narrator empathizes. When the man stumbles, he imitates him and, pretending to avoid 'some trifling, unapparent obstacle in the road',[118] also stumbles. But it seems that the man himself is also acutely aware of the ridicule he is attracting. He carries a walking stick, but, instead of using it for walking, uses it to correct his posture, as a kind of father-figure pressing him to stand upright and, instead of inspecting the ground at his feet, to raise his eyes to the horizon. He presses it 'firmly into the small of his back, and thrusting the curved end under his coat-collar, so that it could be seen standing up like a supporting bar between his neck and the first dorsal vertabra'.[119] 'Yet,' our follower continues, 'I could not keep my anxiety from growing. I knew that as he walked and made ceaseless efforts to appear indifferent and absent-minded, that awful convulsive motion was accumulating in his body.'[120] A strange variation ensues: it seems that the walker can time his convulsive leaps to the convulsions of the traffic:

> At the Place Saint-Michel there were many vehicles and people hurrying hither and thither. We were several times held up between two carriages; he took breath then, and let himself go a little by way of rest, and there would be a slight hopping and a little jerking of the head.[121]

But the 'imprisoned malady' will not be beguiled by this *folie à deux*. When the walker reaches a bridge, it reasserts its power:

> . . . his gait became noticeably uncertain; sometimes he ran a few steps, sometimes he stood. Stood. His left hand gently released the stick and rose, rose, so slowly that I saw it tremble in the air; he thrust his hat back a little, and drew his hand

across his brow. He turned his head slightly, and his gaze wavered over sky, houses and water, without grasping anything. And then he gave in. His stick had gone, he stretched out his arms as if he meant to fly, and then something like a natural force broke out of him, bent him forward and dragged him back, kept him nodding and bowing, and flung him dancing into the midst of the crowd.[122]

CYCLE LANE

According to one pedestrian theorist, the ordinary act of walking embodies something like Viktor Schauberger's 'Cycloid Spiral Space-Curve' – 'open, goal-oriented, structured, concentrated, intensifying, condensing, dynamic, self-organising, self-divesting of the less valuable, rhythmical (cyclical), sinuous, pulsing, in-rolling, centripetal (and out-rolling centrifugal) movement'.[123] No wonder, then, that the man in the street, strait-jacketed by the onerous command to walk in straight lines with a minimum of sway, feels a desire to break out. Don't believe the early manufacturers' posters advertising the pleasures of cycling either. Those gay, abandoned expressions, and pre-Marilyn Monroe uplifted skirts, conceal the fact that, as a form of hyper-walking, reducing the track to a single groove, cycling produced accelerated movement at the cost of the cyclist's enforced immobility. To yield to any 'natural force' was instantly to crash.

Such anxieties were not confined to European capitals. The English writer Flora Thompson recalled the advent of the penny-farthing in 1880s rural Oxfordshire:

Pedestrians backed almost into the hedges when they met one of them, for was there not almost every week in the Sunday newspaper the story of some one being knocked down and killed by a bicycle, and letters from readers saying cyclists ought not to be allowed to use the roads, which, as everybody knew, were provided for people to walk on or to drive on behind horses. 'Bicyclists ought to have roads to themselves, like railway trains' was the general opinion. Yet it was thrilling to see a man hurtling through space on one high wheel, with another tiny wheel wobbling helplessly behind. You wondered how they managed to keep their balance. No wonder they wore an anxious air. 'Bicyclist's face', the expression was called, and the newspapers foretold a hunchbacked and torture-faced future generation as a result of the pastime.[124]

Of the various forms of wheeled transport, cycling was closest to walking. In its undemonstrative way, it embodied the internal inconsistency of a cultural logic that identified progress with traffic. As the mechanical servant of the goal-oriented will, the bicycle clearly allied itself to the interests of the intellectually adventurous and the economically opportunistic. At the same time, to yield (at least on the newly surfaced boulevards of Paris and Vienna) to the sensation of an effortless gliding down the line of least resistance was dangerously like yielding to the drives of the instincts. In this sense, the bicycle was always a tandem: the super-ego and the id both occupied it, and the frightening thing was that they seemed to pump the pedals in perfect concert.

The bicycle made it possible to speed up. It also made it possible to speed away. It encouraged a kind of purposefulness. But it also allowed the cultivation of aloofness. The concentration needed to steer the beast also made narcissism respectable. Inside his mobile envelope, the cyclist is inaccessible. He is like the journalist, an eyewitness to history; he takes no part in it. The bicycle aspires to perfect progress: if it could, it would fly over the ground. As it is, where the ground is metalled, it leaves no trace of its passage. Its passing is dreamlike. Inevitably, though, this ease of motion produces a reaction in the thoughtful cyclist. The removal of the movement inhibition is discerned to be violent. Immaculate journeys produce their contrary: the desire for encounter, the longing to make a mark, the wish to crash.

Peter Gay hints at these possibilities in his memoir of a Berlin childhood. His own household exuded an 'atmosphere of openness'.[125]

He recalls a trivial dishonesty, which produced 'a puzzling and unnerving shattering of a smooth surface'.[126] Perhaps, he implies, this was its object – 'Impatience with my perfection.'[127] A similar motive perhaps made him accident-prone. Once, getting off a streetcar, he was hit by a car; another time, he narrowly avoided being hit after leaving a movie house on the Kurfurstendam. The star of the film had been Richard Tauber: '"Always smiling and always cheerful," he sings, "but what goes on inside is no one's business".'[128] There was another incident:

> In Berlin of the 1920s, children riding the smallest bikes were permitted to use the sidewalk. Happily I would ride my bike from one end of Schweidnerstrasse to another. But one day, chugging along, I noticed an old lady slowly walk toward me. I had plenty of time to stop or swerve round her; instead I ran into her and she fell.[129]

Conscious of no anger towards his carefully directive patients, Gay pondered the 'unconscious rage' expressed in this incident. If it was a hostile feeling towards his parents, then it was successfully projected elsewhere. But it was equally a protest against smoothness. Gay sensed that, at home in the streets as he might be, he was being brought up to miss things. To navigate one's way around obstacles skilfully was also to regret never having encountered them. Gay, it seems, rebelled against the immense spaces, wanting to clutter them up with intimate, even death-defying, encounters. In view of the historical sequel, it is possible to speculate that he dimly grasped a connection between the destructiveness of his own space-opening powers and the terrible destruction to be visited upon his people.

But the forces of progress are seductive: they threaten to immolate you, then they let you off scot-free. The fury of destruction unleashed in the terrors of Kristallnacht filled the young Gay with anger. But one senses that an element of his outrage and frustration stemmed from his own detachment from the scene. Apprised of the sack, he cycled home by a different route, 'through a city that seemed to have been visited by an army of vandals'.[130] Four long blocks of specialty shops in Tauentzienstrasse had had their façades reduced to rubble: 'I kept my head down and bicycled my way home. The aloofness I had cultivated for so long did me good service that morning.'[131]

Going back 40 years, Freud's son, Martin, was a bicycle freak: 'In those days, motor-cars were still rare; and the bicycle which could defeat distance and time had the quality almost of magic, leaving the horse, whether ridden or driven, far behind.'[132] His famous father, though, 'hated bicycles'. One summer, he rejected the Mondsee as a place for a family holiday, because the great number of cyclists on the road made it unsafe for children: 'one had to hate cyclists because of the dust they raised and the number of children they knocked down'.[133] This sounds like the rationalization encountered earlier, in connection with Musil's Ulrich:

> If we ask the [agoraphobic] patients just what danger they stand in dread of, they draw upon all sorts of well-rationalised possibilities: the fear of sudden death, of being stricken with apoplexy, of fainting, and being run over. Often these patients offer statistical proofs of the dangers of the street; some take careful note of every traffic accident, of every collision between streetcars or automobiles.[134]

(And others, we may add, tot up bicycle collisions.)

With his interest in drives, though, perhaps Freud was aware of something far more deep-rooted and obscure. Perhaps part of his desire was to put a spoke in the wheel of a historical progress, conceived as a 'continuously prevented falling'. Such a vision of balance belied its deeper unbalance. Such a self-rationalizing movement had no way of stopping, except by hitting a wall. And it was odd to think of our streets, designed to accommodate ever greater volumes of traffic, as mechanisms of a 'continuously prevented dying'.

Or perhaps Freud foresaw the death of his own greatest critic, Karl Kraus. In February 1936, Kraus 'was struck down in the dark by a bicyclist; he suffered a mild concussion and a severe heart attack as a result. He died on June 12, 1936, of heart failure.'[135]

The man in the street did not, of course, fling himself dancing into the crowd. He kept his hat firmly planted on his head. He used his stick to push rubbish aside and to hail taxis. In general, he repressed his movement inhibitions, like a good actor pretending to get on as if nothing had happened. Nevertheless, the massive effort of reining in his ambulatory fantasies left a trace in the violence of his place names. Having punished himself, he punished his surroundings. In his figures of speech, the lost topography of the city assumed a nightmarish aspect. The lie of the land yielded to a landscape formed of abysses and bridges perilously suspended over them. And the Cartesian observer who watched the chequerboard of rational reality breaking up in front of him was reinvented as a Romantic Robinson Crusoe. As Kant put it, 'The land of the pure intellect . . . is an island, enclosed by nature itself within unalterable boundaries. It is the land of truth . . . surrounded by a vast and stormy ocean.'[136]

Hölderlin expressed the same idea more hysterically:

> The more challenged we are by Nothingness which, like an abyss, yawns all around us, or even dissipated by the thousand-fold Something of society and human activity, which pursues us shapelessly, soullessly and lovelessly, the more passionate and eager and violent must *resistance* come from our side.[137]

Not to resist must have one of two consequences. Either one must plunge into the abyss, a fate which Schopenhauer identified with yielding to the sexual impulse – although, as Safranski notes, 'sex only began to appear abysmal from the perspective of an ego believing itself to be autonomous'.[138] Or one must become a bridge-builder. But this, too, was fraught with dangers and temptations.

> 'Do you know what the closing sentence [of *The Judgment*] means?' Kafka asked Brod – 'Dear parents, I always loved you in spite of everything, and let himself fall. The traffic over the

bridge at that moment was endless.' And he answered, 'I meant by it a strong ejaculation'.[139]

The (literally) suicidal logic which identifies the loss of self-consciousness with death is a symptom of the ego's agoraphobia. In order to ground its stance of autonomy, it has to characterize the world beyond it as groundless. But if the world is groundless, how can the ego be sure that its own ground is not an illusion? Before long, reflection drags the thinking subject into infinite regress. As soon as we attempt to have consciousness of ourselves through ourselves and independently of the objects of cognition, and strive for complete self-reflection (Theodor Adorno wrote, with Schopenhauer in mind), 'we lose ourselves in a bottomless void, find ourselves resembling the hollow glass ball out of whose emptiness a voice speaks that has no cause within the ball, and, in trying to grasp ourselves, we clutch, shuddering, at nothing.'[140]

So much for the ego of the healthy, well-balanced man in the street. But what about his double, the agoraphobe? He does not believe that the abyss is bottomless. He does not believe in abysses. His study is inclinations and intervals. He is interested in the tendency of things to drift together or apart. Of course, in this he is the double of the metropolitan type. After all, as Georg Simmel realized, the withdrawal that occurs in the city, while it makes social encounter more difficult, also charges it with a heightened erotic meaning. When so much effort is directed at keeping people apart, to bump into another person can hardly be accidental. Hence, the three distinctive social commodities sold in the metropolitan marketplace, according to Simmel, are the rendezvous, the adventure and flirtation. Each of these endows the placeless immensity of the modern city with a topography.

The rendezvous 'separates itself out like an island from the continuous course of life's contents'.[141] It achieves a special hold on consciousness and a greater associative effect for recollection. It becomes a focal point of remembrance. The adventure is 'like an island in life which determines its beginning and end according to its own formative powers and not – like the part of a continent – also according to those of adjacent territories'.[142] As for flirtation, it gives to Benjamin's moment of hesitation a bipedal dynamic. It is an endless closing and opening or oscillation between two positions: flirtation is 'the act of taking hold of something only in order to let it fall again, of letting it fall only to take hold of it again, in what could be called the tentative turning towards something on which the shadow of its own denial already falls'.[143] It makes not-having 'tangible for the first time by means of the playful, suggestive illusion of having'.[144] Flirtation towards intellectual subjects 'is the form in which the indecisiveness of life is crystallised into a thoroughly positive way of acting'.[145]

Or, to put it another way, it is the discourse of the other. There is a Greek word for this: *allegory*, derived from *allos + agourein*. *Other-speak*, then, is the language of the agora. Ego-speak, that tortuous mirror-logic described by Adorno, is the language of agoraphobia. And a topography goes with it. Kafka's fall from the bridge may be allegorical, but it suggests an intoxication with great heights and depths. It finds its biographical counterpart in the diving boards, rowing boats and mill weirs he frequented in his carefree twenties. Yet they were not entirely carefree. It seems that the fantasy of self-sacrifice always played around them, the temptation of the abyss. Max Brod recalled how in those water games, Kafka

> had a special trick of leaving one to one's fate in neck-breaking situations with an almost cruel smile which seemed to say something like 'Help yourself.' How I adored that smile, in which, after all, there lay also so much confidence and encouragement. Franz was inexhaustible in finding out new lines of sport, or so it seemed to me. In this too his personality expressed itself, this too he did, as he did everything, with complete abandon.[146]

But abandonment is not love. Nor is the bridge. In love, Simmel has written, 'the I has felt its way across the hiatus to the Thou. The existential will of the I flows to the Thou with complete intimacy. It does not need a bridge, which separates just as it connects.'[147] It does not need a bridge because there was never an abyss, only a gap. And, unlike the abyss, the gap can never be closed: love 'does not nullify the being-for-itself of either the I or the Thou'. Hence, the revelation is always in imminent danger of disappearing. But while it lasts, agoraphobia is conquered. In love, Rilke's Paris is adorable.[148] All of the city is at the lover's disposition, without the least act of will on his part. Its normal indifference is quite overcome and forgotten.

But a different kind of plunging in is needed to grasp this. Perhaps the French verb *s'y abimer* describes it. *To lose oneself there* – as in amorous devotion to a god – the phrase connotes both a place and the act of being damaged by falling into it.[149] Like the agora, an abyss can be both a location and what gathers there.

Besides, what is the prejudice against limpers? A French ball of shot smashing his knee was needed to cure the founder of the Jesuit order, Ignatius de Loyola, of all thoughts of lust and leave his heart serene.[150] As for his follower, Matteo Ricci, it was an injury to his foot which brought him 'limping literally and metaphorically towards the light'.[151]

PROCEED WITH CAUTION

A reader might alight from this stop-start drive through the suburbs of our theme. Why this intense focus on the historical period roughly bounded by the Franco-Prussian War and the outbreak of the Second World War? Why this spotlight on the intellectual fashions of Vienna, Berlin and Paris? The answer is simple and does not depend on the defence that, later on, the field of enquiry is widened and the phenomenon of agoraphobia shown to inform imperialism's colonial adventures, indeed to permeate the West's ancient foundational myths.

The reasoning is somatic and subjective. Depending on the reader's age and the vicissitudes of their parents' and grandparents' lives, as they steered their ways through the obstacles of the twentieth century, the late Victorian period marked the boundary of what came down to us by personal testimony. In my family, what lies beyond the

Relief of Mafeking belongs mainly to writing, letters, newspapers and history books. This side of it, I enter a personally transmitted history, one residing in voices and postures, in which the events of the outside world are mediated through the inside world of domestic space, its intimate topography and history.

An exactly comparable phenomenon applies to our relationship with our built environments: they assume their present configuration mainly in that same historical period. We enter the townscapes of the medieval, Renaissance and Baroque periods as foreign visitors: the streets and public space which constitute our everyday spatial apparel are almost entirely the product of late nineteenth- and early twentieth-century modernization. And they easily permeate our little walls, as interior and exterior design come to resemble each other.

Rilke mused, 'We are incessantly flowing over and over to those who preceded us, to our origins and to those who seemingly come after us.'[152] But this sense that 'in that greatest "open" world all *are*, one cannot say "simultaneous", for the very falling away of time determines that they *are*'[153] applies even more to the experience of buildings and their spaces. Always past, they are only ever present. To revisit the anxieties associated with their grounding is, then, to resist the emptiness to which we are heir. Even to encounter the anxieties loitering in their midst is to take the first step towards recovering a lost community. Bringing to consciousness what was consciously felt then, but which was subsequently repressed in the name of progress, is to get back in touch with the wounded ground under our feet. It is to escape fetishizing our loss in the form of an unnatural attachment to statues. It is to locate ourselves within a history of potential presences, and to make room for them. It is, as Heidegger might have said, to experience the Open as an opening or region, and to have a sense of 'moving-into-nearness'.[154]

But back to the road. The anxiety-ridden landscape of the metropolitan nightmare resembles a post-earthquake scene along the San Andreas Fault. No wonder, then, that the public warms to gap-leapers, acrobats of the abyss and other death-defying acts of the aerial circus. Such folk find a way through the ruins. They master vertigo.

60

They weave invisible, curvilinear lines through each other and come out the other side. They know when and how to leap.

Picasso's saltimbanques learn their art of balance by practice, and, in doing this, they find the formula that banishes agoraphobia. The void, the place that is placeless because it lacks a topography, suddenly becomes a spot. 'And suddenly in this laborious nowhere, suddenly / the unsayable spot where the pure Too-little is transformed / incomprehensibly –, leaps around and changes / into that empty Too-much; / where the difficult calculation becomes numberless and resolved.'[155] When the apprenticeship on the mats and on the wire and the rings is over, the saltimbanques can be compared to lovers with 'their ladders / that have long been standing where there was no ground, leaning / just on each other, trembling . . .'[156]

This taste extended to the stage in general. Funambulists, contortionists and ventriloquists: these honest porters of the theatrical tradition were greeted by the Modernists as the avant-garde of the Unconscious. They seemed to know instinctively what the ethnographers had only recently rediscovered in Africa and Australasia. Their trancelike representation of a higher reality produced an effect not unlike the 'profane illumination' cultivated, said Walter Benjamin, by the Surrealists, 'a materialistic, anthropological inspiration, to which hashish, opium, or whatever else can give an introductory lesson'.[157] The old masters of the gap were now perceived to perform their death-defying gyrations on the brink of an abyss. In this lay their revolutionary potential. Their *lenteur*, their magnification of intervals – a spectacle of giant strides allying their productions with the wide-eyed structuring mechanisms of fairy tales – implies a co-efficient of resistance or a medium possessing its own fluid dynamics. The actors glided about the performance space like a kite sailing its air-currents, tunnelling a mise-en-scène composed of strata or regions of differing density or lightness. Drama as space's chiaroscuro.

The great failure of the new urbanism, according to Sitte, was that it caused disorientation. It was the symmetry of the new squares, the fact that roads radiating from a roundabout looked identical, that caused vertigo.[158] It was as if the new cities performed a lobotomy of the sixth sense upon the poor citizens. The existence of a sixth sense was a topic of lively debate in zoological and anthropological circles of the time; it was the faculty of wayfinding. Migrating birds used it to find their way back to the nest. Being closer to animals in the great evolutionary chain, primitive peoples were also said to possess this faculty. By confirming that modern humans lacked this organ of direction, the progressive urban designer proved how advanced Western peoples were, how removed from their instinctual, animal origins. Agoraphobia was, in this sense, a symptom of regression, a return of the old faculty for returning.

The phenomenon of tropism was widely invoked. True, as an atavistic yearning for the nest, it suggested a less than perfect adaptation to the higher, impersonally devised goals of modernity. On the other hand, just as traffic itself hovered ambiguously between the realm of the instincts and the will of the intellect, so with the sixth sense: in the right head, it could lead to the stars. Mountain guides and aviators, for instance, legitimately cultivated it.[159] Charles Lindbergh was known as 'the Homing Pigeon'.[160] Marcel Proust boasted of a sense analogous to that possessed by pigeons, which enabled him to plumb the general laws of the unconscious unperceived by most. More mundanely, Rémy de Gourmont said that some such faculty prevented him from ever losing his way.[161]

At a micro level, though, it was the juggler and the acrobat who supremely enacted this gift. In their performances, the spot was always found, the actual fulcrum of chaotic forces, which resolved them into a pose. In the miniature geography of their kinetic arrangements, balls could be seen to find their natural places. Rings climbed up to waiting hands, and mysteriously attached themselves. The somersaulter, measuring out the future in the nothingness of his backflip, somehow arrived at the unique point of balance (which was invisible to profane eyes). Responding to an enquiry into tropism hosted by *Nature* in 1873, one contributor suggested that the medium which transmitted information to bees about the correct path home was the same that carried light and electromagnetism, namely the ether.[162] This recalls Munch's image of hair as a telephone wire. Funambulists swarmed up and down these mysterious lines of attraction. As for jugglers, they mastered a movement that did not extend on an axis between stop and go, but in which kinesis and stasis were, like Rilke's Open, both inviolably and simultaneously present. As a child in Berlin, Peter Gay recalled seeing at the Scala 'Rastelli, the world's most remarkable juggler, performing virtual miracles such as balancing three soccer balls, one on top of the other, on one foot.'[163] The clowns, of course, knew exactly what anxieties assailed the crowd. 'At the Scala,' Gay also remembered,

> I saw Grock, the great clown, desperately trying and always failing to construct a human bridge with the dubious help of a confederate. Their ever-repeated announcement that they were about to perform this feat – 'Eine Brücke! Eine Brücke!' – still sounds in my ears.[164]

ACCIDENT BLACKSPOT

If we make the 'movement inhibition' our Ariadne's thread through the labyrinth of agoraphobia, we soon come to the *spot*. The spot is the topographical counterpart of the pose. The agoraphobic city is spotless in theory. The movement of traffic through its rationally ordered grid is immaculate. But the clarity of this vision is intolerable: seeing vanishing points everywhere, it envisages the future as a repeated, and collective, self-sacrifice. No wonder that a psychosomatic reaction sets in against these crystalline expanses, and they begin to buckle, shatter, and the plates underfoot to shudder and slide apart. In addition to their symptoms of vertigo and asphyxiation, Westphal reported that two of his patients 'also complained of seeing shining circles floating before their eyes'.[165] It is as if, in an effort to compose the space, an imaginary troupe of gambollers had been conjured up. The circles were the rings a juggler shuffles so that they dance like gnats in mid-air.

Most men, not to mention women, of the street did not yield to despair. They did not throw themselves off bridges or factory rooftops into the river. Nevertheless, they did descend to the water's edge, finding along its banks the picturesque spot where, temporarily at least, they could legitimately take the weight off their feet. There, beside the gently flowing water, the foot-chain of the stop-go dialectic was relieved. Much has been written about Haussmann's boulevards, Hobrecht's city plan or Wagner's Ringstrasse, and about the effect of the new spaces on their respective citizenries. But far less has been said about these cities' rivers. If the newly linearized expanses of the urban realm induced agoraphobia, what of the new rivers, their periodic floods weired to run evenly at all times, their banks drained, and the obvious gap between them transformed into a perilous abyss safely overcome with bridges? Did they induce a comparable *potamophobia*? Would Paul Célan have committed suicide if, instead of driving him to the brink of the Seine, history's demons had tracked him into the splitting meanders and shallow marshes of Berlin's Spree?

In illustrating the ambiguous appeal of the fluvial spot, one incident will have to stand in for many. Coming from that austere and magnificent testament of exile, Theodor Adorno's *Minima Moralia* (1951), it is particularly eloquent, however. *Minima Moralia* contains a double indictment. It accuses the German intellectual tradition of betraying the spirit of its own origins, and it condemns the post-war materialism of the United States. Canetti had described the dialectical method as the chattering of false teeth. In a book of practical criticism, Adorno reanimates the method; putting flesh back on it, he has, again, to confront the body that history has left out, the subjects of history who remain ethically responsible for their decisions. It is not a forgiving book: a nostalgia for an open society, not dissimilar in constitution to Popper's, alternates with a condemnation of the consumerist phantasmagoria that can be traced back, via Benjamin, to the shop-windows of Baudelaire's Paris.

All the more surprising, then, is Adorno's apparent endorsement of a writer hardly noted for his moral rectitude – that late nineteenth-century chronicler of river life, Guy de Maupassant. Adorno does not even offer the excuse that the frankness of Maupassant's depiction of sexual relations makes him a valuable historical eyewitness, in the manner of Zola. Besides, it was hardly in that spirit that the tales comprising the collection *Sur l'eau* were written. Take the idyllic 'Mouche: Reminiscences of a Rowing Man'. Maupassant thought that it would shock because it represented five men sharing a single mistress. But what really shocks is not the disputed paternity of La Mouche's child, but the manner of her miscarriage: trying to jump ashore from a moving yawl, she missed her footing, 'slipped, struck her belly against the sharp corner, and with a loud cry disappeared into the water. All five of us dived in together, and brought out a poor fainting creature, deathly pale and already suffering terrible pain . . .'[166]

Obviously, this is a brutally rich psychological landscape. A gap turns into an abyss: life was so simple *sur l'eau*, but La Mouche insisted on coming ashore (getting pregnant). The logic is distinctly agoraphobic: La Mouche found her new *gravitas* annoying – 'She could no longer skip around as before, or leap from the boat to the bank as she was used to doing.'[167] Her death-defying leap, then, conceals a desire for self-punishment, a death-wish towards her unborn child. The gap, as opposed to the suspended animation of life on water, is characterized by a mastery of leaps: the genius of La Mouche, her erotic appeal, consists in her ability to keep land and water in touch with each other. But this natural saltimbanque is evidently the convenient projection of male narcissism. It is no accident that her name means *spot*, as she both focuses the will and risks becoming an obstacle to its further traffic.

Maupassant's stories further illuminate the culture of agoraphobia, but what was Adorno's interest in them? In the short essay titled 'Sur l'eau', Adorno entertains the idea of a society that refuses the savagery of progress: 'It is not man's lapse into luxurious indolence that is to be feared, but the savage spread of the social under the mask of universal nature, the collective as a blind fury of activity.'[168] But how to escape this dialectic – this tyrannous imperative to choose between progress and regress. Could it be that 'the true society will grow tired of development and, out of freedom, leave possibilities unused, instead of storming under a confused compulsion to the conquest of strange stars?'[169] Then '*Rien faire come une bête*, lying on water and looking peacefully at the sky, "being, nothing else, without any further definition and fulfilment", might take the place of process, act, satisfaction, and so truly keep the promise of dialectical logic that it would culminate in its origin'.[170]

Rocking, as it were, in the cradle of the dialectic, the daydreamer enjoys the same freedom as the acrobat: he finds the still spot of reflection, immune to the reductive mirror-logic that traps the ego in its own self-consciousness. Open to the sky, he is inoculated against agoraphobia. But nothing in Adorno is without irony; no thesis is without its shadowing antithesis. The allusion to Maupassant cannot be innocent. It is not an idyllic scene that is conjured up. Or, if it is, it is a scene which, like the spot where Simmel's adventures or flirtatious encounters occur, is caught in the grid of historical necessity, and imminently subject to the darker powers of the will.

The Italian novelist and painter Alberto Savinio divided Maupassant's tales into two kinds, those inhabiting the *terra firma* of naturalism, albeit somewhat coastally, (the story of La Mouche would be one) and those in which the author plunges into the abyss of the double life, the realm of stolen names, doubled identities, inexplicably fateful coincidences, warps of ordinary time and space in whose folds the contours of illicit desire rise and fall.[171] Now, among the latter, 'Sur l'eau', the title story of the collection to which Adorno supposedly was alluding, would certainly fit. 'Sur l'eau' is not borderline naturalism, but a frankly phantasmagoric ghost story, a tale of spirit possession. A fisherman goes out at night on the river: sounds, reflected images, their transformation under the influence of his thoughts; a bump against the side of his boat; concern for safety, desire to move on; going to raise anchor, he cannot, the anchor is fixed fast; the consequence of this – panic *au sérieux*, terror, ghastly fancies; gradual return of reason, eventual coming of dawn; friendly fishermen, one, then a second, come to his rescue; together, they succeed in freeing the anchor. Hauling it aboard, however, they find hooked over one of its flukes *une masse noire* – the corpse of an old woman, a large stone tied round her neck.[172]

To recline on the water is also to plumb hidden depths. As La Mouche proves, in the gap between two strides, the historical will makes itself manifest. The division in Maupassant's writing between day-tales of the surface and nightmares of the depths, suggests a fictional agoraphobia, the feuilletonist's inability to impose a unifying design on his environments. But unless this can be done, La Mouche is condemned to become the nameless black mass. *Mouche*: also 'mark', 'stain' and, by extension, 'badge of guilt'. That, wrote Savinio, was the dark attraction water held for Maupassant. It washed him clean. Our fates, Savinio firmly believed, are foreshadowed in our names: Maupassant – *mauvais passant* – the evil traveller. He sought out the touch of water as one with the itch to lave his burning skin.[173]

LIMITED HEADROOM

When Malte Laurids Brigge was following the convulsive leaper down the Boulevard Saint-Michel, he kept crossing to the other side of the street. This was because he wanted to appear normal, unimplicated in the other's motion. He wanted to pass unnoticed, like the man in the street. But who is the man in the street? He is the definitely gendered unit out of which the new 'abstract society' is assembled. He is its willing automaton. His is the opinion that counts, as he is the one who, by a colossal effort of will, or from sheer inertia, can see both sides of the issue. His symmetry of disposition perfectly apes that of the streets. His opinion is inherently public. When he stands up to go out, he puts on a hat. When he is knocked over in the street, it is definitely an accident.

But the man in the street forms part of our story because he is the double of the agoraphobe. The illness of the agoraphobe arises from the fact that the man in the street fails to see this. To overcome the movement inhibition, sessions on the analyst's couch are unnecessary. It is doubtful whether the division of urban spaces into smaller parts would do the trick. It is the rearrangement of parts which is required. But where the rhetoric of commerce has replaced the prosecution of relationships, the more things change, the more they remain the same. The new mobility of the man in the street adds up to nothing. This explains why he is susceptible to the charm of actors, mountebanks and dictators, for they are folk who, in one way or another, promise a decisive change of state.

The man in the street is Musil's New Man Without Qualities:

> Suddenly [in Vienna] the right man was on the spot every-where; and, what is so important, men of practical enterprise joined forces with the men of intellectual enterprise. Talents developed that had previously been choked or had taken no part at all in public life. They were as different from each other as anything well could be, and the contradictions in their aims were unsurpassable. The Superman was adored, and the Subman was adored; health and the sun were worshipped, and the delicacy of consumptive girls was worshipped; people were enthusiastic hero-worshippers and enthusiastic adherents of the social creed of the Man in the Street; one had faith and one was sceptical . . .[174]

So much for his constitution. What of his comportment?

The vital point is that the man in the street wears a hat. This is of the essence. In pre-Freudian days, when the unconscious was poorly developed, it was a moot point where thoughts went when they passed out of consciousness. Evidently, they roosted in the hat. The positivist psychologist T. Ribot reported the case of an epileptic who,

> seized with a sudden paroxysm, fell in a shop, got up, and, eluding the shopman and his friends, ran away, leaving his hat and order-book behind. He was discovered a quarter of a mile away, asking for his hat at all the shops, but not having recovered his senses, nor did he become conscious until he got to the railway ten minutes later.[175]

The epileptic perfectly understood what the hat contained. Besides,

4 Edvard Munch, *Evening on Karl Johan Street,* 1896, hand-coloured lithograph.

the hat introduced a little distance between the walker and the street. It was a portable verandah. Obliging one to proceed erectly, it was an acceptable hand on the shoulder. As no hat comes without its hatpeg, it implied an imminent homecoming. It was a thread through the day's labyrinth. If Ariadne had been a man, she would have handed her lover a hat.

The man who wears a hat is also an actor. His hat is a charm against agoraphobia, but it also signals his vulnerability. It takes only the slightest breeze, and the formerly robust walker feels in danger of losing his head. This seems to be the condition top-hats induce in Munch's paintings. On Oslo's main street – the scene is represented in his 1896 lithograph *Evening on Karl Johan Street* (illus. 4) – Munch wrote, 'I saw all people behind their masks.'[176] It is a scene of anticipated *rencontre*. Yet, walking up and down waiting for the one he loves, the artist feels the immensity of the prospect: '. . . the windows in the Parliament building and in the buildings along Karl Johan reflected yellow from the horizon – they formed lines of shining squares . . . He felt strangely weak the ladies were so beautiful.'[177]

Then she comes towards him, 'pale in the reflection from the horizon': 'She greeted him with a soft smile and walked on . . . Everything became so empty and he felt so alone . . . People who passed by looked so strange and awkward and he felt as if they looked at him stared at him [*sic*] all these faces in the evening light.'[178]

Munch's walker wears a hat. But even this cannot protect him from anxiety. Instead of fitting him, the hat belongs to his mask. It merely conceals his suffering. The modern man in the street is a petrified actor. As for the actor, his role is clear: to unmask the citizen, to confront him with his suffering, to cure him of his stony immobility, to free him up.

TRAFFIC LIGHTS

Stopping, let's look back.

The agoraphobe is an unfortunate young man in 1870s Berlin. He is an armchair statistician of road accidents. He is an over-sexed symbolist whose mother abandoned him far too early. He is a limper, and a critic of modern architecture. He has no use for the telephone,[179] and (a fact I haven't mentioned) he is a confirmed smoker.[180] A masturbator,[181] an ambulatory somnambulist.[182] He is also a woman guiltily obsessed with her father.[183] She is a 'dependent personality'.[184] She suffers physical abuse, and is a specialist in bereavement: by looking at people's faces, she can assess the severity of their loss.[185] She likes to keep the door open, listening for street traffic.[186] Growing up anxious, often asthmatic, she collects doll-houses.[187] And she is a man again (he has a model railway), insecure in the contemporary world's war zone.

The very fact that this list of agoraphobic types and attributes

their *folie à deux*, who turns it into an unconscious *ménage à trois*. He is the environmental witness who whispers in their ear that their agoraclaustrophobic fantasies are not paradoxes of the psyche, but arise from contradictions internal to the constitution of late capitalist spaces. He is the one who, anticipating Tadeusz Kantor's attempts to break out of the mirror-logic used to define the actor's role, might proclaim:

> They do not imitate anything, they do not represent anybody, they do not express anything but themselves, human shells, exhibitionists, con artists, who are separated from and who exhibit their supernatural gifts to the public, who challenge with their individuality and their uncommon behaviour. They are like circus performers, clowns, jugglers, fire-eaters, and acrobats. They solve all the problems, the dilemma of autonomy and representation, with ease. They meet all the demands for new actors.[195]

In the 1934 volume of the *International Journal of Psycho-Analysis*, C. P. Oberndorf reports on a pathologically interlocking family situation which he refers to, colloquially, as a case of *folie à deux*. Mr and Mrs V. 'had been virtually prisoners in their home for about two years – she suffered from a sensation of whirling whenever she left home, he also from whirling and a fear of slipping, or of his automobile skidding whenever the pavement was damp'.[196] They 'practised an unusual sexual perversion – a compulsion which involved the plunging of Mrs V. fully dressed into a bath tub of water'.[197] Oberndorf offers an elaborate Freudian explanation, but from the outside, the history of splash-baths and duckings points in another direction. It recalls the punishment once meted out to alleged witches: if the accused survived ducking, it proved her supernatural powers; if she drowned, it proved (albeit fatally) her innocence. As Antony Wilden has pointed out, such double-bind logic cannot be escaped unless its ideological basis is grasped.[198] The witch is the victim of a misogynistic ideology that classifies women as virgins or whores. Oberndorf's socially isolated couple invite a similar response. It was an unspoken agoraphobia that threw them together. By not acknowledging this, they could only seek their relief in the mirror of each other. Their acrobatic fantasies and their suicidal plunges faithfully mimic the anxieties of society at large. But they can offer no way out.

The agoraphobe is said to overcome his panic when accompanied by a friend. But when his place in the social constellation is remapped and he is found to be the secret sharer in a *ménage à trois*, then perhaps the roles are reversed. Now, the agoraphobe is the strange friend suddenly a few steps ahead. He assumes the role of leading *psychopompos*. He shows the followers timely openings unnoticed before. The man in the street, relieved of the phantasmagoria of shop windows and the cinema of passing vehicles, attends to surfaces, textures, slopes and their co-efficients of friction. As in ancient tomb paintings, and in Botticelli's *La Primavera*, the leader carries a stick. If the one following feels that he is moving as if in a trance, or that he is blindfolded, it is all the better. In the blinding, as he becomes in touch with his surroundings, he measures space differently.

ARCHWAY

To sum up, two Kafkaesque speculations. One relates to a speculative piece of building devised by the writer himself. The other is my own guess about the nature of the fascination Milena Jesenska held for him. When fused, they seemed to produce a walking architecture, a dependent structure, which, if nothing else, delivers us to the next part of *Repressed Spaces*.

First, the serpentine structure Kafka once proposed building across Prague's Old Town Square, a space which, in his *Description of a Struggle*, assumes a disturbingly alien character:

> Today a southwest wind is blowing. The air in the square is agitated. The tip of the Town Hall tower describes small circles . . . What noise! All the window-panes are kicking up a row and the lamp-posts are bending like bamboo. The coat of

St Mary on the column bulges outward and the stormy wind tears at it. Does no one see it? The ladies and gentlemen, who should be walking on the stones, are floating. When the wind draws breath, they stop, say a few words to one another and bow in greeting, but when the wind pushes again, they cannot resist it and they all lift their feet simultaneously. Although they have to hold on to their hats, there is amusement in their eyes, as if the weather were mild. Only I am afraid.[199]

This is already an uncanny evocation of the agoraphobic scene. The agent of incipient panic, the wind, gives a Munch-like warp and animation to normally statuesque things. But the wind is also erotic, threatening to sweep away top-hats and veils of reserve. The wind unbalances, but instead of offering a genuine cure for the agoraphobia it produces, it provides a placebo – the fantasy cure of flight. Kafka's own response to his own fear is altogether more down to earth: 'If one builds such large squares only out of arrogance, why not also build a stone railing that could lead through the square.'[200] Indeed: why not? Such a structure would attract people to it, like iron filings to a magnet. It would be the monumental equivalent of the theatre's Dionysiac troupe winding through the city. It would signify the original function of the agora, which is to gather a crowd and drive it forward.

The first impression that Milena Jesenska made on Kafka was not of 'any particular of your appearance', but 'only the way you walked between the little tables as you left the cafe, your figure, your dress'.[201] It seems that Milena's way of walking was something exceptional, a spiritual gift as well as a phenomenon of physical grace. At the time Kafka knew her, in the full beauty and freedom of her youth,

> the most striking thing about her was her gait; it was never vulgar, she never swayed her hips. That lovely rhythmic gait seemed to cost her no effort at all, she seemed unaware of it. It was not walking, it was gliding to and fro. You couldn't help seeing how spontaneous it was; her movements were not so much 'graceful' as fluid and immaterial.[202]

In short, 'Milena did not walk through life with a sure, firm step. She glided.'[203]

It is still shocking to learn what Kafka did not live to see – the tragic consequences of Milena's marriage to Jaromir Krejcar and her pregnancy in 1929. As a result of septicaemia, she became a cripple, forced at first to hobble round on crutches. 'I couldn't have imagined,' she wrote afterwards, 'not even in my dreams – that I'd ever have a stiff leg.'[204] In her dreams, she moved as before, the embodiment of a security of being which even the most degrading of circumstances could not petrify. When, much later, Margarete Buber-Neumann met Milena on the narrow concentration-camp street at Ravensbruck, Buber-Neumann 'wanted nothing more than to . . . fall back into the prescribed "exercise" rhythm. In years of imprisonment I had adapted to these herd movements.'[205] But Milena was different – 'she ignored the grumbling all around us and prolonged our amenities as much as possible.' Here, Buber-Neumann knew, 'was an unbroken spirit, a free woman in the midst of the insulted and injured'.[206]

The nature of Milena's freedom emerges by implication in a letter Kafka wrote to her:

> . . . the fact is that between this day-world and the 'half hour in bed' that you once spoke of contemptuously as 'men's business' there's an abyss that I can't bridge, probably because I don't want to. The other side is an affair of the night, utterly and in every sense an affair of the night; on this side lies the world I possess, and now you want me to jump across, to leap into the night and take possession of it again.[207]

But in Milena's easy passage from one instantaneously held pose to the next, Kafka's self-inhibiting either–or logic was not so much transcended as sidestepped: 'The existential will of the I flows to the Thou with complete intimacy. It does not need a bridge, which separates just as it connects.'[208]

Transposed back to the urban realm, this mobility of spirit suggests an altogether different kind of architectural form. Superimposed on Kafka's thin wall, the movement-form of Milena yields a rolling outline not dissimilar to the repeated arches of an arcade. Inherently a multiplicity and a repetition, the arcade's form mocks the existential 'Can one take possession of anything again? Wouldn't that be to lose it?'[209] The appeal of the arcade resides precisely in the fact the parts run together to form a *Gestalt* of movement that is inherently stable. The arcades associated with the ancient agora ran uninterruptedly, Camillo Sitte remarked: 'their whole effect is based on continuity, for only by it can the succession of arches become a larger enough unity to create an impact'.[210] If, however, the arcade is regularly cut, it becomes merely an appendage to a building block. Its repeated units add up to nothing. It has no overall coherence.

A related distinction informs Benjamin's Arcades Project (or *Passagen-Werk*). In *One Way Street*, Benjamin places his discussion of dreams (and its critique of Surrealism) inside the Palais-Royal. Margaret Cohen explains the significance of this:

> The eighteenth-century Palais-Royal is constructed somewhat differently from the nineteenth-century arcades dear to [the author of *The Paris Peasant*, Louis] Aragon. While in the nineteenth-century arcades the buildings open onto another interior hall, in the eighteenth century arcades the buildings open onto the street.[211]

As a result, the more recent arcades have to be lit 'by various forms of half-light', a situation which Benjamin associates with the descent of a 'dream-sleep over Europe' or collective phantasmagoria.[212] The 'mental delusion' thus engendered in turn infects architectural practice, especially when it assumes the role of social engineer. Fourier's *phalanstère*, for instance, 'is a city made from arcades. [But here] the construction of the engineer takes on a phantasmagorical character'.[213]

A true arcade establishes the many in the one, and the one in the many. It does not fragment this primary relation, substituting for it the ersatz production of look-alike commodities, which, in the mirror of consumption, reveal the narcissism of their origin. An architecture that redeems agoraphobia is, in this sense, allegorical, making space for the other; an arcade makes space for many others. As Benjamin noted (in Cohen's words),

> the etymology of allegory implying the possibility of redemption contrasts with the etymology of phantasmagoria, allegory's demonic doppelganger. Constructed from *phantasma* and *agoreuein* instead of *allos* and *agoreuein*, [phantasmagoria] substitutes ghosts for the *allos* signifying allegory's transcendence.[214]

Occupying the marketplace, like false desires, these ghosts exclude other forms of traffic.

Reinserting the agoraphobe's historical experience into this analysis softens the dialectic, blurring the distinction between ghost and other. It suggests a more finely stepped relationship between somatic, psychological and spiritual perceptions of our inner-outer environment. In this, the traces of human movement need not trail away into ghostliness. Urban forms, instead of petrifying movement in the interests of commodity-driven traffic, realign themselves as stitched ways, pleated hems and permeable borders marking timely gaps.

2 driving

According to the most up-to-date investigations, the unconscious is a sort of cognitive ghetto – a home for homeless thoughts. Alas, many thoughts are now homesick.

KARL KRAUS [1]

RING-ROAD

After the rather triumphal conclusion to the previous chapter, returning to Freud may come as a disappointment. Readers, like planners, want to get on. But if Freud taught us anything, it is that there is no getting on without going back. There is no intention, though, of plunging deeply into the labyrinth of Freud's psychoanalytic theory, or of attempting to survey all of the suburban roads radiating over the last century from the central citadel of his thought.

Martin Freud reported that his father's luncheon breaks used to include 'a walk which nearly always took in the full circle of the Ringstrasse'.[2] If Vienna's old inner city, formerly enclosed by walls but from the 1860s progressively girded by the Ringstrasse's great polyhedron, corresponds to Freud's many-layered intellectual processes, and if the suburbs outside the Ringstrasse signify their migration, transformation and resettlement elsewhere, then our approach will be to steer a course between the two, following rather more modestly in his footsteps.

The argument for this approach has already been stated. Freud's psychoanalytic theory sprang in part at least from an attempt to relieve his own agoraphobia. In his 'confession of a lingering fear of crossing open places' can be found 'the hidden missing link between his primarily psychological interests and his later occupation with the neuroses'.[3] In the light of agoraphobia's modern history, the interest of this lies not in Freud's neurosis, but in his concealment of it. The concealment seems to have been of two kinds. On the one hand, any possibility that his fear might have had an environmental origin is discounted. On the other, within Freud's own psychological theory, agoraphobia never came to play a significant part.

Psychoanalysis, Freud once remarked, was 'accustomed to divine secret and concealed things from despised or unnoticed features, from the rubbish-heap, as it were, of our observations'.[4] Rilke's hopping man, navigating by way of trifling obstacles and near-invisible objects that others overlook, shares this preoccupation. In this sense, the agoraphobe probes the unconscious of the street just as the analyst uncovers the unconscious associative pathways of the mind. It seems, though, that, in that psychological journey, Freud, at least, care-fully avoided reading the signposts indicating agoraphobia.

Exploring the repressed spaces of Freud's personal and intel-lectual formation puts what might be called psychoanalysis's spatial prehistory back into the picture. More to the point, it suggests that, almost in spite of itself, Freud's interpretation of dreams was, in reality, an allegory of late nineteenth- and early twentieth-century urban anxieties. Far more deeply and empathetically than writers who explicitly addressed the agoraphobia of modern life, Freud implicitly displayed its reality – and this while all the time professing a theory which, more than ever, cut off the development of the ego from any environmental history outside the family's own Ringstrasse, the Oedipal complex.

Perhaps, as Benjamin thought, one can only talk of such matters allegorically.[5] But the allegory puts them out in the marketplace, while, in contrast, as Kraus indicated, consigning 'the unsayable spot' to the fine and private place of the unconscious is to put it back in the ghetto.

SPEED BUMPS

As we're on Vienna's Ringstrasse, let's stay there.

If the inner city was dominated architecturally by symbols of imperial and ecclesiastical authority, the construction of this

84

monumentally scaled, circular road 'celebrated in architecture the triumph of the constitutional *Recht* over imperial *Macht*, of secular culture over religious faith'.[6] It was a celebration of the bourgeoisie that eschewed principles of subordination or primacy:

> The Ringstrasse designers virtually inverted Baroque proce-dure, using the buildings to magnify horizontal space. They organised all the elements in relation to a central broad avenue or corso, without architectonic containment and without visible destination. The street, polyhedral in shape, is literally the only element in the vast complex that leads an independent life, unsubordinated to any other spatial entity. Where a Baroque planner would have sought to join suburb and city – to organise vast vistas oriented toward the central, monumental features – the plan adopted in 1859, with few exceptions, suppressed the vistas in favour of stress on the circular flow. Thus the Ring cut the old centre off from the new suburbs.[7]

No wonder Camillo Sitte hated it: 'For pedestrians such a place is truly hazardous.' Even when a small safety island ('on which a beautiful slender gas light rises like a lighthouse amidst the stormy waves of the ocean of vehicles') was placed in the middle of the road, 'crossing the street [was] advisable only for alert persons; the old and the frail will always by preference take a long detour in order to avoid it.'[8] But if Sitte's attitude towards the Ringstrasse followed logically from his urban design principles, the same cannot be said for Freud. Why would a closet agoraphobe deliberately seek out the place where panic was most likely to overcome him? Why expose himself to danger? One reason might be, as Martin Freud supposed, that there were 'no motor-cars and the crossings were much safer then than they must be now [in the 1950s, when he wrote his memoir]'.[9] Even so, there would have been an abundance of horse-drawn vehicles. Another reason might have been that, despite Sitte's animus, the Ringstrasse was a rather pleasant place: Martin recalled that the Freuds' governess regularly took the children to its public parks.

Yet, 'other dangers lurked'. As the Emperor retained the right to dissolve the parliament, relations between autocracy and democracy, which felt equally insecure, regularly reached a stalemate. Whenever this happened, and the parliament was dissolved, the university and the parliament (both on the Freud children's daily exercise route) were likely to erupt in violence. Once, the children 'found [themselves] between the rioters and some charging dragoons [and] narrowly escaped being trampled down, perambulator and all, under the hooves of the cavalry'.[10] But the principal feature of Sigmund Freud's walks was not their scenery but their style:

> these [did not] take the form of leisurely promenades designed to enjoy the beauty of the Ringstrasse and its flowering trees in springtime. My father marched at terrific speed. The Italian bersaglieri are celebrated for the speed of their marching: when during my travels I saw these highly decorative soldiers tearing along, it occurred to me that each one of them marched like Sigmund Freud.[11]

Others attest to Freud's *speed*. His biographer Ernest Jones said that Freud's 'high-speed military pacing' left most of the younger men who tried to keep up with him 'breathless'.[12] Gathering these ambulatory anecdotes together, the American writer Samuel Rosenberg likens Freud to the biblical Joshua, who by compassing the walls of Jericho seven times brought about its utter destruction. Rosenberg speculates that Freud's

> unvarying route counterclockwise round and round the now-vanished walls [they were destroyed in 1945] of the city he hated and loved . . . past the government and Imperial buildings and churches which reminded him as he raced along of their bitter antagonism to him as a Jew, iconoclast, and ruthless exposer of their inner emotional secrets,[13]

expressed his unconscious desire to penetrate and take his 'Rome'. Rosenberg supports this reading by reference to Freud's well-known empathy with the Romans' great enemy, Hannibal. Freud's 'compulsive encirclements of Vienna's vanished walls' were in part 'a reenactment of Hannibal's long, unsuccessful encirclements of the walls of Rome'.[14]

Further, his reinterpretation of Freud's 'Myops' dream persuades Rosenberg that 'Rome was, to Freud, a Vienna "displaced-downwards".'[15] The conscious repression of the aggression he felt towards the city in which he lived reappeared in the unconscious disguised and displaced. In analysing the 'Myops' dream, Freud himself stated that 'Rome' stood in for another city known to him, and the yoking in the dream of 'Rome' and 'Siena' (obviously rhyming with 'Vienna' – although, of course, not in German) is sufficient for Rosenberg to conclude that the true focus of Freud's anxieties was Vienna, both the professional and cultural temptation it represented, and the historical challenge it symbolized, embodied in an ever-present, if rarely-spoken, anti-Semitism.[16]

Employing the same dream logic it deconstructs, Rosenberg's argument can hardly be refuted. Circumstantially, it is plausible, although whether his ingenious symbol-sleuthing is needed to show what Freud himself knew quite consciously – that, as an upwardly mobile professional Jew in Vienna, Freud's position was always tinged with insecurity, and his person vulnerable to racist slur – is debatable. But more serious limitations of Rosenberg's symbolic topography lie elsewhere.

First, he internalizes the psychoanalytic orthodoxy that the origins of pathology lie in the libidinal and aggressive impulses of the child. On this model, aggression is a sign of neurosis, and, as Morris Eagle put it, there is 'a striking and persistent blindness towards the aggressive and sexual behaviour of adults towards children'.[17] Hence, Rosenberg does not entertain the possibility that the alleged focus of Freud's aggression, 'Vienna', was, *in reality*, an emotionally and physically violent place to be.

Second, focusing on the *drive* behind Freud's speed, Rosenberg discounts the significance of the conscious, proprioceptive control Freud exercised over his own movement.

In *The Interpretation of Dreams*, Freud 'secured the bridge' from his own 'neurosis to the larger continent of general pathology and psychology'.[18] Reik's figure of speech gives the impression that Freud's intellectual breakthrough was also a break *out*. Publishing an original contribution to mental science, Freud eased his agonizing sense of loneliness. But, in another sense, Reik's image is back to front. Professionally, Freud may have been coming out. His theory, though, was travelling in the other direction, from the outer to the inner world. In Freud's interpretation, dreams were the distorted expression of internal processes. The references they contained to the external world were secondary. What counted was the evidence they provided of the turbulent and conflictual life of the unconscious, that 'seething cauldron' of instinctual drives, as he called it.[19] The primary source of conflict, and incipient neurosis, was now located in the libidinal and aggressive instincts of the child. The vicissitudes of a person's biography could fan or quell the flames of incipient conflict, but they could neither spark them nor wholly put them out.

In short, Freud's psychoanalysis rested on the same 'belief that the outside world of things is unreal' to which Richard Sennett attributes the 'bland, neutralising spaces' of the contemporary city.[20] In this logic, a neurosis or phobia originating in *a fear of open spaces* was unthinkable. If the reality of the external world was secondary to what was going on intra-psychically, it could only be comprehended as a displaced anxiety. And once agoraphobia was internalized, it was inevitable that its symptoms should be interpreted as the displaced expressions of unconscious process. Thus Freud in *The Interpretation of Dreams*:

> It is instructive to consider . . . the significance of a hysterical phobia or an agoraphobia. Let us suppose that a neurotic patient is unable to cross the street alone – a condition which we rightly regard as a 'symptom'. If we remove this symptom by compelling him to carry out the act of which he believes

himself incapable, the consequence will be an attack of anxiety; and indeed the occurrence of an anxiety-attack in the street is often the precipitating cause of the onset of an agoraphobia. We see, therefore, that the symptom has been constructed to avoid an outbreak of anxiety; the phobia is erected like a frontier fortification against the anxiety.[21]

Agoraphobia was really only a disguised anxiety. This was the term's first existential downgrade. It suffered a second one in Freud's 1916–17 lecture, 'Anxiety', where he first differentiated between 'realistic' and 'neurotic' anxiety. On the basis of the material I have presented, one might think that agoraphobia was an exemplary 'realistic anxiety', or 'reaction to the perception of an external danger', connected with 'the flight instinct' and the desire of self-preservation.[22] Not according to Freud, who placed it among the 'neurotic' anxieties and, what's more, classified it as the third, least important of these. 'A general apprehensiveness, a kind of freely floating anxiety which is ready to attach itself to any idea that is in any way suitable' or a phobia 'bound psychically, and attached to particular objects or situations'[23] – these may be exaggerated, but they are, according to Freud, at least intelligible. But what are we to make of 'a third group of phobias, which is quite beyond our comprehension'? For instance, 'when a strong, grown-up man is unable owing to anxiety to walk along a street or cross a square in his own familiar home-town'.[24]

By this time, agoraphobia had ceased to have any external referent. 'People,' Freud wrote, 'whose whole existence is restricted by agoraphobia may be entirely free from pessimistic expectant anxiety'[25] – which is code for saying that their behaviour has no basis in reality. To drive home the point: while the second kind of phobia 'seem[s] to have been present from the first', 'agoraphobia and railway phobia – are demonstrably acquired at a fairly mature age' and 'make their appearance rather as eccentricities or whims'.[26] For a theory that locates the origin of hysterical symptoms in the going underground of an original, unemployable libido, a repression belonging to the sufferer's earliest sexual history, the late onset of agoraphobia is another nail in its clinical coffin. It is a curious fact that almost all, if not all, of Freud's patients (including 'Dora', 'Miss Lucy R', 'Little Hans' and the 'nineteen-year-old girl', not to mention two of his thinly disguised autobiographical dreamers, discussed in his correspondence with Fliess) *initially presented symptoms of agoraphobia*. Yet in every case, Freud's first step was to deny the reality of their feelings and to insist that they disguised a deeper, sexually rooted anxiety, which the interpretation of dreams would uncover.

As Freud's theorizing hardened in an effort to achieve internal consistency, agoraphobia was removed ever further from the agora of daily life. In time, he abandoned the position presented in the 'Anxiety' lecture, that neurotic anxiety 'was merely transformed libido'.[27] Rather, 'it was anxiety which produced repression and not, as I formerly believed, repression which produces anxiety.'[28] In this case, the distinction between realistic anxiety caused by an external danger and neurotic anxiety caused by sexual excitation could be given up. The fundamental determinant of anxiety was now said to be 'the occurrence of a traumatic situation', whether external or internal, and the resulting sense of helplessness: 'the majority of phobias go back to an anxiety . . . felt by the ego in regard to the demands of the libido.'[29]

Hence, agoraphobia, Freud remarked in the 1930s (at the same time observing that it was 'a subject that has been less thoroughly studied'), 'seems to be [the ego's] fear of sexual temptation – a fear which, after all, must be connected in its origins with the fear of castration'.[30] 'The agoraphobic patient,' he now explained,

> imposes a restriction on [a person's] ego so as to escape a certain instinctual danger – namely, the danger of giving way to his erotic desires. For if he did so the danger of being castrated, or some similar danger, would once more be conjured up as it was in his childhood. I may cite as an instance the case of a young man who became agoraphobic because he was afraid of

yielding to the solicitations of prostitutes and of contracting syphilitic infection from them as a punishment.[31]

Freud gave another instance: 'An agoraphobic patient may be able to walk in the street provided he is accompanied, like a small child, by someone he knows and trusts.'[32] Or he might 'go out alone provided he remains within a certain distance of his own house and does not go to places which are not familiar to him or where people do not know him'.[33] With unusual lack of qualification, Freud then commented: 'The phobia of being alone is unambiguous in its meaning: it is, ultimately, an endeavour to avoid the temptation to indulge in solitary masturbation.'[34] The inhibitions the ego imposes on itself of being accompanied or staying close to home are 'symptoms'. Anxiety results when these inhibiting conditions are violated.[35]

What does it matter if these last two 'patients' are, in fact, disguised portraits of Freud himself?[36] Isn't the vastly ramified theory of psychoanalysis proof of the fact that he took seriously the injunction 'Physician, heal yourself'? Perhaps. But what is in dispute is the destructive character of his self-help. Suppose, Freud writes in his 1933 lecture,

> that the agoraphobic patient is invariably afraid of feelings of temptation that are aroused in him by meeting people in the street. In his phobia he brings about a displacement and henceforward is afraid of an external situation. What he gains by this is that he thinks he will be able to protect himself better in that way. One can save oneself from external danger by flight; fleeing from an internal danger is a difficult enterprise.[37]

In this – the apotheosis of the belief that the outside world of things is unreal – the person who resists Freud's interpretation of dreams is guilty of an *internal agoraphobia*. Pretending to be afraid of the modern city is a lame excuse for not daring to step over the kerb into the *via regia* of dreams that leads to the raging open spaces of the unconscious and the moving chaos of their traffic.

RAILWAY STATION

Freud's association of agoraphobia with 'railway phobia' in his 'Anxiety' lecture has more to it than meets the eye. While he distanced himself as far as possible from agoraphobia, he *did* admit to an inhibition, connected with making railway journeys. According to Ernest Jones,

> What troubled [Freud] was his susceptibility to attacks of acute anxiety at the moment of embarking on the journey. There were even in later years some traces remaining from this old trouble; he always wanted to be in very good time when catching a train, and by good time he could mean half an hour beforehand.[38]

Jones emphasized that it was not travelling that Freud feared. On the contrary. Once aboard, and once the gravitational pull of Vienna had been escaped, he pursued his travels with a 'restless energy', determined to see everything, each night sleeping somewhere different.[39] Freud toured at the same manic pace at which he circulated the Ringstrasse. Still, it seemed to do him good: on his journeys, 'all the anxieties and moods of depression from which he suffered considerably in those years [the early 1880s] . . . quite vanished'.[40]

What then was the cause of Freud's 'acute anxiety'? Remembering his nervousness in stepping off the kerb into the road, we can guess that it was a movement inhibition associated with bridging the little abyss between the terra firma of the railway platform's edge and the step into the carriage – a little step always potentially slipping away. Such a step was to be taken, but it was not to be thought about. To think about that stride might be to freeze a movement figure in mid-flight. The step outwards, towards another, was a going beyond oneself which, if well timed, delivered the stepper to the spot where he wanted to be. To arrest this rhythmic arcade of unconscious poses in the photograph of thought was to risk falling into panic. Once one asked *how* one foot was placed in front of the other, walking might seem to be a kind of voluntary tottering, a willed and perilous plunge over the edge of one's self.

As the thoroughly pre-Freudian Eduard von Hartmann explained in his *Philosophy of the Unconscious*,

> The intuitive leaps the space to be traversed at a bound; the discursive takes several steps; the space measured is in both cases precisely the same, but the time required for the purpose is different. Each putting of the foot to the ground forms a point of rest, a station, consisting of cerebral vibrations which produce a conscious idea, and for that purpose need time . . . The leaping or stepping itself, on the other hand, is in both cases something momentary, timeless, because empirically falling into the Unconscious; the process proper is thus always unconscious; the difference is only whether, between the conscious stations for halting, greater or lesser tracts be traversed.[41]

Full consciousness, von Hartmann said in effect, is bipedal. To stand in one place, and to understand where one is, involves reasoning: but to get there requires mobilizing a will of which we remain unconscious. The will is the other leg on which we stand, the ground of the ground we occupy.

Needless to say, writers on Freud's railway phobia have not considered such things; instead, they have accepted his own psycho-analytic interpretation. This has not prevented them from unearthing valuable biographical material, throwing light on environmental (social and historical) factors, which might well have contributed to a sense of ontological insecurity. But the archaeological derivation of the ego and its discontents from a series of psychic strata going back to earliest infancy prevents this obvious leap from being taken. Later in life, Freud rationalized his 'railway phobia', his fear of being too late to get on the train and of being left behind, as 'a poverty, or rather a hunger phobia, arising out of my infantile gluttony and called up by the circumstance that my wife had no dowry (of which I am proud)'.[42] Even though this explanation seems whimsical in the extreme, its spirit, if not its letter, has been largely accepted.

As I say, this has not been without biographical spin-offs. Noting that in his correspondence with Fliess, Freud referred to his 'railway phobia' and 'traces it to infantile sources, i.e. the actual loss by migration of a "prehistoric" childhood milieu which had combined life in the Moravian countryside, relative economic safety, and of course, mother and Kinderfrau', Erik Erikson elaborated:

> That the Kinderfrau's mediation between Freud's Jewish milieu and the devoutly Catholic environment had made a deep impression can be seen again from the fact that Freud locates the beginnings of his phobia at age three, when on 'migrating' with his mother, he had in the railroad station of Breslau seen the first gas jets: 'which reminded me of souls burning in Hell'.[43]

Presumably, the three year old Freud was not acquainted with Dante. But from here, Erikson's account spirals inwards:

> It was on the same trip that he remembers having seen his mother 'in nudam' – maybe a somewhat impractical assumption considering Victorian travel, but highly significant for the Oedipal implications of the theme of unveiling Nature.[44]

The Bernfelds also drew together material on Freud's earliest years in Freiberg, 150 miles north-east of Vienna in what is now the Czech Republic. They modified Erikson's image of a prehistoric arcadia. On the contrary, Freud's family were fully heir to the curse of the wandering Jew. By the 1850s, businesses in Freiberg were suffering from the joint effects of industrialization and inflation. Jacob Freud was obliged to move out. If the infant Freud suffered trauma at this time, it was not because of a loss (which in any case could only be grasped in the sequel), but because of his first exposure to mechanized traffic: 'After a long trip by horse-drawn conveyance, he got his first sight of a railway; and, after a ride of many hours, he found himself divorced for good from the beloved home, the pastures, hills and forests of Freiberg.'[45] The Bernfelds placed the migration in the context of post-revolutionary Czech anti-German, anti-Semitic feeling, a pattern of pogroms going back to the expulsion of Jacob's forebears from Cologne in the fourteenth century and their subsequent wanderings to Lithuania, Poland and Moravia.

I am not content with this. Anyone who has missed another person at a railway station will be aware of a painful paradox. At a railway station, meeting seems to be guaranteed. From a great distance, the other's arrival is predestined. According to the schedule, she arrives at this precise time. But the same logic dictates that there is no time to wait. In the event that there is the slightest deviation to one side or other of that ideal instant of meeting, then all is lost. The promised plenitude of lovers meeting transforms itself into an immense and dwarfing void, which no amount of running hither and thither can reclaim.

The railway train and the railway station seem to transcend von Hartmann's bipedal consciousness. At a station, you can see motion slowly coming to a halt; studying the flanks of a railway engine, you can see stillness beginning to slide away. But isn't this a nightmare, when the category of waiting is eliminated, and the timeliness of the encounter no longer counts?

LOW GEAR

Whether or not Freud fantasized that he was a second Joshua or another Hannibal, there is a simple explanation for his high-speed marches round the Ringstrasse: bearing in mind his fear of open spaces, he was practising a self-help desensitization therapy.

Maureen McHugh gives a late twentieth-century example of this therapy's application to a woman who was apparently afraid of going shopping:

> . . . the agoraphobe may first be escorted to the store but not go in. This is followed by several trips in which she goes in and walks through increasing portions of the store quickly and

without purchase. The desensitisation is built up until she can shop alone under normal or even crowded conditions.[46]

Only in America, perhaps, could a return to health be identified with a renewed appetite for conspicuous consumption! Feminist sociologist Gillian Brown has argued that 'agoraphobia epitomises the plight of the individual in a market economy ... we might say that this disorder can be considered, to a certain degree, as a rejection of the commodification of public space made available exclusively for purposes of consumption.'[47] In this case, McHugh's patient has not been cured, simply brainwashed.

Be that as it may, by a self-conscious act of will, Freud overcame what he perceived to be a weakness. Perhaps it was the weakness that Otto Wagner had diagnosed: his 'metropolitan man suffered from only one pathological lack: the need for direction. In his fast-moving world of time and motion, what Wagner called "painful uncertainty" was all too easily felt.' Wagner's solution – the Ringstrasse was a case in point – was to overcome it 'by providing defined lines of movement'.[48] In this case, Freud had self-consciously internalized the urban planner's injunction. In advance of Le Corbusier, he had concluded that the proper behavioural analogue of his determination to realize his professional and intellectual goals was walking, erectly and swiftly, in straight lines. His speed was the escape velocity the imperial ego always needed to overcome its inertia.

To overcome his space anxiety, Freud confronted it full on. He went out of his way to expose himself to anxiety-making situations, in the hope that, by dealing with his anxiety, he could immunize himself against it in future. His enthusiasm for mountaineering seems to illustrate this. Martin Freud reported with admiration his father's solo ascent of the Dachstein in the Alt-Aussee, probably in 1891:

> the southerly route that father took is usually attempted only by experienced climbers, or at least with a guide. The way leads over a wall of steep rocks. There are iron foot-rests,

ladders and steel ropes to make the ascent less difficult in good weather, but when these are covered with ice and snow, they become a hindrance rather than a help to the climber. To climb the Dachstein from the south side, one had to have great powers of perseverance, to be free of vertigo, and to be strong and steady with hand and foot. In a word, that ascent over rocks and ice demanded courage of a high order.[49]

Martin felt that his father failed to grasp the subtleties of mountaineering. He attributed this lack of appreciation for 'the rigour of the game', and for his beginner's unduly 'optimistic attitude of mind towards snowbridges, towards hidden crevasses in glaciers, to exposed ravines upon which rocks can crash and towards shrubs growing out from steep rock faces,'[50] to the fact that his father took up climbing rather late in life. Martin himself had started when he was only eight. But perhaps Freud's inattention to details, his urge to get on, was of a piece with the furious pace he kept up in the Ringstrasse. In the mountains, he confronted his agoraphobic vertigo in a heightened form, but this only produced in him a greater resolution than ever to control and subdue it.

Circumstantial support for this interpretation can perhaps be found in the short story 'In the Mountains' by the late nineteenth-century Polish novelist Boleslaw Prus. Prus was an agoraphobia sufferer, and his tale of a man who cures himself of his vertigo by exposing himself to it is undoubtedly autobiographical. The vertigo-sufferer in the story is a 'German' but, just as Rilke's hopping man communicates his symptoms to the author, so Prus's narrator finds himself imitating the other:

> Once, when I forgot for a moment that I was in the mountains, I had the impression that I was standing on a plain that suddenly tilted under my feet; at one end it rose right into the sky, while the other end sloped away into the bowels of the earth. My head began to spin, and to prevent myself from stumbling I seized the arm of the German . . . Symptomatically the German interprets this gesture of panic as a sign of strength designed to encourage *him*![51]

They climb to their goal, then turn to begin the descent, whereupon mist engulfs them, blotting the vast spaces that surround them from view. The party is aware of a precipice below, but can no longer fix its exact position. The climbers therefore come to a standstill and decide to wait for the mist to lift. The cocooning mist does not comfort the German: unable to see actual vast spaces, he imagines them everywhere, claustrophobically bearing down on him. He runs into the mist and throws himself over the edge. Instead of killing himself, as he expects, the vertigo-sufferer falls a few feet onto rocks. He emerges from the mist onto a new path. Finding that his panic has gone, he calls up to his companions, who follow him down. Back at their hotel, the would-be suicide turns out to be cured of his fear of heights: 'He even joined a mountain-climbing club, and recently I've seen his name on the list of those climbers who have conquered the highest peaks.'[52]

There is no exact parallel between this and Freud's progress in the Alps. And yet two anecdotes Martin Freud tells suggest the emotional and physical cost of staying upright, balanced, and of holding one's place. On one occasion, climbing a near perpendicular meadow above the village of Koenigsee, Freud lost his footing and began falling backwards. Instead of allowing himself to slither down, 'much to our admiration, father achieved a beautifully co-ordinated movement of his body which produced a back somersault, like a diver leaving a springboard'. Freud was in his forties when this occurred. He came out of the somersault and 'landed safely on his feet'.[53]

The other event occurred on a road near the summer spa resort of Reichenhall. A group of locals who had been shadowing the party during the day 'began shouting anti-Semitic abuse'. Freud behaved with great courage. 'Keeping to the middle of the road, [he] marched towards the hostile crowd [which numbered about ten men, "armed with sticks and umbrellas"]', then, 'swinging his stick, [he] charged the hostile crowd, which gave way before him and promptly dispersed, allowing him a free passage.'[54]

Martin remembered 'these crusaders in racial hatred' 55 years later; his father, he said, never once referred to the incident. Yet, while superficially different, both events represented confrontations for which Freud *was always prepared*. Nowhere was it harder to place one foot in front of the other than on a steep mountain slope. Freud was coiled like a tense spring: when the unlooked-for crisis occurred, that energy released itself. In the beauty of his backward somersault, in embracing a timeliness that did not obey the law of the railway timetable, he overcame the abyss, transforming it into a harmonious gap. What's more, he achieved this prodigious feat on an incline where no acrobat would dare to perform. In the same way, years of striding blindly forward prepared him for driving a wedge through the crowd. The Ringstrasse, although apparently empty, was, in his fancy, filled with obstacles to progress, which only an energy – considerably greater than that of the athlete who lifts a huge weight once a day – and a marvellous self-control could vanquish.

SLOW DOWN

The image of Freud marching round the Ringstrasse is a partial one. There were day walks, but there were also night walks. If the day walks round the Ringstrasse ran on rails, as it were, keeping to the same route and the same timetable, the night walks tended to run off the rails. As Hanns Sachs, his disciple, put it:

> In spite of his sedentary life, Freud was an indefatigable walker, and the way home was extended to long promenades through the silent streets. (Vienna, except for a few nightspots, went to bed before eleven.) On these promenades the subjects that had been debated at [our] meetings, and many others, were discussed and reexamined . . . We learned how it happened that he was progressing restlessly, never coming to a standstill . . . I learned in these nightly hours many things about the 'via regia to the understanding of the Unconscious,' as Freud called it, which I had not been able to get out of his book.[55]

Sachs added: 'In the relaxed mood of these nightly promenades Freud indulged more freely than at other times in his habit of illustrating a difficult point with a story. When he found in his rich treasure of anecdotes one that answered the purpose, he did not care if it was not "quite nice".'[56]

Parallels have often been drawn between the place where Freud lived and worked and aspects of his life and ideas. For instance, Sachs wrote of Freud's Berggasse address:

> The street deserved its name (Hill Street), since a part of it was, even for the uneven ground of Vienna, exceptionally steep. As often happens in old cities, the two ends of the street belonged to different worlds. It started at the Tandelmarket, Vienna's historic flea market, and ended at the Votivkirche, a modern Gothic cathedral, which dominated one of the most notable ornamental squares of Vienna, flanked by the university and other public buildings.[57]

If we interpret this topography symbolically, Freud might be said to have lived between two agoras, the crowded agora of the instincts and the lonely modern one of the spirit. In a similar way, Rosenberg speculates that the Berggasse, 'once a rural path . . . a steep, sloping lane', is the 'arena' of the so-called 'Hagen–Siegfried' dream, which Jung dreamt at the time of his traumatic split with Freud:

> In his account of that Freudicidal nightmare Jung refers to his place of ambush as a 'narrow path' at the 'crest of a mountain', and as a 'precipitous slope'. These dream-exaggerated images match perfectly those associated with Vienna's (Freud's) *Berggasse* or *mountain lane*.[58]

This is symbolic overkill. It is the reductive outcome of Freud's suggestion that 'the frequency with which buildings, localities and landscapes are employed as symbolic representations of the body, in particular (with constant reiteration) of the genitals would certainly deserve a comprehensive study.'[59] Here, I agree with Gaston Bachelard.

A curfew on metaphorical explanations is overdue.[60] Freud's night-time walks, for instance, were not a form of ambulatory automatism, unconsciously beating the bounds of the unconscious. They were highly self-conscious, and orchestrated, images of a different route to knowledge. They improvised a process. They were map-making exercises. Anna Bernays recalls,

> During the Franco-Prussian war of 1870 the fourteen-year-old Sigmund had a large map on his writing desk and followed the campaigns by means of small flags. While he did this, he lectured to me and my sister Rose about the war in general and the importance of the various moves of the combatants.[61]

This habit continued into Freud's professional practice:

> He had a great zest for details in associations and dreams. When names of places were mentioned he would go into the library and ask to be shown the place on the map, which he would then study. He had to understand thoroughly locations and relationships of houses and rooms, frequently asking that diagrams be drawn.[62]

The Romantic psychologist Gustav Theodor Fechner was one of very few commentators on dreams whom Freud deigned to quote in *The Interpretation of Dreams*. He liked Fechner's suggestion that waking and dreaming occurred, as it were, in two different places:

> a man may conduct a quite different life in town than in the country, and when passing from one of his residences to the other he can always come back again to the same coherent way of life; but it would be impossible for him to change his way of life while staying in the same place.[63]

Paraphrasing this – 'the psychical territory on which the dream process is played out is a different one' – Freud commented, 'It has been left to me to draw a crude map of it.'[64] Perhaps his drawing of the unconscious as a war zone of catastrophic impulses owed something to the Franco-Prussian War.

To return to Freud's night-time walks. They were not a tour of the symbolic topography of his life, nor even a study of the genitalia of buildings. Developing Gustav Fechner's suggestion, Freud explained that the journey from the town of the conscious to the 'country' could only occur *'via the preconscious'*,[65] whose terrain was characterized by a dense network of 'paths' or 'unconscious wishes'.[66] The beginning of the dream process, which occurs when the preconscious is 'aroused', is 'no doubt a simultaneous exploring of one path and another, a swinging of the excitation now this way and now that, until at last [the dream-wish] accumulates in the direction that is most opportune.'[67] In another passage, the route to the unconscious sources of emotion is likened to a mountain region where floods have cut off the major roads 'but where communications are still maintained over inconvenient and steep paths normally used only by the hunter.'[68] Its way is a 'zigzag journey',[69] a system of ramifying and converging lines with nodal points where two threads may flow together.[70]

Freud's late-night walks, in which he progressed restlessly, never coming to standstill, in which he looked for the *via regia* to the understanding of the Unconscious, were not symbolic at all: they were locomotory and topographical embodiments of preconscious (or subconscious) process. In these Viennese promenades, exploring the older, lower quarters of the city inside the royal high road of the Ringstrasse, whose labyrinthine night-time set of alleys, passages, area gates and stairways Arthur Schnitzler describes in *Traumnovelle* (1931), Freud developed something akin to Benjamin's 'art of straying'.[71]

DRIVE IN

Freud's night walks were akin to Benjamin's Parisian adventures, but by no means identical. If Benjamin's drifting brought him to the occupants of the small brothel in the rue de la Harpe, Freud's peregrinations were *evasive*. If it's true that he avoided the street because 'he was afraid of yielding to the solicitations of prostitutes',[72] then his late-night ambles must have been a form of desensitization therapy. Respectable Vienna may have been in bed by eleven, but not its

condemned to wander without shelter. The new territory of the unconscious is, after all, a place where previously outcast emotions can gather, where thoughts that were refugees in dreams can be given an identity and reintegrated within the greater community of Western ideas.

The prevalence of architectural metaphors in Freud's description of the psyche may illustrate this, as may his archaeological analogies. Rudolf Arnheim has suggested that the building parallel goes even deeper. He points out that, while Freud broke with older ideas of hereditarily defined psychic constitution, his conception of the Id surrounded by a protective Ego that mediates the self's relations with the outer world retains an ancient idea of the self as a sphere, enclosed and at a distance from its environment. Arnheim likens this passive and reactive conception of the self's place in the world to 'the basic perceptual pattern of figure and ground', tracing it back to the Milesian philosophers, especially Anaximander, who made a distinction 'between a geometrically shaped world, constituted of the four elements, and the boundless, limitless, undefined matter (*apeiron*) creating it and surrounding it'.[85]

Arnheim comments that the distinction between figure and ground produces 'an object, defined and more or less structured . . . set off against a separate ground, which is boundless, shapeless, homogeneous, secondary in importance, and often entirely ignored'.[86] This ignored ground corresponds to our environmental unconscious. But Arnheim also makes the point that this way of thinking was critical for the emergence of the Hippodamian grid. As the nineteenth-century urban designs all involved, in one form or another, the final triumph of rectilinear grid thinking, the plans of Haussmann, Wagner and Hobrecht did not simply embody the ideology of the imperial ego: they also repressed the ground, the boundless extension without which their figures could not be set off. Hence, the environmental unconscious producing agoraphobia also stemmed from the violence done to the lie of the land.

In this sense, Freud's static conception of individual and societal well-being doesn't depart much from Kant's. 'By the word people (*populus*) we mean a multitude of men assembled within a tract of land, insofar as they comprise a *whole*,'[87] Kant explains in his *Anthropology from a Pragmatic Point of View* (1798). The corollary is that anyone given to movement for its own sake must be deranged. Kant even identifies an illness known as 'crossing the line'.[88] The same principles apply to personal comportment. In instructions that might have been addressed to Freud, Kant allows the value of a daily constitutional. A walk clears the head after 'persistent pondering on one and the same subject'.[89] However, the distraction should, as it were, be purposeful. If a person goes for a walk, it is not in order to imitate the wanderer, that type who 'is useless to society, since he blindly follows his imagination in its free play';[90] it is to place a framing distance between himself and his thoughts so that they come more clearly into focus. The important thing is homecoming; the art consists in not getting lost, in learning 'to distract oneself without being distracted'.[91]

One begins to see the intellectual prejudice wrapped up in the 'wandering Jew' stereotype, one that Freud no doubt confronted at the outset of his career. Anthony Vidler reports that Charcot, for instance, cited as an instance of the vagabond

> the case of a Hungarian Jew who suffered from a 'manie des voyages' . . . as perhaps indicating the hereditary nature of this 'Israelite' disease: 'He is Israelite, you see it well, and the sole fact of his bizarre peregrinations presents itself to us as mentally submitted to the regimen of instincts'.[92]

But it went beyond this: after all, what was the ambition of the soul doctors, if not to cure the psychological equivalent of the wandering Jew symptom, hysteria? Hysteria, the argument went, was an illness of the wandering womb:

> the uterus had an ardent desire to create children. If the womb remained empty for too long after its owner's puberty, it became unhappy and angry and began to travel throughout the

body. In its wanderings it pressed against various bodily organs, creating 'hysterical' – that is, uterus-related – symptoms.[93]

In her study of Freud's treatment of 'Dora', Hannah Decker lays bare a systemic misogyny. But she also shows that the disgust a patriarchal culture incubated against women extended to those thought to associate with them. Woman – and her wandering womb proved the point – was considered to be 'so passive as to be unformed unless she became moulded by the subtle hand of a masterful, self-controlled man'.[94] Women were regarded as childlike. Popular iconography reinforced the learned medical opinion that women were the creatures of their instincts. The conventional art of the day, Decker notes,

> so frequently depicted women as scantily clad tree nymphs, dancing or sprawled on the ground that one would think the woods were truly full of them . . . the nymphs of the woods and streams sent the 'scientific' message that once women escaped from civilised man's rule, they reverted to their wild and sex-crazed nature.[95]

And, she adds, 'misogyny was linked with anti-Semitism. The satyrs and fauns – men who were part animals – with whom the nymphs caroused, were drawn like the caricatured Jews of cartoons: dark, hairy, and with long, curved noses.'[96]

In this cultural environment, to confess one's agoraphobia was tantamount to admitting one's Semitic identity. It aligned one with weaklings and wanderers. It was to behave effeminately. It was to reveal atavistic tendencies to vagabondage. But perhaps most threateningly, it was to mirror the late nineteenth-century nation-state's own unspoken desire to break out of its individual claustrophobia and collective isolation. The stereotyped Jew, coming from nowhere, both mirrored this desire and was its scapegoat. His wandering was both a source of envy and fear. He was both the demagogue working on the crowd's basest instincts and the witness to this who must be destroyed.

This is why his glance is always sly. It reveals to the Gentile his repressed desire. In *The Spell I* (1976), Hermann Broch's fable of fascist psychology, the Doctor puts it this way:

> the man whom we meet does not come from this or that region, he doesn't come from a space that has width and depth and height, yea, not even animals originate in such space, but man comes from much farther away than he himself knows, and the glance that emerges from his body betrays its origin in that inconceivable infinity of space in which both body and space are constantly being reborn and in which being is joined to being, so that man never again can live without infinity and fancies himself a traitor to ineffable eternity . . . when he is called upon to abandon and turn his back on the wanderer who, with his glance, has granted him a shimmer of his own innermost being.[97]

In Lyotard's view, the European is dimly aware of (and made anxious by) the fact that 'the Jews represent *something that Europe does not want to or cannot know anything about* . . . Europe is seized for an instant by the horror and terror of *confronting its own desire.*'[98] By relocating the wandering illness inside the collective psychic body, Freud *germanized* it. Alternatively, he reformulated the German-speaking unconscious as a *Volk* ghetto. Either way, the effect was to provide the anti-Semite with an alibi for his 'treachery'. Henceforth, it was the Jew-within whose homelessness he would care for. But by the same token, to be cured of his anxiety was also to be rid of 'the Jews'.

SHOPPING COMPLEX

Freud's agoraphobia stemmed from his consciousness of an environment whose name could never be spoken. It could not be named because it had done nothing, it had committed no crime. At the same time, it exercised a palpable, if indefinable, influence. Perhaps it was responsible for a sense of existential homelessness. Perhaps it better explained the 'general apprehensiveness, a kind of freely floating anxiety' which Freud attributed to the trauma of birth.[99] Such an agoraphobia was by no means the same as R. D. Laing's ontological insecurity. It possessed a definite historical character, a will if you like. In this sense, it oppressed the sufferer with a feeling of foreboding. It might make the long-term resident feel like a wanderer. It pursued the man in the street with strange fantasies. A sense of entrapment went with a sense of exposure. But nothing was actually said. And, if one had spoken one's fears, there was no-one to listen. Karl Kraus summed it up: 'Prussia: freedom of movement with the mouth taped shut. Austria: a padded cell where screaming is permitted.'[100]

If this account has any value, it should enable us to reinterpret Freud's interpretation of dreams. For example, it would suggest that the famous 'complex' from which Oedipus suffered is not to be found in that 'universal event in early childhood' (as Freud put it in an 1897 letter to Fliess) which he had himself experienced as 'being in love with my mother and jealous of my father',[101] but somewhere else. It's often been pointed out that, in order to make Sophocles' character fit his thesis, Freud greatly misrepresented his history. Robert Eisner has been particularly sarcastic about this. For instance, in psychoanalysis, 'forgetting is symptomatic of neurosis. But Oedipus never forgot, because he never knew, what the Freudian neurotic is supposed to have suppressed.'[102] Or, again, isn't Oedipus the one figure who doesn't suffer from an Oedipus complex? 'If Oedipus had had an Oedipus complex, he would have killed Polybus and married Merope.'[103]

Eisner thinks Freud manipulated the play out of pure self-interest. He interpreted Sophocles' trilogy (incorrectly) as a drama of fate. He had an investment in representing his own Oedipus complex as a discovery that entitled him to be regarded as one of the discoverer's of Nature's secrets. The logic of this is explained by Paul Ricoeur: 'Being honest with oneself coincides with grasping a universal drama.'[104] Then, as Eisner comments, 'Self-knowledge stiffened into oracular drama as the analysand stepped out of the shaky role of Oedipus the murderer and into that more secure one of Oedipus the mouthpiece of the gods.'[105] This train of thought had two consequences. The truth must lie in the past, and it needs a skilled interpreter to uncover it: but here, too, Freud misrepresented the classical tradition. 'By replacing the oracle and the prophet with the analyst, Freud reversed the direction of ancient prophecies, examining only the entrails of the past and neglecting the flight of the future.'[106]

Freud's unreliability as an interpreter of the classics is often taken as proof of the unscrupulousness of psychoanalytical appropriations of myth in general. But in this case at least, perhaps there was a more interesting motive. Freud may have been mistaken in attributing an Oedipus complex to Oedipus. There was, though, a neurosis that Freud *could* legitimately backdate to him:

> Oedipus, by his devotion to the search for the truth, was bound to be an exile. Incest provides the excuse why home can never be home to post-lapsarian man. He has asked the questions which, whether or not he ever gets the answers, make it impossible for him to remain a member of any society, for stability requires ignorance, native or self-imposed . . . Oedipus was doomed from his birth to wander across rocky and chaotic intervals between the secure walls of cities, the wild country that first received him. In a countryside ruled by the grudge and the vendetta, no act of murder could be more isolating and more dangerous than patricide.[107]

Doesn't this suggest the obvious, that Oedipus was a victim of *agoraphobia*? He was afraid of the marketplace and the abode of men. His fear of exposure originated in a violently imposed movement inhibition. Oedipus Swellfoot was a limper all his life. Exposed as a three-day-old babe on Mount Cithaeron, his ankles pierced and tied, his fate was to pass through the world shelterless and incapable of escape. This must have bred two things: a heroic determination to stand on his own feet and, alternating with this, an overwhelming need to cleave to a mothering ground, place or person. In this regard, Oedipus combines characteristics of both Balint's ocnophilic and philobatic types. Unable to escape, he experiences encounters with the other as unbearably claustrophobic. His lack of agility makes him vulnerable to fear. He is seized with a desire to break out of the situation, and yet feels rooted to the spot. He has the sensation of being driven by powers (instincts or fate) over which he has no control.

If Oedipus had lived in Vienna, he would have had a profound fear of the street. In particular, an ungovernable panic would have overcome him when he tried to step off the pavement's edge to take a tram, or off the platform to board a train. Once in those smoothly gliding interiors, however, he would have felt elation, a surging power and sense of release. Eisner has reconstructed the fatal meeting between Oedipus and Laius thus:

> Oedipus was travelling on foot; Laius was riding in a chariot, accompanied by an entourage and preceded by a herald – obviously a royal personage. The road was probably a rutted one, like most ancient Greek roads; only the wheel ruts, cut for axles of a standard size, were leveled, rather like railroad tracks in reverse. If two vehicles met head on, one of them would have to back up to a siding; clearly a traveler on foot should yield to one in a wagon or chariot. Oedipus did not.[108]

This may not have been pure intellectual pride. As a limper, Oedipus may have found it difficult to back up. In any case, limping was his key to Nature's secrets. It cannot be an accident that the riddle the Sphinx asks him – What goes first on four, then on two and finally on three legs? – refers to three modes of human locomotion which Oedipus, because of his disability, had personally experienced. The Sphinx plunges from her rock not least because, unmasked of her illusion of power, she, too, feels her loneliness and exposure.

Oedipus' knowledge of the world is agoraphobic. His familiarity with the rocky and chaotic intervals between the secure walls of cities contributes to his understanding of the city. As we shall see in the next chapter, the etymological constellation of which *agora* forms a part includes the *agros*, the wilderness where the shepherd goes with his flock. It is from the wilderness that the hunter returns, bringing what he has captured to the gathering place. Oedipus' knowledge of humanity stems from his infant exposure to the *agros*: and it is to shepherds that he applies when he seeks self-knowledge. It is these men, exiled from the cities of men, who enable him to retrace the path that leads him to his central position in the political life of Thebes.

Oedipus, as the encounter with the king proves, is afraid that he will kill men if exposed to them. He will find their nearness so threatening that he will not be able to control his desire to make space for himself. Like the destructive character, he has to remove all obstacles to progress. His fear of open places is a fear of yielding to this aggressive impulse – although that fear has historical roots in the traumatic fact that he was exposed in a shelterless place (by his own father and mother). Hence he keeps to himself, avoiding the 'street', staying indoors, a private place equivalent to the solitude of the wilderness. It is in these respects that Oedipus faithfully anticipates Freud. The parallels are close. For instance, Peter Rudnytsky has pointed out that Freud's 'discovery' of the Oedipal complex was associated with the analysis of two key patients, E. and 'Another man (who dares not go out in the street because of homicidal tendencies)'.[109] This latter reasoned that, if he was 'capable of wanting to push his own father over a precipice from the top of a mountain, [he] was not to be trusted to respect the rights of those less closely related to him; he was quite right to shut himself up in his room'.[110] Both of these patients were agoraphobic. According to Rudnytsky, they may or may not have existed, but were in any case pivotal doubles or alter-egos of Freud himself.

Freud not only repressed his own agoraphobia: he repressed the agoraphobia of the mythical figure with whom he chose to identify. Insisting that Oedipus was responsible for everything in his life and must learn to stand on his own two feet, Freud prepared the way for his own emergence from the shadow of his Jewish migrant home – Y. S. Feldman makes the point that, after all, Freud enjoyed a 'typically Jewish relationship' with his father, one which followed 'an archetype of the relations between immigrant Jewish fathers and their talented sons in modern times'.[111] And it wasn't Oedipal at all: 'All such sons have been, in a sense, father-slayers. But unlike the Primeval father of Freudian mythology, these Jewish fathers have been more than willing victims, eager to be slain.'[112] But the tactical value of Freud's interpretation was obvious. It gave him control over himself, and it gave him control over his patient, for the Freudian concept of the unconscious follows directly from his decision to 'ignore the striking fact that Laius, the father, ordered that the infant Oedipus be put to death'.[113]

Ignoring the family history, the external causes of distress, how can Oedipus' desires be explained except by supposing that they originated internally? But how can they be 'mental states' if Oedipus is unaware of them? To explain this, it is necessary to give a newly dynamic and autonomous role to the unconscious – Freud (1919): 'It is in the years of childhood between the ages of two and four that the congenital libidinal factors are first awakened by actual experiences and become attached to certain complexes.'[114] The unconscious by definition cannot be known directly – its existence, and its structure, are indicated in dreams. As Oedipus is now able to generate the history of his own neurosis out of himself, it follows that the contents of the unconscious must be historically the earliest, having been laid down when the infant was as yet incapable of reflection. This lends the unconscious an interesting character. Carrying it around like a life-support system, Oedipus can, in fact, stake out a history of his own. The unconscious is a dynamic psychic territory (of instincts) that is not derived from mother or father, even though it is pervaded by conflicting feelings towards them. It is 'congenital' and hence constitutional, not environmental, in origin.

By chaining Oedipus to a new past that is his own, the unconscious creates a new psychic space out of which he can generate himself. It is a myth of psychic autochthony that is played out. A new subject is born, his history defined and the tripartite structure of his self-consciousness more or less stabilized. But the ground slips further and further away, boundless, shapeless, ignored.

3 alighting

One of the universal laws of semantic change
is that all basic verbs easily end up with the
meaning 'fuck'.

RAIMO ANTTILA[1]

BACK WAY

Our attempt to keep up with Freud on the Ringstrasse fleshed out the proposition that, whatever else it is, agoraphobia is a movement inhibition. The movement inhibition originates in an intuition of the environmental unconscious. As that intuition is a historical one, the next step is perhaps another backward one. Although clinical descriptions of agoraphobia postdate the mid-Victorian era, the phenomenon itself is not necessarily an exclusively modern, metropolitan disease. Camillo Sitte thought that Roman and medieval architects and urban designers had consciously avoided large, exposed open spaces because they were well aware of the dangers of triggering space-fear. Wilhelm Worringer went much further, arguing that agoraphobia was the universal condition of primitive people – the march of civilization was, on his definition, the process of making oneself feel at home in the world and, through an empathetic identification with one's natural surroundings, the overcoming of agoraphobia.

However, these speculations had no historical foundation. As for Oedipus, one classical figure who undoubtedly manifested all the symptoms of agoraphobia, in his modern recension these symptoms are ignored. To escape, then, from this rather claustrophobic ring of self-reinforcing definitions, and to place agoraphobia on a more ample footing, it's worth looking at the ancient history of the term. That it might have such a history is implicit in the Greek provenance of the terms *agora* and *phobia*. Both deserve excavation, but, taking the broad sense of *phobia* as given (Greek *phobos* means 'fear' or 'dread' or 'antipathy towards'), I concentrate here on the first element.

The result of exploring the various connotations of the word *agora* is not to provide the modern condition with a genealogy. What this phenomenological approach does do, however, is to *normalize* the condition – not by Freud's method of annexing it to a history of the neuroses in general, but by showing that it was a dread with a real object. When the significations of the agora are sifted rather more finely, it also turns out that a fear of the agora is not simply to be upgraded to the category of a 'realistic anxiety'. It is a critical way of inhabiting the environment, one standing at a dissident angle to the orthodoxy which identifies stability (mental, political and architectural) with stasis. It signifies a mobile measure of environmental well-being, one predicated on a 'thick' description of the inside-outside space of many bodies interacting.

As might be expected, different ways of recovering the significance of the classical agora produce different agoras. Drawing on the ancient literary record, one naturally finds out about the agora as an assembly of people. The charming figure of the *agoraios*, or agora-loiterer, comes into focus. And it turns out that there are many kinds of agora, not simply one. Turning to the physical evidence from surviving (or archaeologically reconstructed) sites, it is the agora as a place of assembly that can be studied. But in gaining an insight into the unconscious associations the word may have carried, the best tool is probably etymology – especially as, in the case of *agora*, an excellent study is to hand in the form of Raimo Anttila's scholarly polemic, *Greek and Indo-European Etymology in Action* (2000).

The result of combining these approaches is the discovery that the movement inhibition, repeatedly invoked in earlier pages, is the disorder of a primary pose or movement figure. That figure is not the expression of an individual whim or eccentricity, but serves to define the dynamic character of the assembly. It combines the movement towards with the movement away, centripetal with centrifugal impulses. And this double movement is, in turn, proto-urban, suggesting the clearing and its relation to the wilderness.

This line of thought manages, among other things, to give back to the word *alighting* its double signification. As the clearing in which reason finds its voice, the agora has long been associated with enlightenment. But the place in which, through the power of allegorical speech to lay out ideas, individuals are fused into a politically self-conscious public is also the 'unsayable spot' where a foot alights by chance, perhaps, and, springing down, is relieved of its weight. When this happens, 'to light' is, as the dictionary indicates, both 'to provide a person with light to see the way' *and* 'to make lighter or more free in movement'.

CLOSED TO TRAFFIC

Agoraphobia was, for Sitte, an oxymoron. In his view, 'fear of the agora' was a contradiction in terms. The agora's distinguishing qualities were its sociability and homeliness. Why would anyone feel afraid there? The 'very new and modern ailment', agoraphobia, was, in this respect, misnamed. As an anxiety or discomfort experienced in traversing vast open places, the new nervous disorder was an *anti-agora* phobia, a panic associated with a new species of non-place. In any case, Sitte's purpose was to inculcate *agoraphilia* in town planners, by which he meant far more than a respect for old squares and winding streets. Sitte's object was to create in the mind of the urban designer the possibility of places produced, not according to compass, square and ruler, but through a synthesis of the building with plastic and graphic arts.

Modernist city theorists savaged Sitte's ideas – witness Le Corbusier dismissive reference to the pack-donkey's meanders – as naïvely backward-looking. In doing this, they ignored Sitte's historical self-awareness, as well as the forward-looking character of his programme. His aim was not to turn back the clock: noting that plazas in his day rarely harboured popular festivities or even markets, he commented, 'today not an open plaza but closed halls would be used for such purposes'.[2] This comment anticipated Benjamin's critique of the nineteenth-century arcades of Paris which, being closed off from the outdoors, encouraged a phantasmagoric existence. In a similar way, Sitte was a city-doctor, analyzing symptoms with a view to relieving them.

His rather Wagnerian vision of the synthetic *Gesamtwerk* may be dated, especially in its reliance on monumental effect, but his critique (in advance) of the psychological alienation produced by Brasilia-like conceptions of town planning continues to haunt us. In essence, what Sitte objected to in the new urban gigantism was the divorce of figure from ground – in the realm of psychology, Freud's image of the Id imprisoned inside the walls of the Ego had the same effect. As James Holston has reminded us, it is this divorce that characterizes Brasilia, where 'vast areas of continuous space *without exception* form the perceptual ground against which the solids of buildings emerge as sculptural figures',[3] and 'every building now vies to be recognised as a monument'.[4] In contrast, Holston identifies in Brazil's older colonial cities 'a structure of signification maintained over a very long period of time by professional education and practice in architecture'[5] – in effect restating Sitte's claim that the old architects were aware of the dangers of agoraphobia and consciously designed their cities to prevent it.

Holston's phrase applies to Sitte, who was primarily interested in the agora as a 'structure of signification'. Sitte was no architectural determinist. He understood perfectly well that public spaces created a sense of communal well-being when memories gathered there. It was not the size of the square that counted, but the richness of human associations it harboured. In this regard, the way to represent urban space correctly was not in plan but perspectively, and the rules of perspective, of convergence and divergence, were the same associative ones that operated in memory. When observed, in fact, these rules invert large and small:

> One naturally feels very cozy in small, old plazas, and only in our memory do they loom gigantic, because in our imagination

5 J. Buhlmann's 'ideal restoration' of the Athenian agora (marketplace), reproduced in Camillo Sitte's *Der Städte-Bau* (City Building, 1889).

that magnitude of the artistic effect takes the place of actual size. On our modern gigantic plaza, with their yawning emptiness and oppressive ennui, the inhabitants of snug old towns suffer attacks of this fashionable agoraphobia. On recollection, however, our image of these squares shrinks until only a tiny residue remains.[6]

In short, although Sitte's conception, and illustration, of the Greek agora and the Roman forum in *Der Städte-Bau* are, on his own admission, idealized, they are not superficial or adventitious. They partly represent the state of archaeological knowledge at the time, but they also reflect Sitte's programme: to prevent the ruin of the future by a study of ancient ruins. To disentangle the other agoras repressed in Sitte's idealizations is not only to enrich the history of a term, but to enlarge the scope of future design. For one thing, it might suggest a radically different kind of public art.

Sitte's ideal agora (illus. 5) is a conflation of at least four urban forms and venues. He would have known from Jacob Burckhardt's lectures, posthumously published in his two-volume *History of Greek Culture* (1898–1902), that the ancient Athenian agora changed function over time. If it began as a place of political assembly, coeval with the emergence of Athenian democracy, it soon developed into a marketplace, which, crowded with stalls, more resembled an 'Oriental *souk*' than Sitte's dream vision of porticoes, stairs and harmoniously disposed temples. Alluding to this corruption of function, Aristotle distinguished an agora for free men, where nothing might be bought, and where no farmer or labourer might enter except on command of the authorities, and another agora for the purpose of buying and selling.[7]

Sitte also presumed that the Greek agora and the Roman forum could be lumped together. The Forum Romanum and the excavations at Pompeii revealed the 'unusual quantity of columns, monuments, statues and other artistic treasures . . . lavished on this place . . . displayed in an orderly fashion, leaving the centre free so that one could survey the richness of them'[8] – plausible ancient support for his notion of the modern square as a *Gesamtwerk*. Less plausible, but driven by the same city-as-collective-artwork principle, was his assimilation of the Athenian agora to the Acropolis:

> There architecture, sculpture, and painting are united into an artistic synthesis [*Gesamtwerk*] that has the sublimity and grandeur of a great tragedy or a mighty symphony . . . The most elevated poetry and thought has found spatial embodiment here at this hallowed spot.[9]

What happens when these different, if functionally overlapping, venues are disentangled from one another? The first effect is to reveal the existence of different *speaking places*, we might say, different ways of moving the crowd. As an assembly of the people, the agora develops the gift of (public) speaking. The word *agoreusis* means 'speech' or 'oration' or 'proclamation'.[10] Early in its evolution in Athens, the agora changed function. Robert Flacelière noted that the political assemblies and dramatic festivals originally held in the agora were soon pushed out, retreating respectively to the Pnyx and the sanctuary of Dionysus. After this, 'only the market remained in situ at the *agora*', along with a few specialized, and intermittent, political functions: 'the members of the Council and the *prytaneis* used it as their meeting-place, and a Citizen Assembly could always be held there if occasion demanded'.[11]

When oratory migrated from the agora, what replaced it? One slightly radical answer might be: philosophy. Arriving too late to hear the orator Gorgias, Socrates excuses himself, saying that his companion, Chaerophon, is to blame – 'he compelled us to loiter in the market place'.[12] But Socrates' self-deprecation is ironic: the implication is that there is more to be learned by loitering in the marketplace than by listening to oratory. So what is to be gained there? In the *Laws*, Plato lays down the notion that 'the seller of any article in the market must never name two prices for his goods, but only one, and if he doesn't get it, he will (quite rightly) remove his wares without raising or lowering his price that day.'[13] Socrates applied the same principle to the purchase of truth. His effort was directed towards detecting fraud – when a man holds contradictory views of a concept, he is guilty, in effect, of presenting the idea at more than one price. Further, as in the marketplace, if the seller of an idea cannot convince the purchaser that the right value has been set on it, then he will have no choice but to withdraw it from the agora of discourse.

It seems that the agora attracted a particular type – the *agoraios*, the person who hangs around the marketplace. The verb *agorazo* means roughly 'to frequent the market', 'to buy in the market', 'to haunt the agora'. This type of person was specifically a product of this new social space. He was attached to the goings-on there. Aristophanes satirized him as the man eager for the latest news, gossip and anecdote.[14] He was a kind of *attached flâneur*. Even if he didn't actively take part in the business of buying and selling, he felt himself to be part of the urban scene. He was a drifter, but he drifted down well-established driftlanes. He could easily change mask and become a shopkeeper. He was like the pedlar and the North African street seller. He was the occupant of the café, and the one who leant against the post. An indication of the communal (non-alienated) nature of his presence is suggested by the fact that a particular part of the day (the forenoon) was set aside for frequenting the agora. Aristophanes may have disparaged the *agoraios*, but not Socrates. When he explained, 'I'm a lover of learning, and trees and open country won't teach me anything, whereas men in the town do,'[15] he presumably had the *agoraios* in mind. After all, Socrates was a philosophical *agoraios* himself.

Gossip, hearsay and rumour dominated the agora, and there went with them a repertoire of gestures, poses and habits of movement. The *agoraios* was a constitutional leaner. He was extravagant with his hand gestures. He was also a stroller, his gait seeming to be softly sprung, so that he took the uneven surface of the agora, its kerbs and drains, in his stride. By contrast, at the Pnyx, the crudely fashioned amphitheatre nearby, oratory dominated, also producing its actorly repertoire. Among these, if the conclusions of archaeologist Christopher Lyle Johnstone are to be believed, must have been a pose signifying the pretence of hearing:

> . . . the acoustical defects of the Pnyx in its first phase (i.e. during the fifth century) made it likely that speakers could not be adequately heard by a significant portion of their audience, and thus that our understanding of the role of oratory in Athenian public deliberation must be revised.[16]

Could it be that the Pnyx produced, in some listeners at least, a kind of auditory agoraphobia? A *polis* where few if any could hear what was being said, whose democracy was born of crisis, which was bent on imperial expansion, colonization and enslavement, which lurched from one political and military dysfunction to the next, and which harboured an intellectual and artistic culture without peer – why, it might have been Vienna or Musil's Kakania:

There was the parliament which made such vigorous use of its liberty that it was usually kept shut; but there was also the Emergency Powers Act by means of which it was possible to manage without parliament. And each time that everyone was just beginning to rejoice in absolutism, the Crown decreed that there must now be a return to parliamentary government.[17]

Socrates' critique of the over-wordy Sophists finds its modern counterpart in Wittgenstein's conviction 'that all that really matters in human life is precisely what . . . we must be silent about'.[18]

In proportion to the hollowness of the rhetoric, the orator affected uprightness. The verb *katagorein*, etymologically *kata* + *agora*, 'to speak in the assembly', means 'to accuse'. The orator stands tall as the agent of justice. His accusation is intended to bring about the fall of his opponent. In his commentary on the *Parmenides*, Heidegger maintains that the Latin word *falsum* is connected with the verb 'to fall'. This, after all, leads to a profound observation, that 'felling' brought about in this way creates, as it were, a low place (in contradistinction to the high place occupied by the feller). Once 'brought down', the 'dominated are not kept down, nor simply despised, but, rather . . . they themselves are permitted within the territory of command, to offer their services for the continuation of domination'.[19] These words, written in 1944, might be a reflection on the 'Jewish Question'. They also ponder the philosopher's own situation.

They also remind me that the modern father of agoraphobic reasoning, Descartes, borrowed his famous dictum from St Augustine. 'Cogito, ergo sum,' and the massive argument which depends from it, is a reworking of a passage from Augustine's *Civitas Dei* which begins 'Fallor, ergo sum':

> . . . for if I am deceived, I am. For he who is not, cannot be deceived; and if I am deceived, by this same token I am. And since I am if I am deceived, how am I deceived in believing that I am? for it is certain that I am if I am deceived.[20]

To speak in this agora is not to idle, drift and wander, but to stand rooted to the spot. As for that spot, it is arranged in tiers, stepped against slipping away. In this sense, Savinio's remark about Maupassant, that our fates are foreshadowed in our names, also applies to Descartes, whose title 'du Perron' meant 'a staircase or flight of steps'.[21]

DIVIDED ROAD

Other divisions open up in the agora when its character as a *place* of assembly falls under discussion. The antithetical positions adopted by the French cultural historian Henri Lefebvre in his *The Production of Space* (1974) and the American architectural historian Peter Zucker in his book *Town and Square: From the Agora to the Village Green* (1970) show this. They also illustrate the question mark that hangs over any attempt to treat the Roman forum and the Greek agora as variants on the same fundamental urban form. If Lefebvre makes the Greek agora a high point in civil design, regarding the Roman forum as at best an academic copy of it, Zucker reverses the hierarchy, treating the older agora as merely groping towards the unified conception of space apparent in Rome.

Thus Lefebvre attributes to the ancient Greeks a 'completely rational unity of form, function, and structure', at least as regards monumentality in the temple, stadium or agora.[22] He maintains that the design of the Greek temple showed that 'in its ancient Greek version, absolute space may contain nothing.'[23] He accepts a Heideggerian vision of the *polis* as a gathering of that absolute space:

> The founding image of Greek space was a space already fully formed and carefully populated; a space in which each focal point, whether that of each house or that of the *polis* as a whole, was ideally placed . . . At once means and end, at once knowledge and action, at once natural and political, this space was occupied by people and monuments. Its centre – the agora – served as focus, as gathering-place.[24]

128

Lefebvre contrasts the empty space of the agora with the Roman forum, in which Being had been shattered into a host of beings: 'The Roman Forum, by contrast, contains state monuments, the tribune, temples, rostra, and later a prison: it is a place occupied and filled by objects and things, and as such it stands in contradiction to the space of the Greeks.'[25]

Zucker takes a very different view. Acknowledging the growing cohesion of the agora's articulation, the way in which public buildings, temples around (and occasionally on) it, become 'anchored in some system of mutual reference, as are the stoas and porticoes', he nonetheless asserts:

> The shape of the free open space, the form of the three-dimensional void, was . . . not yet felt as absolute form but rather as a by-product . . . To the Greeks, space meant only a medium to define and set off the shaped volume – sculpture as well as the individual architectural structure.[26]

Reversing Lefebvre's genealogy, Zucker attributes the invention of absolute space to the Romans. They and they alone contributed to the history of city planning 'the feeling for the shape of the void space, for its artistic meaning, and for its modification by specific proportions and by a superhuman scale'.[27] Contradicting Lefebvre, he writes, '. . . this central area was much less interspersed with statues, altars, and shrines than it had been on the Greek agora'.[28]

Probably, these antithetical views cannot be reconciled. If clutter is associated with agoraphobia, then Lefebvre finds the Roman forum agoraphobic. Zucker would, on the same basis, find the Greek agora residually abstract – and thus, according to Worringer, also agoraphobic. Assuming a direct correlation between a society's built forms and its political institutions, the writers' assessments probably reflect their own different political leanings. More to the point here is the fact that the same assumption informs both accounts. Both Lefebvre and Zucker take it for granted that the genius of the agora/forum is to give spatial expression to a metaphysical sense of being, one that translates, in a social and physical sense, into a feeling of well-being. Being is the quality of 'absolute space'. In achieving this quality, the ancient builders fused intellectual and physical vision. The ancient Greeks, according to Richard Sennett, thought with their eyes. They could design their buildings and public spaces to express intellectual and moral values. By contrast, modern urban dwellers experience a tragic divorce between the complexly nuanced place they imagine inhabiting and the blandly soulless conglomeration of apartment blocks, motorways and shopping malls which in fact form their physical environment. Or, as Sennett summed it up, 'What once were the experiences of places appear now as floating mental operations.'[29]

For Zucker and Lefebvre, it is in the agora/forum that men first became fully present to themselves: in the presence of an architecturally instantiated Being, they felt for the first time that empathy with their surroundings which, Worringer states, differentiates Western culture from others.[30] The absolute space of the agora/forum was no Modernist void. Its harmonized emptiness disclosed the plenitude of Being. The kin of Pan, the demi-gods, the fauns and satyrs associated with the wilderness, retreated in the face of this all-seeing stare. They could not withstand its overpowering enlightenment. And with their rout and dispersal, panic also was banished from the public places of Athens and Rome. This is the cultural myth invested in the symbolic value attributed to the agora: that there, agoraphobia was categorized as unreal, a species of non-being, a pseudo-spirit.[31]

The difficulty with this conception is, though, obvious. It identifies Being with stasis. It implants a massive movement inhibition as the condition of civility. Its centrist, all-seeing gaze *looks down* on others and, freezing them like rabbits in a car's headlights, instantly subjugates or destroys them. It is not the neighbourly bipedal well-being of the *agoraios* that is celebrated here, but the estranged pinnacle-stance of the imperial ego, one that cannot abide the prospect of difference, except as a prelude to its enslavement. 'We could never recover the Greek past,' Sennett wrote, 'even if we wished and we would not wish to; their city was founded on massive slavery. But the clarity with which they could literally see the fullness of life raises at least the question of why we cannot see as fully.'[32] Perhaps, though, it raises another question: What kind of clarity is it that founds the fullness of life on a massive slavery?

TWO WAY

In a general sense, this question has already been answered. The vision associated with the upper agora is a conquering one. The agora idealized by Lefebvre, Zucker's forum, and Sennett's clarity of vision embodied in these places are the expressions of societies whose sense of unity rested on a successfully prosecuted policy of territorial expansion. The gathering together which the agora allowed and encouraged was the in-breath of a collective body whose out-breath was an expanding frontier of armies and navies, trailing in their conquering wake new trade routes, new ideas – and new stimulants to *pothos*, that type of *eros* which, at least in Alexander the Great's all-conquering soul, produced an irresistable desire to go on going beyond the horizon.[33]

In other words, rather than representing a state of Oneness or Being, the agora was the expression of a double movement, outwards and inwards. It was a moment of poise in a history of becoming. Its illusion of oneness was the outcome of a widened knowledge of the world's multiplicity. As Alexander's appeal to *pothos* indicates, this double movement depended on a motive force. The counterpoise to the inertia of the imperial ego was *eros*. Love mobilized empire. In this sense, every imperial adventure had its Helen, not just the siege of Troy.

A key moment in this history occurred when the orator Alcibiades stood up in the agora and argued for the conquest of Sicily. Thucydides reported that his words so inflamed the crowd that old and young alike were seized with an erotic passion to invade the island.[34] The agora was able to kindle this desire to *go beyond* because of the historical experience of the Athenians, who, during the second Persian invasion, had themselves suffered exile. Ousted from their city, becoming 'men without place, the Athenians severed in some way their connections with all the fixed things that the life of a city normally revolves around, that normally serve as its stable, conservative base'.[35] Forced to abandon their holy places, the abodes of their gods, and their ancestral graves, the Athenians displayed the greatest courage, but also 'a certain tincture of impiety' that 'might go beyond what is permitted to human courage. It is audacity; it is daring.'[36]

It has been suggested that the legend of Atlantis, which Plato retells in the *Timaeus*, is a fable about the folly of the Sicilian expedition. In Plato's telling, Atlantis is founded in the many, while the constitution of Athens is a unity: 'In the beginning . . . Atlantis was of the earth, and Poseidon, lord of the island, was a divinity of the soul.'[37] The doubleness or duality of this foundation is reflected in the fact that two springs (as opposed to Athens's one) rise in the island's centre: 'the structure of Atlantis is constituted by the play of *apeiron*, of non-identity'.[38] Atlantis, unlike Athens, is in a state of continuous becoming and expansion. The kings build bridges and open the land to the sea. They improve the plain by means of a grandiose system of canals. They provide themselves with a large army. They lay out in the centre of the island a monumental area complete with a palace, a sanctuary of Poseidon and even a horse-racing circuit, as one might expect on an island consecrated to that god. The next step is inevitable: 'Atlantis became an imperial power "which had rule over the whole island and several others, and over parts of the continent",'[39] finally launching overseas expeditions against Athens.

These expeditions proved to be the nemesis of Atlantis: defeated by the Athenians, the nation-state sank (in a night and a day) beneath the sea. But who is 'Atlantis' in this fable, who 'Athens'? In the catastrophic Sicilian expedition, Athens suffered a fate comparable to that of Atlantis. Consider what was needed to defeat Atlantis. In the story,

> Athens is triumphant. The city of Unity defeats the city that has allowed itself to be taken over by disunity and heterogeneity.

The waters close over Atlantis. Their absolute victory halts the advance of non-identity. But Athens loses her foundation in earth and becomes Atlantis.[40]

That is, the myth of Athenian Oneness, whose urban expression and microcosm is the agora, rests on a prior experience of the Many. And, of course, the constitution of Athens was double, being a joint foundation of Pallas Athene and Poseidon. If Athens became Atlantis, it was because Atlantis was always Athens, for we are told that, after the prehistoric city was washed away in a night of rain, 'the whole country [became] only a long promontory extending far into the sea away from the rest of the continent'.[41]

The Greek term *apeiron* recalls Arnheim's comparison of Freud's conception of the self's place in the world to the cast of thinking behind the emergence of the Greek colonial (or Hippodamian) grid. In both instances, a more or less defined object is made to stand out from a ground that is boundless and largely neglected.[42] Thucydides' account of the reaction to Alcibiades' speech, and Plato's Atlantis fable, enable us to say something about the nature of that neglect. The centralist myth of the agora's constitution does not simply ignore the multiplicity of the world's remainder: it seeks to repress the movement back and forth between the One and the Many. And, returning to Sennett's own admission, that clarity of intellectual vision went hand in hand with slavery, it means suppressing the history of the agora's fabrication, its physical construction and maintenance.

It would seem to be a matter of philosophical belief whether the 'absolute space' of the agora represents a presencing of Being, or whether it is what it looks like, a product of the destructive character's determination to clear away every obstacle. This is the ambiguity that a binary definition of the agora produces. Law courts, Montaigne once observed in connection with a case of disputed identity, are most prone to misjudgement because they are constituted to judge.[43] So it was with the agora: as a place of accusation, it left everyone vulnerable to accusation and misidentification. It meant that everyone could fall and be enslaved. Speculating that the first slaves were not born of slaves, but were most likely overpowered in brigandage or war, the early Christian author Dio Chrysostom commented that they would not only be justified in escaping from slavery, but would be very likely, if the occasion arose, to enslave their former masters: whence ' "at the flip of a shell", as the saying goes, their positions are completely reversed'.[44]

So the many, the slaves, are absent from the picture because their presence would threaten the illusion of unity: 'The slave made the social game feasible, not because he performed all the manual labour (that was never true) but because his condition as the anti-citizen, the utter foreigner, allowed citizen status to define itself.'[45] The practical founders of urban space were the unacknowledged founders of its history: '. . . for the slave-holding city a time without slaves is outside of history; it is in a pre-civic *earlier* or a post-civic *later* and even, to a great extent, before or after civilization itself.'[46] This forest of foreigners, then, was not absent from the agora. It was just that their comings and goings represented a blind spot in the Athenian's intellectual vision.

In this sense, the characterization of the agora as a unified space perpetuates a form of cultural agoraphobia. As its unity depends on banishing the many from it, the resulting space looks rather empty. It might, in any visitor sensitive to the labour that must have gone into its construction, induce a sense of dread, a foreboding of violent expulsion. It is in order to forestall that anxiety that the architectural metaphysicians have pretended that the void is metaphysically peopled, filled with Being.

In any case, it is clear that the modern counterpart of the slave is the agoraphobe, the double of the man in the street. This is proved by the fact that he is also invisible.

BEWARE OF CARS

Actually, there is rather more direct evidence of ancient agoraphobia, but it is mythic rather than historical. It derives from the two best-known stories associated with the voyage of the Argo: Jason and the Golden Fleece, and Theseus and the Minotaur.[47] To judge from later literary treatments of these stories, ancient dramatists and poets may have known nothing about agoraphobia, but they readily understood *argophobia*.

Euripides' *Medea* famously opens with the Nurse's lament. Reflecting on the fateful chain of events that has brought her mistress to her present plight, the Nurse imagines how things might have turned out differently. She has no doubt about the event that forged the first link in the chain. Medea's fate would have been avoided if the Argo had never set sail. It did not simply produce family tragedies in Colchis and (now) in Corinth. Nor was it simply the vessel of a repetition of these events in Crete and Athens. The effect of the Argo's voyage was to bring about the fall of the old tribal organization of society. This Seneca makes plain when, in his own version of Medea's story, he has his Chorus lament: 'Rightly the laws of nature fenced the world off. / But Argo tore down / fences, made the world one.' The Argo inaugurated imperialism – 'Boundaries have all moved; cities now build walls / in lands just discovered. // Nothing is left where it once was: the world is / open to travel.'[48]

By displacing and amalgamating formerly separate peoples, the Argo also inaugurated Karl Popper's open society. Centred on the agora, it is mythically founded in these two adventures. The challenges Theseus and Jason face overseas, and whose legacy they bring home, in the form of an inexorable chain of misfortune, are symptoms of the anxieties associated with the establishment of a new social and political order. To gain the Fleece, Jason must traverse the wide open space of the wilderness, the *agros* of wild beasts, soldiers and shepherds. His task is to tame the beasts, to plough the land and to subdue the crowd. What is his reaction? Unprotected, in open country, he is seized by panic. Where can he hide from the bulls, where in this open plain can he stalk the warriors? The earth from which they will spring is untamed. The ground protests against his footsteps. Medea comes to the rescue. With her spells, Jason yokes the bulls, ploughs the land

and sows it with dragon's teeth. On her advice, he throws a rock into the midst of the giants. They spring up like corn in the furrows and slaughter one another.

The terrain of Theseus's adventure is, of course, entirely different. To find, attack and kill the Minotaur, he must plunge underground, into the cloying darkness of the Labyrinth. He, too, is helpless. On the Labyrinth's threshold, would he not have felt 'a panic fear of bring alone in a closed space, a sensation of being able to go neither forward nor back'?[49] But Ariadne came to his aid, giving him her magic ball of thread, capable of rolling along, 'diminishing as it went and making, with devious turns and twists, for the innermost recess where the Minotaur was lodged'.[50] Thus armed, the hero could contain his panic. Like Samuel Beckett's nameless prisoner, he might even see in it his destiny:

> Spite of the dark he does not grope his way, arms outstretched, hands agape and the feet held back just before the ground. With the result he must often, namely at every turn, strike against the walls that hem his path, against the right-hand when he turns left, the left-hand when he turns right, now with his foot, now with the crown of his head.

There are places where the walls almost meet, but he will squeeze through. Who knows? 'All may yet grow light, at any moment, first dimly and then – how can one say? – then more and more, till all is flooded with light, the way, the ground, the walls, the vault, without his being one whit the wiser.'[51]

With their pharmocopoeias, Medea and Ariadne minister respectively to their lovers' agoraphobia and claustrophobia, and, if we allow that Jason and Theseus are doubles, as Jason himself recognizes in Apollonius of Rhodes' poem,[52] then the psychological legacy of the voyage is clear. On the death of the King of Attica, Plutarch wrote, 'Theseus conceived a wonderful and far-reaching plan, which was nothing less than to concentrate the inhabitants of Attica into a capital. In this way he transformed them into one people belonging to one city.'[53] On top of this, 'there was to be a democracy,' and, to this end, he 'proceeded to abolish the town halls, council chambers, and magistracies in the various districts. To replace them he built a single town-hall and senate house for the whole community on the site of the present Acropolis.'[54] In other words, as the Argo had made the world one, so Theseus, internalizing this process, made Attica one, in the process confronting the same psycho-spatial challenges.

The conclusion of this is that Athenian democracy, and the place of its birth, the agora, sprang from a repressed history of scattering and destruction. Its unity was constructed like Freud's Ego. But the historical landscape that sprawled beyond it, and crawled up to its walls, was haunted by the ghosts of agora-claustrophobia.

FOOTPATH CLOSED

The fiction 'the man in the street' implies a hat: any sentence beginning 'Every schoolboy knows' implies a knowledge of Latin. As both literary sub-species have largely died out, the name Mettius Curtius probably needs to be explained. Mettius Curtius was the self-sacrificing youth who, in 362 BC, threw himself into an abyss that had opened up in the Roman Forum, thus satisfying the soothsayers' declaration that the hole could only be filled up by 'throwing into it Rome's greatest treasure'[55] I mention Mettius Curtius here for this reason: if the agora was a coming together born of a violent spreading apart, then it's reasonable to expect evidences of that original violence to survive *within* the agora/forum, as well as in the mayhem caused along foreign shores. It is possible that a thoughtful citizen who contemplated the collective willpower embodied in that public space might well feel giddy. But, if he felt that the ground was slipping from under his feet, and that what had seemed solid was now melting into air, it would not necessarily have been a symptom of inner conflict. It might refer to the violence done to the lie of the land.

Say that the new public space of imperial democracy internalized the double-movement out of which it had emerged. If gathering together, or assembly, preserved a memory of spreading and splitting apart, this dynamic was likely to be reproduced internally. It can be imagined that the space of gathering would have harboured within it opposite forces, tending to rend it asunder, producing a double crowd and a floor cracking up like drought-stricken soil. In this case, the sensations of Westphal's patients begin to make more sense. One of them compared his feeling to that 'of a swimmer crossing a lake, uncertain whether he will be able to reach the other side'.[56] On the basis of his observations of agoraphobic patients, a certain Dr Cordes summarized the dominant idea: 'You can't get across, you will fall, you are paralysed.'[57] This could be interpreted as a reaction to a space without measure. Where the sensation of movement is negated by such spatial qualities as immensity, symmetry and lack of orientation, panic attends the act of putting one foot in front of another: it is like walking up a stairway of sand if, taking a step, you feel you are getting nowhere at all. You might feel like a patient described by Edmund Bergler: 'she felt as though everything about her were swaying and turning round and the ground seemed made of rubber. Sometimes she had the sensation of being aboard a steamer upon stormy seas. "I reel about as if drunk."'[58]

This is one sensation, but an agoraphobe might feel exactly the opposite. He might feel that the ground before him was so fissured that any advance through it was impossible. The everyday equivalent of this sensation is the familiar one associated with avoiding the cracks in the pavement or the gaps between paving flags. Those cracks and gaps could multiply and ramify to the point where there was nowhere one could safely put one's foot. The agoraphobe who said he could not reach the other side was not necessarily complaining about the distance: he may have felt that a 'gulf' was opening up between him and his destination. In this case, to advance into that melting, fissuring field was to ensure his own destruction, to plunge in and drown.

Mettius Curtius' legend not only attests to the collective experience of such tensions, it also roots them in a return of the repressed environmental unconscious. The 'lie of the land', which makes its protesting presence felt when the clearing of the agora/ forum occurs, is not a semi-mystical psycho-topographical category. It is the realm of the many that the new order seeks to unify and enslave. It has its own economy of exchange, its own politics and erotics. The cultural and historical medium of its survey is the social foot. It is that 'momentary kinetic coincidence [that] enables us to understand the lie of the land as a process of enclosure, in the "open sense" of giving to the elements a form which does not rupture their dependence on their surroundings'.[59]

The ideological character of the exchange is reflected in the fact that two stories were told about Mettius Curtius' great leap. Both were related by the Roman grammarian Varro. In the first, already summarized,

> [in the Forum] the earth yawned open, and the matter was by decree of the senate referred to the haruspices; they gave the answer that the God of the Dead demanded the fulfilment of a forgotten vow, namely that the bravest citizen be sent down to him. Then a certain Curtius, a brave man, put on his war gear, mounted his horse, and turning away from the Temple of Concord, plunged into the gap, horse and all; upon which the place closed up, and gave his body a burial divinely approved, and left to his clan a lasting memorial.[60]

Mettius' behaviour finds an entirely different explanation in the second version of the legend. According to this,

> . . . in the Sabine War between Romulus and Tatius, a Sabine hero named Mettius Curtius, when Romulus with his men had charged down from higher ground and driven in the Sabines, got away into a swampy spot which at that time was in the Forum, before the sewers had been made, and escaped from there to his own men on the Capitoline.[61]

What was the 'forgotten vow' that the God of the Dead demanded should be fulfilled? Possibly it was an undertaking to sacrifice to the *genii loci*, whose homes the construction of the Forum had violated. In particular, perhaps, it was a call to appease the water spirit whose realm the Via Sacra traversed. In her book *Janus and the Bridge* (1961), Louise Holland emphasizes that, in its unenclosed, pre-Forum state, the Forum (Varro's 'swampy spot') could easily have accommodated a disappearance:

> we are not dealing with a brook brimming level with the meadow through which it runs, but with a deep gash dropping abruptly below reed and willow-covered banks, except where tributaries entered it . . . a Mettius Curtius indiscreet enough to try to gallop across such unpromising terrain might seem to have been swallowed, horse and all, as in the legend.[62]

Holland speculates that the sudden disappearance of Curtius 'might be a distorted reminiscence of the cleft through which the brook ran in its natural state, a hard thing for Romans of historical times to visualise across the pavement of the Forum'.[63]

Bridging the brook involved a significant engineering process. More importantly, it involved a religious transgression. Making the point that running water was among Mediterranean peoples, and perhaps universally, recognized as strong magic, Holland adds, 'The power of a stream to neutralise or wash away the magical power of those who cross it has important consequences in Roman ritual.'[64] The ritual associated with crossing the living body of the Forum brook centred, Holland argues, on the figure of Janus. According to her, the original Janus, said to have been established by Numa Pompilius, was a water crossing. Specifically, it was the crossing which traversed the Forum brook running south-west into the Tiber, thus dividing the Quirinal and Capitoline hills to the north-west from the Viminal, Esquiline, Palatine, Caelian and Aventine hills to the south and east, thereby unifying 'the double city': 'The Forum brook cut straight across the Sacred Way where priests and magistrates passed back and forth upon the business of the gods, from the arx and the Comitium on one side, to the Regia and the temple of Vesta on the other.'[65]

Holland speculates further that the importance of the Janus ritual was directly proportional to the supposed potency of the topography at that place:

> The gap closed by the Sacra Via represents the point of weakness characteristic of the old confluence sites. It may be that the name of the road . . . has some relation to its boundary function, for the 'flow' of traffic on a road makes it according to folk superstition a line of cleavage similar to that set up by the flow of water in a perennial stream. Ghosts and witches find in it a similar obstacle, and an intersection of roads has an uncanny character analogous to that of a confluence of rivers. Processions or races along the road would increase its effectiveness.[66]

In any case, the primary meaning of Janus was not the one familiar to us, that of gateway guardian. It centred on a crossing which carried a road: 'through a religious ceremony in which an augur played an official part, [the Janus on the Forum brook] had become a "locus effatus", a place over which the proper formula had been spoken to separate it with the god's consent from the rest of the earth as a templum.'[67] That is to say, 'where the Sacred Way met the strong magic of running water, the Janus formed an inaugurated crossing point . . . a privileged bridge where priests and magistrates could cross freely under the sanction of auspices taken once for all at the initial dedication.'[68]

What has this to do with our topic? First, Holland's account of Janus suggests how the two stories Varro told might be reconciled. The Roman version depends on repressing the lie of the land. As a consequence of that repression, the subsidence of the Forum, perhaps undermined by seepage, caused panic. The opening in the ground was classified as an 'abyss' and characterized as a chaotic gulf inhabited by turbulent, instinctual forces. The sequel is obvious: only an equal and opposite act of violence could make it close up again. Mettius Curtius, however, as the other story indicates, possessed a knowledge of the double character of the ground, of its upper and lower levels, and of its mingling of elements. The Romans could pretend that the closing up of the Forum (which left no trace of Mettius behind, and hence concealed even the act of disappearance) confirmed their hold on the land, but Mettius knew better. He escaped to take command of forces that resisted the Romans' imperial progress. In taking military control of the resistant Sabines, he asserted the emptiness of the political formulas being worked out in the Forum.

In the context of our meditation on agoraphobia as a movement inhibition, however, a second point is more important. As a hero who operated under the protection of Janus, Mettius Curtius embodied a different conception of movement. Instead of assimilating himself to the linear, imperial traffic moving back and forth across the bridge, Mettius remembered the cross-flowing water underneath. He knew the warp of lengthwise movement, but he also understood the weft of crosswise movement. Holland makes the persuasive point that the law attributed to Numa, that the Janus should be *opened* in time of war, closed in peacetime – a regulation that makes no sense so long as Janus is identified with a door or gate – refers to Janus as a waterway. In times of war, when the enemy's access to the city must be prevented, 'the approaches were cut, and the god of the crossing poured his waters across the road to hinder the enemy.' In time of peace, when the bridge was restored, 'this would close the Janus'.[69]

Thus in this early usage, the word *Janus* referred to a two-faced concept. It meant the crossing of the river both as a bridge over flowing water, and as water crossing over an inaugurated place. But when the Forum was consolidated, and the dominance of the Via Sacra over the Forum brook seemed to be assured, the original weaving of the place was forgotten, and the crosswise movement inhibited. It seems reasonable to relate this history of violent 'closure' to certain symptoms of modern agoraphobia. Why is Kafka's character so afraid of 'the traffic over the bridge' that he plunges to his death? Why does the 'imprisoned malady' which afflicts Rilke's hopping walker finally break out on the bridge? On the bridge, the height is a monument to what lies buried underneath, a cross-flow. It could be the stream that Maupassant's characters haunt. It could be the ghosts of that flow. In any case, it is no surprise that there, more than anywhere, 'something like a natural force' breaks over them.

SUBWAY

So much for historical and mythic surmise: what of the 'unconscious associations' of the word *agora* revealed to us by etymology? Perhaps, first, the significance of this allusion to Freud's own way of interpreting dreams needs to be brought out. At the same time, this is an opportunity, before plunging into our own ancient word analysis, to say something about method, not for the sake of pedantry, but to set the tone for the next chapter, in which the poetics of agoraphobia are discussed.

Reading Freud's interpretation of his dreams is sometimes to have the impression that a parody is being attempted. The discourse being parodied is nineteenth-century philology with its tendency to etymological speculation. Verbal free associationism reveals, according to Freud, the genealogy of repressed desires. It displays a rule-governed unconscious. The means of association are poetic. Homophones and puns unlock hidden semantic connections. Etymology operated similarly, and the attempt to bring reason to the search for semantic lines of descent, through the identification of roots, finds an exact analogy in Freud's assumption that verbal displacements can be sheeted back to a verbal form.[70] Linguistically, Freud's unconscious obeys Ernst Haeckel's embryological dictum. Ontogeny repeats phylogeny in this realm too.

Another parallel: Freud's followers liked to call the process of analysis 'anamnesis'.[71] The analysand recovered her lost memories. The dreamwork was shown to be a one-way street leading down and back into the realm of infantile sexuality. The recovery of this hidden stratum of instinctual drives was held to constitute knowledge. But this was (or should have been) only a curious variant on the 'hermeneutic task' which characterizes the interpretation of the past in general. As Anttila has commented, 'hermeneutics and semiosis share the same structure and goal, we also find that anamnesis is the essence in both, or creation of knowledge, whether "new" or re-enacted.'[72]

The question is – and it's a question of poetics – What are the rules of Freud's verbal associations? Are the patterns he discerned evidence of repressed wishes, or are they intrinsic to the structure of new meanings in language? If the latter, then his internalization of the poetic process represents another kind of agoraphobia or retreat from the marketplace of exchange. The apparent ingenuity of his interpretations represents, in relation to the rich historical texture of the language he used, a kind of autism or withdrawal. An ersatz economy of meaning production was substituted for the historical realm in which the hermeneutic task normally operated.

I don't know whether Freud ever read Fritz Mauthner's *Sprach und Psychologie* (1901), although he was no doubt familiar with Max Müller's researches into Indo-European languages and emphasis on the interdependence of thinking and speaking. Mauthner's central thesis was that both language and thinking were metaphorical, and he defined metaphor as 'thought association', believing, as Gershom Weiler put it, that 'metaphor and association are concepts which, under certain circumstances, can be substituted for each other'.[73] Thus, 'if we want to highlight the fact that the act of comparison is unusual, we shall refer to it as metaphorical. If we want to direct attention to the psychological mechanism involved, we shall speak of association'.[74]

This pretty closely glosses Freud's 'method', and the degree of metaphoricity, the unusualness of the leap, becomes in Freud an index of the powerful conflict between the repressed wish and the forces repressing it. Freud presented his data as a detective following up clues. He was a cryptographer telling a story about a crime. But suppose that he was actually giving us a stream of consciousness, a mirror to the unthinkable currents of life running in the street. Then, his discourse was agoraphobic and revealing in a different way. For instance, it might unconsciously have enslaved those very voices it intended to unchain. A slave, wrote Euripides, is he who cannot speak. But if he can only speak when the words he uses are shown to be anchored in instincts that lie outside his control, then he has gained little: his anamnesis only inhibits further his freedom of thought.

Of course, the criticism of Freud's method applies even more forcibly to most etymology – a category of thought which, 50 years ago, Ernst Curtius influentially dismissed as poetic license or else foolish and trifling.[75] Even 'scientific' etymology, as recommended by Otto Jespersen, entirely ignores the world of the word, in which it operates metaphorically, punningly and even, perhaps, by the ironic inversion of meaning.[76] This is the pleasure of Anttila's book, mentioned before. Recognizing the low esteem in which etymological studies are held, he proposes to reinvigorate them by discovering the historical relations of words in the semantic clusters they form. Inverting the usual search for the pure root, he focuses instead on the subsequent, exploded state of the linguistic universe. The cultural resonances of words are indicated by the size – the historical longevity, geographical spread and semantic fertility – of the semantic cluster to which they belong.

In this view, words are no longer links in a chain, but nodal points in a spider's web. The elaborateness of the semantic constellation is not proof of some kind of historical self-censoring. It attests to language's capacity to act, and not simply, as happens in Freud's interpetations, to be acted upon.

DRIVEWAY

In Anttila's linguistic celestial chart, the term *agora* is a star in the 'gathering force' cluster.[77] This cluster belongs to the 'aggression and substance' nebula.[78] (The entire universe, by the way, is an expression of a proto-Indo-European root, *Ag, meaning 'action' in general.[79]) Once fixed in this way, there then, as Anttila remarks, 'seems to be no end' to the connotations of *agora*: there is 'assembly of the people, place of assembly, market-place', not to mention 'its rich derivatives in the meanings of the business of the agora, viz. public speaking, marketing, and selling'.[80] But we have met all of these meanings already. The question is whether an etymological enquiry can yield any information about the nature of the 'gathering' that occurs there.

Freud once remarked that there was no more urgent need in psychology than for a securely founded theory of the *drives* or instincts.[81] But this may be exactly what etymology delivers, as, according to Anttila, once we look into the background of *agora*, we find that the proto Indo-European *Ag means to 'drive, lead (particularly cattle)'.[82] By a natural extension of meaning, the term comes to name the path the driven herd takes, and paths or roads generally – 'and where such paths are the densest, we do get towns, *aguiai*'[83] – the scenario of certain early twentieth-century German 'street films' (illus. 6) might almost be derived from such an etymology. The idea of drawing a line not only suggests a path: in the context of establishing a permanent settlement, it might mean marking a boundary. The Greek *ago* 'is the term for constructing walls and digging ditches'.[84] This is interesting, as it redefines the agora as a dynamic process of gathering or driving together. But it is only one part of the story, one phase of the movement the term implies.

Within *agora*'s own constellation, there occurs a word that apparently bears an opposite sense. *Agros* originally meant 'countryside', even 'faraway places'. It is where animals may be driven. It implies pastoral rather than agricultural activity. It is untilled land, even wilderness, and is sharply contrasted with the camp, village or settlement. By extension, the term is applied to those who frequent such desert places – wild animals, soldiers and shepherds – those people whom Oedipus had to consult in order to find out about his origins. What possible connection can the untilled and forested wilderness have with the cultivated clearing of the agora? The answer is that they are both places associated with driving. An accelerated volume of traffic is common to both.

In this sense, an early Greek hunting term, *agra*, mediates between them. Referring to the hunt, to booty, or game, it covers the ideas of catching, seizing, grabbing, and comprehends the act of taking

6 A still from Paul Wegener and Carl Boese's 'street film', *Der Golem, wie er in die Welt kam* (1920).

and the thing taken.[85] Thus the dissipation of forces associated with hunting – which the Italian Renaissance master Paolo Uccello captured in his great painting – turns round to produce a convergence and an event: animals employed in the hunt are driven; the quarry is also driven, perhaps by beating the bushes: 'In a hunting-and-gathering situation the collection point is at the end of the activity, the prey is the goal.'[86] From this, it is a short step to the idea of the raid, and not only on the unconscious. A further short step produces the head raider, who must also be the leader of his community – a meaning attested by the Greek term *agerochos* meaning 'lordly', 'noble'.[87]

Agora and *agros* are linked by a shared idea of driving together, but so are many other words. Does anything in their semantic field suggest a dynamic relationship? Could the agora become at certain times wilderness-like? Is it imaginable that a lover of learning like Socrates could ever feel that trees and open country might teach him something? Anttila has suggested two ways in which this kind of enquiry might be pursued. One way is through a speculative reconstruction of the history of the people using the terms. The other involves asking what 'action' means. What is the fundamental condition of action which driving fulfils?

Taking the first approach, pre-Greek *aga* may have signified both a 'drive' and 'a driven group of people (*oikos*-size)'.[88] (A Germanic parallel is the word *drift*, meaning both 'hunt' and 'herd'.) Either way, there is a dynamic impression of a community forming, driven together by a commanding Driver. The primary meaning of Greek *agathos* is 'a quality of excellence pertaining to leading families', 'the drivers, the active ones, the achievers'[89] – 'Social action was *aga* action and the *agathoi* controlled it . . . *aga* gentry was also landed gentry by entailment.'[90] In this phase, driving gathers. But it can also disperse. 'The Aryans were now typically people on the go,' Anttila has observed.[91] And he has drawn attention to a 'fairly deep-reaching parallel' between *aga* and Greek *eri. The latter is related to the Vedic term *ari*, which is glossed as 'stranger' or 'guest', but which is 'no foreigner' and a 'permanent condition'. It may designate 'the majority of the people and not a single traveller.'[92] The term can then mean other groups of the same population, the context suggesting friendly or unfriendly rivalry and competition. A further semantic step produces 'a separate or separating part of the tribe', on the principle in herding cultures that an excess in the population is dealt with by driving part of it away.[93] By this means, a gathering term also comes to mean 'go apart'.[94]

A similar result is produced if the action inherent in 'action' is spelled out. The apparently different acts of driving out and gathering in belong under one sign because, fundamentally, to act is to produce a change at some point. Imparting energy, it is to change the local topography. An action that did not produce a qualitative change of this kind would not count as such. It would produce no event. Giambattista Vico visualized the force of cumulative change as a wedge, or *cuneus*;[95] the latter word is another member of the **ag/akka* family.[96] The wedge both drives outwards and, as its own shape indicates, signifies a force that concentrates energy at a point. This is important, because it suggests that any active gathering also possesses the power either to gather more and excel or, no less dramatically, to explode and dissipate.

From both of these enquiries, it appears that there is gathered and focused in a group an energy that did not exist before. Hence, we can talk of an assembly as a crowd, and the crowd is understood to be a new kind of social organism. *Agon* in Greek signifies a special kind of meeting, one dedicated to the celebration of driving, and, by extension, a festival dedicated to competitive races.[97] Like the agora, the *agon* is both an assembly and the place of assembly. Architecturally, it is the drive translated into a length of ground. The driving forth of animals has here been ritualized. Measuring out the course introduces the notion of repetition and the possibility of a shared history. The gathering and physical inscription of ideal paths naturally makes it possible to bring out into the open the best of drivers – the enhancing particle *aga* seems to be related to *mega*, meaning 'great'.[98] The drives now magnified and raised up are not only physical, but emotional. Emotion gathers where the crowd gathers. An air of mounting excitement brings about its psychological sequel, a massive discharge of feeling. The crowd drives on the charioteers, just as the charioteers drive on the horses. Taking part in this, the crowd both drives and is driven. It is both fused together and flung apart.

Doesn't this double provenance explain the mingled awe and terror the agora produces? Its traffic both transforms and uplifts, but it also threatens to sweep away and destroy. In driving men together, it drives a man apart from himself. Not simply an assembly of people, but a crowd drawn or driven together, it is an image of power. It is a unit in which inflation and deflation dangerously stalk each other. In a time of monetary inflation, Elias Canetti observed, a double devaluation is experienced: 'The *individual* feels depreciated because the unit on which he relied, and with which he had equated himself, starts sliding; and the crowd feels depreciated because the *million* is.'[99] Inflated speech both revalues concepts and devalues them. Similarly, in the marketplace, one can talk up products, but there is always the danger that the bottom will drop out of the market.

These dynamics follow directly from the violent, coercive and ecstatic drive of the crowd-forming. Destruction is inherent in the crowd's construction. Even in good times, the dynamic crowd is never simply an assembly, but a gathering of hunting paths; it is a potential 'hunting pack', it is also a potential 'baiting crowd'; it is a situation in which the seizing urge is given maximum stimulus. This is why *pothos*, the desire to seize, or be seized by, flourishes there. It also explains why a fear of exposure and estrangement *has* to oscillate with a fear of immersion and suffocation, agora-claustrophobia.

VACANT SPACE

As a site of action, the agora both gathers and dissipates. Its imperialism is two-faced. In its centripetal mode, it displaces, enslaves and amalgamates. In its centrifugal aspect, it colonizes, spreading its ideas, preoccupations and anxieties beyond the horizon. It follows that it also exports, as well as imports, its space fears. If an agora-claustrophobia is coeval with its foundation, then the same anxiety is likely to dog the footsteps of the military commanders, explorers and settlers sent out to civilize the world. I think a persuasive account of Alexander the Great's campaigns could be made in these terms, but in order to steer the argument back towards the modern history of agoraphobia, let's consider the nature of nineteenth-century colonial geography.

In Australia, in South Africa, in British Guiana or along the western marches of the United States and Canada, explorers and surveyors (not necessarily the same creature) had as their object the haussmannization of the interior. Their rhetoric, as well as the linear progress they practised, described colonization in terms of opening up, breaking through, clearing a way. Camillo Sitte's attack on open spaces was, according to Vidler, 'a commonplace of the aesthetic criticism of urbanism since the brothers Goncourt had complained of the "American deserts" created by the cutting of the modern boulevards'.[100] The British naturalist Alfred Russel Wallace extended this critique to the bush:

> In all the newer States there are no roads or paths whatever beyond the limits of the townships, and the only lines of communication for foot or horsemen or vehicles of any kind are along these rectangular section-lines, often going up and down hill, over bog or stream, and almost always compelling the traveller to go a much greater distance than the form of the surface rendered necessary.[101]

Like their Northern European urban contemporaries, these geographical travellers wanted to modernize the land, to make it fit for traffic. And that meant replacing the lines of least resistance – Le Corbusier's meandering pack-donkey trails – with straight, purposeful ones.

The implicit scene was a disorganized spread of doubtfully bounded objects, peoples and topography. The Australia of the early nineteenth-century gentleman-explorer was Attica before Theseus had made his mark. It was as dense in its impenetrability, and in its host of motley tongues, as a medieval town complete with its ghetto. It was also as mentally dysfunctional as a modern city where ambulatory automatism was tolerated, and vagabonds haunted the public space. When the evangelical Samuel Marsden wrote (in the 1820s),

> [The Australian Aborigines] appear to have no reflection, no fore-thought, they never provide for tomorrow, they have neither Store-house or Barn, they independently range the Woods in the day, like the fowls of the air or the beasts of the field, and lie down in the Bush wherever night overtakes them,[102]

he was creating the rural, colonial precursor of Charcot's urban vagabonds, 'who often sleep under bridges, in quarries or lime kilns and who are exposed at any instant to the blows of the police'.[103]

The purposeful traveller with his compass and quadrant did not survey the thick space of encounter: he cleared it away. Like the destructive character, he made space. To continue the analogy, it follows that, in opening up immense spaces, he also created the conditions of agoraphobia. The Australian record shows that he carried that anxiety with him: it was implicit in his desire to reduce space to a grid-like order and an agora-like flatness. He only saw space as immense because he wanted to control it. He only felt dwarfed because of his ambition, and, unlike Le Corbusier, he rarely had an Eiffel Tower he could climb in order to command the view, and, invert-ing the optic, to reduce great distances to nothing. On the ground, as it were, the emptiness he was creating came back to haunt him. It grew uncanny in a classically Freudian sense. Having evacuated his surroundings of affect, he found them filling up again with dreams that bore witness to destructive drives of which he was unconscious. And, all the time perhaps, he was aware of a vague feeling of being followed.

The admittedly susceptible explorer Ernest Giles found, some-where on the south-east edge of the Gibson Desert, a 'very singular little glen' in which there were

> several small mounds of stones placed at even distances apart, and, though the ground was originally all stones, places like paths have been cleared between them. There was also a large,

bare, flat rock in the centre of these strange heaps, which were not more than two and a half feet high . . .

We now can see why Giles was immediately led to conclude

> that these are small kinds of *teocallis* [ancient Mexican places of worship], and that on the bare rock already mentioned the natives have performed, and will again perform, their horrid rites of human butchery, and that the drippings of the pellucid fountains from the rocky basins above have been echoed and re-echoed by the dripping fountains of human gore from the veins and arteries of their bound and helpless victims.[104]

This is a textbook case of Freud's proposition that 'the repression of a desire gives rise to a vague sense of disquiet . . . [this *flottierende Angst*] is consciously felt as something unendurable, and is at once attached to a special object, as in obedience to an impulse which counts as "protective"', although the relief afforded may be anything but complete. The fears of water, of the dark, of certain animals, of meeting people, of crowds, of church and theatre, and so on through all their multitudinous forms, are made up in part, according to this view, of fears of ourselves.[105] On this logic, Giles was protecting himself from his repressed desire by projecting the resulting sense of disquiet onto a bunch of cairns. But the repressed came back to haunt him, as his vision of bloody sacrifice accurately represents his own desire to clear the path of obstacles and, in particular, to remove the Aborigines by force of arms.

Note, though, that this 'Freudian' account does not need a Freudian unconscious to support it. It is an environmental unconscious whose uncontrollable presence Giles sensed and to which he reacted. His agora-claustrophobia arose directly from his determination to open a path. How could the land be opened up if it wasn't 'closed' before? The explorer experiences the same anxiety as Moses when he drove his people to the Promised Land through a gap miraculously opened up in the Red Sea: there is always the fear that, at his back, the land closes ranks. He opens a path but behind him its sides, like those of a ship's waves, are cleaving together again. Hence, together with a feeling of immense spaces, there comes a sensation of space contracting, a feeling that there is less and less ground on which to stand.

Modern agoraphobes can face open spaces when accompanied by a friend they trust. In the absence of a friend, some other indication of direction must do. In the old days, a leisurely horse-drawn carriage might be followed. A walking stick could give support too. The exact geographical counterpart of this aid in Australian exploration is the coastline which Edward J. Eyre followed round the Great Australian Bight. The coastline both divided the immense space and lent it an edge or kerb. At the same time, its narrowness continued to oppress him. Even if he trod a high wire suspended only a foot above the ground, he had the sensation of being poised over an abyss, especially when travelling in the dark: 'There appeared to be a disastrous fatality attending all our movements in this wretched region, which was quite inexplicable.'[106] If topography let the explorer down, another companion was invoked, 'when I sat down beside the waters of the beautiful channel to which Providence in its goodness had been pleased to direct my steps.'[107]

Whatever other pleasures exploration might deliver, it could never be an easy stroll. It was axiomatic that the explorer battled an intransigent environment, one bent on inhibiting movement. It was a heroic step to advance into it, and despair at the crushing immensity of the task was never far away. The explorer's progress might be steady, but it was never light or dance-like. The ground could never be taken for granted. Even walking across 'plains' could be dangerous. Land north of what was to become Melbourne presented the explorer William Hovell with 'frequent chasms, wide and deep'.[108] His unofficial journal added, more graphically, 'some of the cracks were large enough to admit of the leg going down them'.[109] Travelling habitually alternated between illusions of high speed, in which the travellers seemed to suffer from ambulatory automatism and flit along in a dream, and periods of inertia, when all willpower drained away. As Eyre put it, '[I] could have sat quietly and contentedly, and let the glass of life glide away to its last sand. There was a dreamy kind of pleasure, which made me forgetful or careless of the circumstances and difficulties by which I was surrounded.'[110]

In a remarkable image, Hovell wrote of progress across the Werribee Plains, immediately south-west of Melbourne, that 'since approaching this Country it has appeared (*sic*) to us as if we had been transported from one Cloud to another'.[111] Although he was referring to the strength of the wind and the clouds scudding before it, their speed and sense of direction seem to have communicated themselves to his own journey and sense of getting on. Thrusting himself forward, he avoided the panic of indecision; he repressed his anxiety about cracks opening up in the pavement ahead. He avoided meeting others' eyes. His high-speed perambulation contrasted with the rebelliously slow gait of the convict-servant or the ambulatory automatism of the Aborigine, so given to taking a nap and drifting on. For the explorer, as for Kafka's Alexander, the greatest nightmare is to come to a standstill.

Comparing colonial exploration to the haussmannization of Paris, Berlin or Vienna indicates its agoraphobic character. It also throws light on the cult of the Picturesque. Picturesque views were window-dressing. They transformed the route into an arcade, in which one shop-window view after another presented itself to the prospective buyer. These 'views' were projections of the land speculator's imagination: one step to the left or the right and they might dissolve. They veiled the barrenness of the grid being laid over the land; they did not spring from any engagement with the environment and its structuring principles. The spurious clarity of their views was of the same order as the image produced by the magic lantern. The light was an inner light, and the images it produced had no necessary connection with reality. The very barrenness of much of the land seemed to assist this impression:

> a vast sheet of water appeared to intervene between us and the shore, whilst the Mount Deception ranges, which I knew to be at least thirty-five miles distant, seemed to rise out of the

bed of the lake itself, the mock waters of which were laving their base, and reflecting the inverted outline of their rugged summits. The whole scene partook more of enchantment than reality.[112]

In this way, it was not only over mid-nineteenth-century Europe that a 'dream-sleep' fell. The arcades the Victorian explorer made for his colonial arcadia also had a 'phantasmagorical character'.

STAND BACK

Agoraphobia also accompanied more sternly scientific surveyors. This was not due to personal disposition, but was inherent in the survey. The straight lines that the surveyor used to compass the country arbitrarily segmented the lie of the land. They created a country every-where split down the middle, composed of opposite views and asymmetrical distances. The survey lines cut through hills, bisected lakes, ignored the meanders of rivers. Hence, wherever the progressive line intersected with landscape features, it halved and doubled them, creating a jigsaw of part forms without any geomorphological reason of their own. In other words, the incoherence of the environment that the surveyor entered, and its seeming failure to gather into pleasing assemblages, was a direct consequence of his own vocation. By drawing lines, he cut up the environment into a rectilinear jigsaw that bore no resemblance to the ground's spatio-temporal continuum.

The surveyor's divisionism was both conceptual and visual, both cartographic and poetic. Associated with his roads was the produc-tion of views and viewpoints. A ridge-top track produced two opposite valley views. A line drawn across the plain produced two plains and two edges. And so on. The survey of the land, like the Picturesque view, proceeded by way of constructing edges or frames. These were the (non-) places or baselines of the survey, but their impact on the land's legibility was fundamental. By introducing a system of arbitrary edges, starting points and horizons, they introduced a movement inhibition into the fluid, dynamic geometries that naturally informed the environment. The sense of a landscape that failed to gather was a direct result of the grid's sectarian logic. With his chain and theodolite, the surveyor had a 'walking stick' that enabled him to overcome his space fear. The convicts, settler women and shepherds who followed were often less well protected.

This is not the place to attempt even a short history of land clearing. But it seems that the Haussmanization of the interior inaugurated by the survey must have created in the settlers who followed the surveyors something like Rilke's 'twinge of incipient fear'. Instead of acknowledging their unease on entering a country already cleared of much of its native topography (because of the way the grid was laid through it), they blamed the land for their sense of disquiet. Feeling that the land did not face them or speak to them, they experienced an unbearable isolation, even perhaps a kind of rural anomie. They felt hemmed in by their own self-appointed fate. They wanted to break out.

In the passage already quoted, Kant explains that 'Persistent pondering on one and the same subject leaves behind an echo, so to speak . . . [which] can be stopped only by distracting our attention and applying it to other objects.'[113] In a similar way, repressing the sense of homelessness that haunted their efforts to make a home, the colonial settlers turned the resulting anxiety outwards, expressing it as an aggression towards the land. As a result, they shared the ironic fate of the destructive character: clearing the land only intensified its agoraphobic charge. The more they tried to drive the symptom out, the more they reproduced it. In the process of removing trees and over-grazing, they advanced towards self-destruction. Yet the panic to produce an ideal flatness from which every ghost of the environmental unconscious had been removed seems to have been irresistible.

It is the dubious privilege of the present generation of Australians to witness this mass panic in its terminal stages. As far back as the 1850s (despite popular wisdom), the consequences of bad farming practices were perfectly well known: over-grazing and tree clearance, especially on humus-poor and nutrient-deficient soils, inevitably produced erosion and salination. Perhaps as late as the 1950s, the land-plundering cattle barons were fooled by their own 'opening up the land' developmental rhetoric, not to mention their impressive short-term profits. But the current rage for land clearing (which is no fly-by-night operation, but is condoned, even subsidized, by federal and state governments) now proceeds without any economic, environmental or even cultural rationalization. Only a pure and limitless space panic, whose cultural and historical origins go back at least as far as the modernization agenda of colonial geography, can begin to explain it.

UNEVEN SURFACE

Surveying the ancient agora, its types, myths and histories, illuminates the nature of the movement inhibition associated with agoraphobia. The sensation the agoraphobe feels of being rooted to the spot arrests a double impulse, a movement out of oneself towards the other, and a movement away from the other towards oneself. As Colin Davis puts it, paraphrasing Levinas, 'only by discovering the irreducibility of the Other can I understand that I am neither solipsistically alone in the world nor part of a totality to which all others belong'.[114] It is a mistake to conceptualize this movement only from the Ego's viewpoint. From another's angle, or from the mass of the many (Canetti's 'million'), it is equally true to talk of gathering and dissipation. They are two phases of a single pose. Or, to put it another way, they are what happens to the pose when it is conceptualized bipedally and kinetically, rather than statically and inertially.

Conceptualized in this way, the repressed movement is also a repressed space of human relations, one which only a 'thick' description of everyday life can recover. And such a description will still fall flat, if it fails to take account of the topology of encounter, the intuitive meshing and interflowing of many 'cycloid spiral space-curves'. For the act of walking, an 'in-rolling, centripetal (and out-rolling centrifugal) movement', as Schauberger's description reminds us,[115] offers a microcosm of the double-drive instantiated in the agora. Benjamin's hesitation at the edge of the pavement, his 'obstinate and voluptuous hovering on the brink,'[116] recognizes the double impulse of the agoraphobe, to shrink back or to rush ahead, but the resulting aesthetic pose is attenuated and highly personal.

Less exquisitely isolated individuals might find their agoraphobia defined *regionally*, in the ambiguity of those meetings which are not meetings, although they pose as such, but which are, in reality, a reiterated parting and retreat – an experience captured in our phrase *bumping into someone*. Meeting someone unexpectedly, we say we bumped into them. By this we mean that we *nearly* made *involuntary* physical contact. Figuratively, we bumped into them; physically, we avoided contact. To bump into someone is to be unpleasantly reminded of a former connection; it is to be mentally jolted, distracted from one's present train of thought. To bump into a stranger might be to embark on an adventure or a flirtation, but to spring a ghost from one's past is always to turn away. Bumping into someone or, more accurately, not bumping into someone, is to have the sensation of inhabiting a space of conflicting desires. It is these desires which define the patterns of mobility in any social space. They squeeze and push; they draw together and push apart. They score the emotional choreography of the crowd.

As the Gestalt psychologist Kurt Lewin observed,

> One thinks generally of a medium as a region which offers no resistance to a movement, whereas a thing seems dynamically compact and solid. However, one must realise that regions may offer all possible degrees of resistance. There are regions which can be crossed but which still act as obstacles to movement. For bodily locomotion for instance, a thick underbrush is a medium which offers definite 'friction'. This friction can increase until it is impossible to advance farther. Then one is no longer dealing with a space of free movement but with a boundary of this space. This example shows clearly that there all possible transitions between the dynamical properties of thing and medium.[117]

It also shows that the agoraphobe who feels herself swimming, or treading a rubbery floor, is alive to this fact. What others see as immense empty spaces, she finds dense and difficult to 'go through'.[118]

A final lesson to be drawn from an ancient history of agoraphobia is that the organizing principle of the movement which is inhibited is erotic. The speech of Alcibiades and the language of Alexander both identify spatial conquest with erotic desire. Etymology also supports this identification. The German word for 'drive' is *Trieb*. Originally referring to the physical driving of animals, it came to signify 'inner driving force'.[119] *Aja*, in Finnish, ultimately derived from the Indo-European **Ag*, makes the sexual connection explicit, as it means both driver and he-goat.[120] In German, we have *Triebleben*, 'sexual life', and the strong verb *treiben*, 'to masturbate'.[121] Further, 'when the goal of this striving, *Drang*, is mentioned we get the meaning "instinct", picked up by psychology.'[122] *Drang* means a craving, but it also signifies a crowd. Hence, in German, to yield to the instincts is to join the throng. But, less auspiciously, it is to be driven in droves. Driving 'can be looked at from two angles: the ease and speed of it, or the difficulties provided (by the driven)'.[123]

If Socrates' etymology is to be believed, this ambiguity is inherent in *eros* itself, which, according to him, 'is so called because flowing in (*esron*) from without'.[124] That is, *eros* is constitutionally a relationship and a region. In this sense, the agora that pretends to be a unity represses the in-going, out-going drives that inform its vitality. In this connection, there is an important passage in Plato's *Laws* in which the Athenian advises against building a wall round the city. The city that boasts of being able to defend itself has no need of stone defences, the Athenian explains. Indeed, it partly draws its strength from the lawless countryside. And besides, being open to what lies beyond encourages a kind of virtue or readiness akin to the opportunism for which Athens was renowned: a wall

> invites [inhabitants] to take refuge behind it instead of tackling
> the enemy and ensuring their own safety by mounting guard

160

day and night; it tempts them to suppose that a foolproof way of protecting themselves is to barricade themselves behind their walls and gates, and then drop off to sleep, as if they were brought into the world for a life of luxury. It never occurs to them that comfort is really to be won by the sweat of the brow.[125]

In other words, walls encourage citizens to be afraid of what lies beyond, and to resist its in-coming. They encourage citizens to feel agoraphobic because they block the erotic intercourse between agora and *agros*. The Athenian also makes the point that the value of this encounter with the other is recognized in the city's own religious and military practices: 'What fools people would take us for, and rightly, if we sent our young men out each year to excavate trenches and ditches and various structures to ward off the enemy and stop them coming over the boundaries at all – and then were to build a wall round the city.'[126]

The young men referred to here are presumably *ephebes* of the type described by Vidal-Naquet:

a light-armed soldier, an anti-hoplite who ensured the perpetuation, often unseen, of a mode of fighting that is both pre- and anti-hoplite, and that reappears in the light of day (and of history) during the Peloponnesian War and in the fourth century BC. Creature of the frontier area, of the *eschatia*, he guarantees in his hoplite oath to protect the boundary-stones of his country, and with them, the cultivated fields, the wheat, barley, olive trees, vines, and figs.[127]

Perhaps these keepers of in-between regions had an insight into the 'ethical agoraphobia' identified by Emmanuel Levinas. Ethical agoraphobia is a response to the marketplace of self-interest, in which good will barely disguises hatred. It is a sense of responsibility that transcends any rules of exchange. It cannot be escaped by escaping from the agora into the *ager* (Latin: 'field'). Levinas thinks that Socrates' disparagement of the countryside ('trees and and open country won't teach me anything, whereas men in the town do'[128]) proves that the only escape is not through the freedom of a heroically persistent egological will, but through a speaking in which I am bound by the other who teaches me more than I can learn from the country which, although outside the city wall, is more hermetically enclosed than the *agora*.[129]

But Socrates' situation was more ambiguous. He was the *agoraios*. Like Gustav Fechner's man, however, who conducted quite a different life in town than in the country (and whose two states Freud compared to the difference between waking and dreaming[130]), Socrates had another existence. He was also, like the ephebe, a *peripolos*, 'one who circles round' or goes on patrol.[131] Diotima described him as without an *oikos*, although not without a *polis*. According to her, Socrates was 'really hardened, unkempt, barefoot, homeless, always sleeping rough and without a blanket, bedding down in doorways and on the streets under the stars, and impoverished'.[132] There is also the story of Socrates' military service at Potidea. The fact that he went barefoot allied him with the daimon Eros.[133] And in the *Phaedrus*, Socrates locates his discourse outside the walls of Athens in a liminal region (the Ilissus) adjacent to his own deme and therefore well known to him.[134]

In other words, Socrates located his ethics in and against the beyond of love. It is no accident that he invoked the Delphic injunction, 'Know Thyself', in the encounter with a sacred place. Sidestepping the truth value of the myth associated with the nearby Sanctuary of Agra, Socrates remarked that, in view of his ignorance about himself, it would have been premature to pronounce on such matters. Levinas thinks that the 'u-topic exteriority' of the agora and the *ager* would be further proved if they could be shown to have a shared etymological root.[135] (In fact, they do.[136]) More telling is the connection Anttila makes between *agora* and *agra*. In the *agra*, one both seizes and is seized, one is both the hunter and the one who, responding to the call of the hunter, is killed. At the *agra*, an accident occurs, a gathering that can mimic extinction. The *agra*, on this account, is the other scene that haunts Levinas, the 'other "other" scene beyond the psychoanalytic unconscious'.[137]

4 meeting

A labyrinth made of all the paths one has taken.

Elias Canetti[1]

LOW BEAM

Obviously, the psychoanalysts of Berlin and Vienna avoided the cinema. Otherwise, they could have studied 'street fear' in the comfort of the dark. The 'street films' emanating from Berlin in the 1920s and '30s – Siegfried Kracauer goes so far as to describe them as a distinct genre – add up to a modern anatomy of agoraphobia. And they manage this without recourse to a hypothesis of the unconscious. Perhaps this was inherent in the medium, whose moving images were, from the earliest days, and particularly in the period of the silent movie, compared to the experience of dreaming. Nothing in film was displaced, unless through the conscious intervention of montage – and even this only served to reinforce the impression of a free association governed by invisible laws. Freed of psychologism, film was able to explore the poetics of agoraphobia, to show that the principles of agoraphobic behaviour were aesthetically coherent.

Psychoanalysis came to recognize that the street was not merely feared: it was also desired. But what the analyst regarded as a conflict to be resolved, the film-maker grasped as the catalyst of a narrative, and, as in the consulting room, so in the cinema, the attractions of the street sometimes outweighed its perils. In Karl Grune's *Die Strasse* (*The Street*, 1923), the street represents 'the region of chaos'.[2] By contrast, in Rudolf Pabst's *Die Freudlose Gasse* (*The Joyless Street*, 1925) and Bruno Rahn's *Dirnentragödie* (*Tragedy of the Street*, 1927), the street is no longer 'the dreadful jungle', but 'a region harbouring virtues that had deserted bourgeois society'.[3] In these, and in films like Joe May's *Asphalt* (1929), '"die Strasse" of brothels' is glorified and, Siegfried Kracauer thought, a discontent with the stabilized Weimar Republic expressed.[4] In a further twist of the dialectic, Erno Metzner's *Überfall* (*Accident*, 1929) dispenses with both the negative and positive connotations of the street: the characters and motifs of *Tragedy of the Street* and *Asphalt* reappear, but with changed meanings: '. . . it neither glorifies the petty bourgeois as a rebel nor transforms the chaotic street into a haven for genuine love.'[5]

A visual vocabulary evolved to communicate the ambiguous appeal of the modern street. At the beginning of *The Street*, when the man is cocooned in the claustrophobic respectability of his parlour, 'the ceiling becomes luminous with lights reflecting those of the street outside.' Looking out, he sees

> not the street itself, but a hallucinated street. Shots of rushing cars, fireworks and crowds form, along with shots taken from a speeding roller coaster, a confusing whole, made still more confusing by the use of multiple exposures and the insertion of transparent close-ups of a circus clown, a woman and an organ-grinder.

By these means, 'the irrational alternations in the sphere of instinctive life' are symbolised. And Kracauer makes the additional interesting point, 'The circle usually serving as a symbol of chaos has yielded to the straight line of a city street; since chaos here is not so much an end in itself as a passage ending in the realm of authority, this change of symbols is well-founded.'[6] It's a comment that might also be applied to Le Corbusier's urbanism.

In street films, the street became an actor in its own right. There developed a metonymic sign language of motifs and gestures representing its perils and temptations. In Rahn's *Tragedy of the Street*, the street is mainly characterized by a close-up of 'the feet that walk over its stones', a motif Kracauer traces back to a close shot in Grune's

The Street in which the philistine's legs are shown 'following a wavy line on the pavement'.[7] Legs also figure largely in Walter Ruttmann's *Berlin, die Symphonie einer Grossstadt* (Berlin, Symphony of a Great City, 1927): in the last sequence, for example, 'the legs of girl dancers perform; Chaplin's legs stumble across a screen; two lovers, or rather two pairs of legs, make for the nearest hotel; and finally a true pandaemonium of legs breaks loose: the six day race going on and on without interruption.'[8] The motif of the 'feet that walk' is also emphasized in May's *Heimkehr* (*Homecoming*, 1928): 'Marching soldier boots change into slippers which in turn give way to foot-bandages that are finally superseded by the naked and dusty feet themselves.'[9] Finally, in *Asphalt*, the pavement itself is a central motif. The prologue to this film illustrates, after the manner of a documentary, how asphalt is produced and how it voraciously swallows open land to pave the way for city traffic.[10]

Such films implicitly addressed the scene of agoraphobia. They could also represent its symptoms explicitly. A typical agoraphobe, as described in 1930 by Emanuel Miller, first develops a fear of crowded streets, tall buildings and open spaces, then personifies these zones. She associates the tall building with her father 'so tall and big as he stood in the bedroom', and a disused mill – 'gaunt and grey . . . it seemed to point at her like a judge' – with her mother.[11] In *Accident*, released in the same year as Miller wrote his report, the 'hero', after winning money at the gambling table and walking away, finds himself followed at a steadily diminishing distance by a thug: 'The man is scared. No sooner does he take to his heels than all the objects about him make common cause with his pursuer. The dark railway underpass turns into a sinister trap; frozen threats, the dilapidated slum houses close rank and stare at him.'[12]

Kracauer makes a far larger claim for film. It is not due to the personal interests and creative ingenuity of film directors that the medium uniquely captures the anxieties of 'metropolitan man': film's expressive superiority in this regard is, he argues, intrinsic to it. Just to list its aesthetic qualities bears this out. Film specializes in capturing the unstaged and the fortuitous. In this sense (Kracauer again), it enjoys an elective affinity with that 'centre of fleeting impressions', the street – 'a region where the accidental prevails over the providential, and happenings in the nature of unexpected incidents are all but the rule'.[13] The street is

> not only the arena of fleeting impressions and chance encounters but a place where the flow of life is bound to assert itself . . . the city street [possesses] ever-moving anonymous crowds. The kaleidoscopic sights mingle with unidentified shapes and fragmentary visual complexes and cancel each other out . . . It remains an unfixable flow which carries fearful uncertainties and alluring excitements.[14]

These are the qualities of the agoraphobe's nightmare. Yet film does not merely mimic them: it analyzes them. Giving concrete expression to repressed sensations, its poetics of representation is therapeutic.

An even grander claim follows from this. In *Abstraction and Empathy* (1908), the aesthetician Wilhelm Worringer had identified abstraction with a kind of 'spiritual agoraphobia in the face of the motley disorder and caprice of the phenomenal world'.[15] Transposing this notion to the modern world, Karl Popper also identified the emergence of 'abstract society' with a loss of focus – the crowd no longer furnishing the citizen with friendly faces.[16] In his *Theory of Film*, Kracauer takes up this theme, but gives it a decidedly different twist. Instead of rejecting the motley disorder, he perceives in film a way to redeem it. As a result, Worringer's spiritual agoraphobe, who, 'dependent upon the deceptive and ever-changing play of phenomena, that robs him of all assurance and all feeling of spiritual tranquility, [feels] a profound trust of the glittering veil of Maya which conceals from him the true being of things',[17] is replaced by the ardent filmgoer.

Modern, or post-Second World War, society, wrote Kracauer, is abstract. Science, including social science, is irremediably abstract, concerned with quantities not qualities. The values that attach to sensations are psychologized away; relativism is the rule of the day. Neither progressive ideology nor religion carries conviction any longer.

Modern people drift rudderless: '[Man] lacks the guidance of binding norms. He touches reality only with the fingertips.'[18] But it is just here, in extending vestigial human contact with the world, that film finds a therapeutic role. It uniquely cuts through the prevailing abstractness, grasping the given and yet ungiven physical phenomena of concrete reality:

> Film exposes to view a world never seen before, a world as elusive as Poe's purloined letter, which cannot be found because it is within everyone's reach. What is meant here is . . . not any of those extensions of the everyday world which are being annexed by science but our ordinary physical environment itself. Strange as it may seem, although streets, faces, railway stations, etc., lie before our eyes, they have remained largely invisible so far.[19]

Film is the *redemptive art of estrangement*. It puts us back in touch with reality:

> It effectively assists us in discovering the material world with its psychophysical correspondences. We literally redeem this world from its dormant state, its state of virtual nonexistence, by endeavouring to experience it through the camera. And we are free to experience it because we are fragmentized.[20]

In effect, Kracauer argues that film addresses itself to space fear on condition that it is recognized as a well-founded reaction to objective conditions. Space or street fear *is* symptomatic, but not of a displaced phobia. It springs from a blocked *agoraphilia*, a desire to re-member what has been dismembered – to make concrete what has grown abstract. The film medium and its compositional techniques show that reparation occurs not by way of a nostalgic, Sitte-inspired restoration of lost urban topography, but through mobilizing the movement inhibition differently. This is why film is therapeutic.

Film may excel in exploiting an agoraphobic poetics, but, despite the brilliance of Kracauer's presentation, it hardly constitutes a *poetics of agoraphobia*. It may surpass painting, sculpture or the dance as a medium for the representation of agoraphobic experience. Like any form of mimesis, its effects will be cathartic. But it remains detached from the scene of that experience. The womb-like darkroom of the cinema resembles the smoke-veiled interior of the analyst's consulting room. Many street fantasies are conjured up there – in *Nadja* (1928), André Breton relates seeing a woman divest herself of her coat and walk nude up and down the aisles of the Electric-Palace in Paris. The paragraph where this is reported begins, 'I have always wished . . . to encounter at night, in a wood, a beautiful nude woman.'[21] Who hasn't? In Breton's free association, the cinema represents the urban counterpart of the *agros*, or wilderness. But in comparison with the agora, the illusion of reality the picture-house provides is phantasmagoric.

As an agoraphobic poetics, film is one among many. In this regard, the johnny-come-lately discourse of psychoanalysis is hardly inferior. Adam Phillips has made the point that psychoanalysis began 'as a kind of virtuoso improvisation within the science of medicine; and free association – the heart of psychoanalytic treatment – is itself ritualised'.[22] The improvisations psychoanalysis performs on language remarkably resemble the operations film undertakes on visual phenomena. There is the same privileging of the overlooked, the accidental and the instinctual. If we remove the self-legitimizing myth of the unconscious and its equally mythic structures, the authority of the analyst depends entirely on a gift for presenting free association as a poetically coherent technique of recall.

As Esther da Costa Meyer has noted, when it is pathologized in this way, agoraphobia emerges as 'a language with a syntax of its own'; it is (following Julia Kristeva) a form of 'body talk'; in short, 'a coherent signifying system [in which] its victims stand to gain something from their extreme stance'.[23] This coherence, though, depends on ignoring both the fact that agoraphobia has been constructed as a woman's disease and its corollary: 'If gender is the product of social practices and institutions (disciplines), we must historicise and contextualise agoraphobia, not just pathologise it.'[24]

And the same applies to film: its gaze is not innocent (or for that matter ungendered), but voyeuristic. The film eye is always a detective in search of a clue. Wherever it looks is the scene of a crime. It is undeniable that, like the pathologizing discourse of psychoanalysis, the exposure which film promotes exacerbates the condition which Kracauer claimed it cures. In this sense, the agoraphobic poetics of film may be said to pathologize the poetics of agoraphobia. A significant literature has grown up around the definition of the movement image in film. But even those who argue that film gives a post-phenomenologically accurate image of perception don't claim that it can model the proprioceptive sensation of moving *towards another* among an assembly of objects, faces and planes.

Gilles Deleuze argues that Henri Bergson's suspicion of cinematography was misplaced: in claiming that image is matter, and matter luminous by itself, Bergson's universe resembled a *metacinema* – 'The *movement-image* and *flowing matter* are strictly the same thing.'[25] Emmanuel Levinas discerned in Bergson's concept of *durée* a movement injunction that is both physical and psychic. *Durée* is, he said, the 'to-God of time'.[26] Its qualitative, concrete conception of temporality not only escapes the 'nothing new' of clockwork, scientific time, but points individuals towards their fates – which Levinas identified ethically, as an engagement with the other.[27] But evidently, film cannot *participate* in these processes.

At least in the early days, the flickering screen caused by the rapid succession of one frozen frame after another attested not to an image of mobility, but to a residual movement inhibition. And if, as Kracauer maintains, the technical properties of film give it a privileged grip on 'psychophysical correspondences',[28] then its limitations are equally telling. Rendering the invisible visible, it may yet conceal another reality, one bound up with a bipedal and kinetic perception of spatial relations. Then, instead of allaying anxiety, film might produce it, creating an uneasiness, which for Robert Musil's young Törless creates an experience analogous to

> watching cinematographic pictures, when, for all the illusion the whole thing creates, one is . . . unable to shake off a vague awareness that behind the image one perceives there are hundreds of other images flashing past, and each of them utterly different from the picture as a whole.[29]

Now, a near-absolute smoothness of flow has been achieved: but the suspicion remains that the very evenness of change conceals another terrain. What Kracauer says of the street also applies to film: 'chaos is not so much an end in itself as a passage ending in the realm of authority'.[30] Film can be said to resemble a street even when a street is not depicted. Even the motionless camera is in motion, looking for something to happen, and, in this sense, traffics with time. It is hard to imagine a camera resting: as a rule, film halts only in order to move on. Like the idling motorcar at a traffic signal, it anticipates red turning to green. These structural analogies explain why a genre of *square films* is hard to envisage. When squares *do* make their appearance in early film, it is under the aegis of the crowd, treated as a moving human street. This, too, is implicit in the constitution of the medium. Film replaces the transcendental pose of the ancients with the arbitrary cut in time represented by the frame. This is not merely an empirical advance. As the pose is dissected, its thin parts begin to totter, and fall over one another. A violent rejoining of parts, fusing them into a massed whole, or *procession*, is the condition of creating an illusion of equilibrium.

In the films of Sergei Eisenstein, it seems that processions of images were a means of glorifying processions in general. According to Alexander Etkind, Eisenstein was 'drawn to cosmic forms of total union inaccessible to the limited individual'[31] and felt that the unconscious 'was the reflection of the earliest undifferentiated social existence'.[32] Eisenstein

> had experienced first hand the magnetic pull of the masses, and for him the return to a former state was not merely a topic for cocktail-party conversation, but a real possibility in life. All one had to do was to step out into the street, into the heart of a seething crowd.[33]

In Eisenstein's work, 'the "Age of the Mob" discovered its most exceptional artist,' and totalitarianism found its aesthetic'.[34] (The cocktail-party reference is to the Russian Symbolist Vyacheslav Ivanov and his circle, whose new religion centred on 'the suffering god' Dionysus and a 'quest for a national, orgiastic, collective and conciliatory culture'.[35])

This is not to indict film, as it were, but to underline the fact that an agoraphobic poetics is by no means the same thing as a poetics of agoraphobia. The interests of Dionysus are not those of Oedipus. Etkind reports that Freud, who had absolutely no sympathy either for Dionysus or for his latter-day followers, became disillusioned with Jung precisely because of the latter's attempt to combine Oedipus and Dionysus.[36] Oedipus is not Pentheus, but he resists the procession and the crowd. He avoids the street and the square, seeking access to lost terrains by different routes. This is not to say that he is a recluse or lacks political conviction, but he sees the pathways of fate grouping differently. Oedipus (and Freud) would have agreed with Hannah Arendt's wise remark that 'the public realm, as the common world, gathers us together and yet *prevents our falling over each other*, so to speak'.[37]

LOOK-OUT

So long as agoraphobia is regarded as a kind of ambit-claim anxiety characteristic of modernity, its impact on the arts can be discerned almost wherever one looks. Perhaps its symptoms are intrinsic to the film medium. In the popular imagination, though, it is artists like Edvard Munch or Giorgio di Chirico whose paintings are typically identified as depicting agoraphobic panic. Munch wasn't agoraphobic.

Nor was di Chirico – when, like Musil's Törless, he famously experienced a breakdown of visual associationism at Versailles, his sense of the enigma of his surroundings may have resembled what German psychiatry calls *die Wahrnehmungstarre*, or 'truth-taking stare'.[38] But this did not prove that he was clinically ill. (As we shall see, the same applies to the sculptor Alberto Giacometti, who, at one point in his life, was assailed by a similar sense of environmental estrangement.)

Perhaps these artists misrepresented agoraphobia because they depicted it too overtly as an aesthetic stance. Munch's vertiginous streets and di Chirico's abandoned squares represent the hostile forces contributing to a feeling of unease, but they do not render something subtler, the apparent *normality* (or lack of enigma) of ordinary urban appearances, the apparent *absence* of external reasons for feeling dread. Here, other less obviously agoraphobic artists and art movements may be more reliable. Consider the Impressionists. Sitte's editors make a suggestive point when they compare his preference for limited panoramas to Pissarro's taste for city vistas, which, by displacing the axis to the side of the observer, close off a distance that, here too, is perhaps felt to end in the realm of authority.[39] The arcadian quality of Impressionist paintings indicates their estrangement from the urban scene. Their cultivation of fleeting effects – the tremulous play of light on water or foliage which, by rendering permanent an ephemeral effect, makes it phantasmagoric – is the stylistic counterpart of Simmel's flirtation. Even Monet's Le Havre scenes approach their subject from an infinite distance. The acrobatics of the dabbing, scarcely lingering brush emphasize detachment.

As I mentioned earlier, in 'Friendly Expanses – Horrid Empty Spaces' (1955), the psychoanalyst Michael Balint tried to identify two antithetical forms of movement inhibition. With characteristic clinical zeal, he improvised two new words to describe them. Philobatism is, literally, a love of walking on one's toes. A philobat enjoys open spaces. The thrill experienced there is 'the greater the longer his exposure, the more tenuous his connection with the safety zone [the safe earth], and the less equipment he uses to cope with the danger'.[40] In contrast,

7 Chaim Soutine, *Village Square, Céret*, c.1921, oil on canvas.

ocnophilia is a desire of shrinking, hesitating, hanging back. Accordingly, the ocnophilic world consists of objects, separated by horrid empty spaces. The ocnophilic individual 'lives from object to object, cutting his sojourns in the empty spaces as short as possible. Fear is provoked by leaving the objects, and allayed by rejoining them'.[41]

Philobatism is, in effect, claustrophobia recast in dynamic terms. Ocnophilia is, likewise, agoraphobia defined mobilely. Isn't

Impressionism's preoccupation with thrills – amusements, races, flirtatious situations of every kind – indeed, with every psycho-visual epiphany that charmingly distances us from the tedium of routine and the inertia of responsibility, philobatic in tendency? Equally, isn't Cubism's desire to reconfigure external reality in terms of a manifold of surfaces that renders empty spaces in between an unnecessary hypothesis *ocnophilic*?

Clearly, there is no end of this kind of speculation – and I am not saying that drawing parallels between styles of painting and states of anxiety fails to produce intriguing results. In the *inverted vortex* at least, it throws up a form close to the core of the agoraphobic experience. In its period of influence, Cubism spawned masters of movement as well as stillness. Picasso and Braque had their dynamic counterparts in Fernand Léger, Robert Delaunay and Chaim Soutine. These latter applied prin-ciples of Cubist composition to the representation of streets, squares and monuments. In such paintings as Delaunay's *Eiffel Tower* (1914) or almost any of Soutine's Céret series, all that is empty turns solid. And the solid has a particular form, whirlpool-like, torpedo-shaped or predominantly vortical. In Soutine's *Village Square, Céret* (*c.* 1921) (illus. 7), it is as if the ground of the void has been ploughed up into mighty ridges. The ploughshares are rooflines, and the torque emanating from their furrows produces a rotation in the environment. In Delaunay's painting of the Eiffel Tower, it is, in Apollinaire's words, as if an earthquake has been depicted. Force-lines fuse the monument back into a curvilinear environment in whose elastic envelope it now appears as a deepening fissure, the slowly rotating arm of a black nebula.

The inverted vortex is a whirling dervish stalking the inter-stices of the urban scene. It is a gathering track, a figure of the agoraphobe's desire to steer a path among others, while not falling over them. If nothing else, tracing this unconscious figure breaches some groupings of art-historical orthodoxy. For instance, it was the Futurist Umberto Boccioni who not only gave the vortex its clearest representation but who also theorized it in terms of a curvilinear

8 Umberto Boccioni, *La Città che sale*, 1910, oil on canvas.

Cubism. The energy of the vortices of *La Città che sale* (illus. 8), *Le Forze di una Strada* or *Rissa in galleria* (all dating from 1910) is ambiguous. Their furious traffic suggests a world 'gone mad', in which to cross the threshold is to risk possible sacrifice. But, to continue Le Corbusier's conversion account, it also celebrates the 'rapture of power' and 'the simple and ingenuous pleasure of being in the centre of so much power, so much speed'. And the condition of this plastic fusion, in which inverted tornados skate up petrified rapids, is the disappearance of Euclidean space – 'Lo spazio non esiste più,' as Boccioni put it in the 'Futurist Painters' Manifesto, April 1910'.[42]

Perhaps predictably, architects theorized modern space differently. They could not afford to have the void coagulate into a tangled mass of intersecting curves, lines, immanent planes and sections. They could not underwrite an earthquake. Nor was it practical to run roads through living rooms or to litter the path of traffic with bedroom furniture. Nevertheless, they, too, developed an agoraphobic poetics. The Munich sculptor Adolf Hildebrand's notion of kinetic vision or vision-in-motion (presented in his 1893 essay, 'Problem of Form') not only influenced the Futurists; it also inspired the Munich Secessionist architect August Endell, who, in 1908, described the street in terms of choreography. Endell noted that 'already one human being, one moving point is sufficient, to distort the impression of a regular, symmetrical street. It receives a human axis, an a-symmetrical one; the free space is bisected by moving bodies,' explaining further that 'the human being creates with his body, what the architect and painter call space.'[43] True, 'the street as architectural space is in itself a distressing product,' but 'moving people bisect it anew . . . expand it, fill it with the music of a rhythmically alternating spatial life.'[44] As for the group perception of this rhythmically ordered space, it is vortical, as 'the dimension of depth can only be experienced by approximation, by swirling and by waving . . .'[45]

In short, an agoraphobic poetics can be ascribed to many early Modernist painters, architects and sculptors, as well as film-makers. It can also be discerned in avant-garde performance. Cocteau and Satie's *Parade* (1919) is a live montage of the semi-popular world of acting, cabaret and film, in which a great part of the *élan vital* consists in *stopping* the action and leaping from one unlikely truncated pose to the next. Thus, introducing the 'Steamship Rag', the Little American Girl 'in rapid succession . . . mimes the action of catching a train, driving a car, swimming, acting in a movie, and foiling a hold-up – with sound effects for each'.[46] Nor have we mentioned animated films. But in light of what was said earlier about the man in the street, anxiously repressing his anxiety with the help of a hat, who can mistake the psychological satire Hans Richter intended when, in *Vormittagsspuk* (*Ghosts Before Breakfast*, 1928), he showed 'inanimate objects in full revolt against the conventional use we make of them. Bowlers mocking

178

their possessors fly through the air, while a number of persons completely disappear behind a thin lamp post'?[47]

These notes may correct any impression formed after reading the earlier parts of this book: agoraphobia was not only a preoccupation of urban aesthetes or devotees of the unconscious. In a generalized way, space anxiety infiltrates many cultural forms and styles characteristic of modernity and Modernism, and another book could no doubt be devoted to making good this claim. But at the risk of labouring the point, to represent agoraphobic sensations, even if it is cathartic, is not the same as a poetics of agoraphobia. A practice of place-making that truly fulfils Kracauer's ambition of putting people back in touch with the environmental unconscious needs, first, to resist agoraphobia's metaphorical overinterpretation. Agoraphobia cannot be shorthand for civilization's every anxiety. It has a precise locus – the agora. Any design it has on spaces lost and found begins and ends there.

Two stories are told about Umberto Boccioni. In one, he nearly perished in a street accident. He had run across a piazza to post a letter to his mother and was returning at a fast pace when he suddenly stopped and, glancing up at a balcony, uttered some joyous word or other. Just at that moment, while he was distracted, a tram came rumbling and squeaking towards him. At the last moment, hearing the bell, the artist leapt out of its path – and into the path of an oncoming car. Fortunately, there was just time enough to leap a second time, onto the pavement.[48] That is one story. The other story is about his death. It seems that the artist died, while serving on the Italian front (17 August 1916), as a result of falling off his horse.[49] These tragicomic anecdotes are a parable for us. It is one thing brilliantly to represent the tumultuous rhapsody of modern life, but quite another to get out of the way of the destructive character striding to its rhythms.

AVOID THE TRACKS

Three conclusions seem reasonably clear. Agoraphobia is a movement inhibition. The inhibition is a symptom of the repressed spaces of imperial life and points to the existence of an environmental unconscious. It is not the inhibition of *any* movement, but the arrest of a double impulse, a movement out of oneself towards the other, and a movement away from the other towards oneself. These conclusions may still be general. They insist, though, that agoraphobia is an ailment specific to the other, or allegorical, space of public places and their discontents. Agoraphobia is *a place-making anxiety*. If it is also a disguised form of agoraphilia, a desire of *other* other places, it follows that the arena of its poetics is public space and its re-imagining.

Public space, Rosalind Deutsche has argued, is a 'phantom'. It has to be because it is a product of a form of society, democracy, that is open, not closed, 'where meaning continuously appears and continuously fades'.[50] To be afraid of the phantom, to want to invent a 'lost public sphere . . . where private individuals gather and, from the point of view of reason, seek to know the world objectively'[51] represents a kind of ideological agoraphobia. It attempts to settle relations between self and others which, by definition, must remain unsettled. For Deutsche, good town planning, let alone architecture, doesn't come into it. In this regard, she shares the scepticism of Esther da Costa Meyer, who, at the end of her Foucauldian account of agoraphobia asks: Are buildings and urban spaces 'empty husks to which repressed pathologic (*sic*) behaviour attaches itself', or 'is there some underlying reason that leads victims of agoraphobia to cast their scenarios of fear and foreboding in architectural terms?'[52] Costa Meyer dismisses her own question with Denis Hollier's remark that 'architecture is society's authorised superego'.[53] Buildings and their spaces are, then, simply signifiers of patriarchal order. Thus pathologized, the discourse of urban space once again slips out of consciousness.

Agoraphobic space may not represent a longing for the nostalgically imagined piazzas and winding streets of Camillo Sitte. But it impoverishes the argument to deny to the design of spaces a role in the formation of psychic, social and political dispositions. The question is: What do such spaces signify, what psychophysical correspondences do they suggest? The usual response, best articulated by Adrian Stokes, is that they offer a satisfying body image, one rooted in our earliest experiences. Adolf Loos liked to quote Kant – 'all our consciousness is grounded in spatial consciousness'[54] – and Colin St John Wilson, under the influence of Stokes, commented:

> From the moment of being born we spend our lives in a state of comfort or discomfort on a scale of sensibility that stretches between claustrophobia and agoraphobia. We are inside or outside; or on the threshold between. There are no other places to be.[55]

The role of architecture is therapeutic: forms of envelopment (room and roof) and forms of exposure (façade) minister to our incipient agora-claustro-phobic panic.

The trouble with this argument is that it pathologizes space. It perpetuates the myth of the immobile observer. It mistakes balance for possession of a pedestal, and passage from one state to another as a sign of instability. Kinetic vision and axialization of space experience have no roles to play. In this sense, the psychological idealization offered here is open to the same criticism that Henri Lefebvre levelled against architectural reveries written from a phenomenological stance. Both ignore the social and historical production of space. They share the perspective of the space theoretician who defines a centre as the point made by a pencil on a blank sheet of paper, and for whom 'the marking-out of space has no aim or meaning beyond that of an *aide-memoire* for the (subjective) recognition of places.'[56]

Such space theoreticians – they include most architects and landscape designers – produce an illusory space, as they pay no attention to the drawing out of the line (or indeed to the line itself). They do not consider the *tracks* they are making in terrains that exist outside their blank page as densely woven human environments. They do not differentiate between representational spaces and representations of space.

This puts us on the scent of our final theme. The agoraphobe is not afraid of clearings. It is not even their immensity that causes her to panic. Her place-making anxiety focuses on the preconditions of clearing away. It is not the destructive character's demolition of fondly regarded streets and buildings that overwhelms her with a sense of unfoundedness, but the presupposition driving it, that the representational space of the modern designer is an adequate representation of the spaces she inhabits. The focus of her anxiety is not a lost topography as such, *but the assumption of tracklessness*. This is the condition of the blank page, to erase the past from the representation of the present. The point made by the pencil and the line projected from it spring from the immense act of will needed to overcome the void's inertia. They are possessed by the same self-mastering rapidity as Freud's walk, the same involuntary aggression as Kafka's ejaculatory plunge from the bridge. Their illusory space of straight lines or geometrically derived curvilinear arabesques represses the agoraphobia of the blank page. Encountering these tactics in the transformation of the urban scene, the agoraphobe sees under the rationalizing gaze of the new Pallas Athene a Medusa's head of wounded tracks, coiling, uncoiling.

The *set* of these tracks is, perhaps, Walter Benjamin's 'labyrinth'. Benjamin clearly understood the ideological nature of the blank page. The lines drawn on it, like the lines of Haussmann's Paris, signified the character of progress all too accurately: coming from nowhere, they went nowhere. Appearing neutral, they brutally erased a spatial history demarcated in terms of memory places and their poses. They eradicated neighbourhoods. They eliminated meeting: 'The concept of progress is to be grounded in the idea of catastrophe. That things are that *status quo* is the catastrophe. It is not that which is approaching but that which is.'[57] To counteract the ideology of the pencil point marking the centre, Benjamin cultivated a kind of spatial *tachisme*, or a random art of the blot, an 'art of straying [that] fulfilled a dream that had shown its first traces in the labyrinths on the blotting pages of my school exercise books'.[58]

Anthony Vidler argues that Benjamin's 'labyrinth' represents the synthesis of two road systems, the pre-modern 'nomadic route', associated with the 'terrors of wandering', and the modern urban street, engendering its own terror, that of boredom inspired by 'the monotonous ribbon of asphalt'. In his labyrinth, a site of endless and monotonous wandering, these two terrors are synthesized and are 'still to be found buried in the subterranean routes of the modern city'.[59] This accounts for Benjamin's almost filmic fascination with

> the passages, architectures where we live again oneirically the life of our parents and our grand-parents, like the embryo in the womb of its mother repeats phylogenesis. Existence flows in these places without particular accentuation, as in the episodes of dreams. Flânerie gives its rhythm to this somnolence.[60]

But this is perhaps too passive. Assuaging his agoraphobia, the *flâneur* explores as well as wanders. He seeks, or tracks, crossing-places, 'where ghostly signals flash from the traffic [*Verkehr*], and inconceivable analogies and connections between events are the order of the day'.[61]

But what actually happens at these crossing-places? Adrian Rifkin is deeply suspicious of Benjamin's analogies, believing that his so-called demystification of Baudelaire's Paris is an act of sentimental mystification, testifying to 'the *anomie* of modernity'.[62] The proto-fascist Surrealist *flâneur*, the intellectual as rag-picker: these are utopian inventions. What then? Rifkin concludes that sites of public memory have to be as eagerly contested as Deutsche's public space. The site of contestation is wherever something is being cleared away as, in that ambiguous zone between past and future, the politics of remembering and forgetting surface:

> In 'Le Cygne' Baudelaire's mind's-eye images of old Paris could be a vision of the future as if it were already a ruin, its compositional elements like so many shards. The 'huts, rough-hewn capitals and shafts' can hardly be told apart as building sites or relics – 'for me everything becomes allegory'.[63]

Allegory, as we know, is the discourse of public space. Hence, the public space that emerges at the crossroads, where past and future momentarily speak to each other, is constitutionally a site of *contradiction*.

Reflecting on the migration of memories from one recently destroyed place to another, Rifkin concludes that much 'depends on where your memories begin. The points at which the past becomes felt as loss, in emotion or topography, can be the focus for quite contradictory perceptions of the city.'[64]

SIDETRACK

Agoraphobia is an anxiety about *meeting* places. Modern places of encounter, crossroads, cancel out the trajectories converging on them and passing through them. They are constructed in terms of binary opposites, which have no business morphing into each other. Traffic signals are installed to prevent meeting, as meetings in the modern city are regarded as unpleasant accidents. The agoraphobe, by contrast, imagines another place of meeting, constructed differently. Contradictions and differences may breed there, but so may chiasmatic phenomena, cross-over events. There is nothing particularly mysterious about *chiasmus* except the word itself. Most feedback mechanisms operate chiasmatically. The incremental, and sometimes surprisingly unpredictable, changes characteristic of fractal systems are another instance. Dialogue, in which, as Plutarch said, the actions of receiver and thrower must be in perfect harmony, as in a game of ball, is also an art of cross-over that does not cross out.[65]

Simmel described the emotional quality of spaces imagined as places of possible meeting. According to him, metropolitan man's sensation of estrangement presupposed this intuition: 'The "empty space" between people was, he asserted, not empty at all but filled and animated by their reciprocal relations.' Space defined social boundaries in terms of territorial groupings: 'Spatial unities might be identified within borders coincident with the locations of particular social groups.' And 'such borders, the spatial expression of sociological and functional unity alike, intersected social space like a network of imaginary lines, articulating the activity of society as a frame isolates a picture from its background.'[66] Simmel's idea of flirtation was the emotional steady state characteristic of this network. Here, 'the act of taking hold of something only in order to let it fall again, of letting it fall only to take hold of it again, in what could be called the tentative turning towards something on which the shadow of its own denial already falls'[67] was institutionalized. But it didn't count as meeting.

Meeting seemed to require certain environmental hints. But these, after all, were embedded in the nature of the public space (agora). To judge from Hannah Arendt, the ancient agora, no less than Deutsche's contemporary public realm, was a site dedicated to meeting. It was not simply a gathering place, but had as its object a mutual recognition, including the recognition of otherness (and the discourse of allegory). The *polis* of ancient Greek democracy emerged from a desire to share words and deeds; it 'was supposed to multiply the occasions to win "immortal fame", that is, to multiply the chances for everyone to distinguish himself, to show in deed and word who he was in his unique distinctness'.[68] Most importantly, the *polis* offered 'a remedy for the futility of action and speech'.[69] In this sense, the gathering place only existed in the repeated performances for which it was set aside, and these performances represented historical and geographical trajectories, the ways by which those present had come there and deserved to be distinguished.

These trajectories were, it seems, inscribed in the physical prehistory of the agora. Peter Zucker reports that both the agora and the acropolis originated as 'more or less monumental enlargements of a general thoroughfare'.[70] But whereas the acropolis tended to become an enclosure, and was characteristically sited on high ground, the agora remained open, and resisted 'the principle of the axis'.[71] Under the influence of the Hippodamian revolution, the agora came to be conceived as a distinct *Gestalt*, but it was never enclosed 'and resemble[d] a horseshoe'.[72] Stoas, or porticos, helped to set the agora off from adjacent streets, but its site and the irregular orientation of axes reflected the prehistory of the site, its earlier buildings and tracks. In other words, the genius of this space lay in *resisting* geometrical idealization. The agora's 'group design'[73] – incidentally, neither 'square' nor 'street', but a chiasmatic passage-place in which both were transformed – embodied a history of tracks meeting and passing through each other. Remembering Freud's characterization of the terrain of the pre-conscious, it brought the wilderness to town. Paths did not simply meet in the agora. A surplus of paths boomeranged there, their collective energy scouring out the space.

The opening which the grooves of arrival and parting produced was presumably composed of wedge-shaped islands, turning circles, terraces – in short, every kind of locomotory trace. Ancient evidence of this is obviously hard to come by. The kind of thing I have in mind, though, is described by William Cobbett, who, in one of his rural rides made into England's Wiltshire, reported visiting Ashton Keines, 'now a straggling village [but formerly] a large market town': 'There is a market-cross still standing in an open place in it; and, there are such numerous lanes, crossing each other, and cutting the land up into such little bits, that it must, at one time, have been a large town.'[74] In his picturesque way, Camillo Sitte also recognized the 'unconscious artistry' of such tracks. If you want to know, he wrote, where to place statues in a public square, watch where children build their snowmen –

> Imagine the open square of a small market town in the country, covered with deep snow and criss-crossed by several roads and paths that, shaped by the traffic, form the natural lines of communication. Between them are left irregularly distributed patches untouched by traffic; on these stand our snowmen, because the necessary clean snow was to be found only there.[75]

Have such ephemeral meeting places been entirely asphalted away? Not according to anthropologist Kathleen Stewart, who finds the *other* other place in a space by the side of the road in West Virginia's post-industrial landscape. Her interviews with people inhabiting this marginalized landscape suggests to her that a different discursive space is being produced there. Here is a people who make the debris of modernity their dwelling place. They are the human rubbish of progress. There is no place for them in the Le Corbusier plan of the future. In this situation of having been forgotten, the act of place-making is a vital act of collective self-remembering, and it takes place in language.

The critical feature of this historically and physically sidelined space is that it came into being through social encounter. Perhaps an 'accidental event' acts as a catalyst;[76] in any case, from it there emerges the fundamental scene of speaker and listener, and the beginning of story. The story is making itself in the site of encounter; hence, it has to be *followed*. The listeners, too, 'place themselves in the scene of the story and follow along its track so that they too [can] be somehow marked with its impression'.[77] Speaking from within the scene of their history, the participants both recall the past and perform that recall. In a vernacular performance whose motivation is not so different from the ancient Athenian Greek seeking 'a remedy for the futility of action and speech' in the agora, Stewart's story-tellers are 'makin' somethin' of thangs'.[78]

The qualities Stewart ascribes to the world these stories make are clearly a cure for agoraphobia. Unlike Freud or Benjamin, reduced to wordlessness on the kerb, the story of finding oneself at the side of the road 'is a conventional opening that posits, among other things, that things happen, that *places* mark the space of lingering impacts and unseen forces'.[79] In contrast with Simmel's totalizing network, connections here are partial: '. . . there is always something more to say, always an uncaptured excess that provokes further questions, new associations that just come, and fresh gaps in understanding.'[80] The result is a 'storehouse for local ways of talkin' and ways of doin'' which provide a kind of protection from 'the feared and despised ways of the city'.[81]

A poetics of agoraphobia, then, stems from a recognition that the agora begins as a happening produced by the meeting and momentary knotting of two or more tracks. It grows through the networking of these passages to make them more dense and interwoven. Being instinct with topological properties (left and right, up and down, near and far), it is not tempted into the metaphysical miasma of attempting to unify itself under the aegis of a centralized gaze: it remains a grouping of units, a mobile arrangement of parts whose pattern can never be fully represented. It exhibits what Edward Casey has evoked as a provisional topology that expresses not so much identity as the constitutive performances of everyday life.[82] These place-making performances locate, according to Casey, a middle path, a dimension attuned to the lived dynamism of mundane practices like walking.[83]

GIVE WAY

The agoraphobe is not just an inhibited walker. He is haunted by a fear of the 'rhythmic or throbbing' crowd. He wants to mingle, to be swept up in its dionysiac traffic, but not at the cost of his sanity. Rather than be dismembered, he wants to remember. Canetti thinks that the rhythmic crowd originated in hunter-gatherer societies as a self-empowering, magical response to the other 'crowd' of wild animals, known by the traces they left in the form of footprints or tracks. This was the hunter's

> oldest knowledge. He learnt to know the animals by the rhythm of their movement. The earliest writing he learnt to read was that of their tracks; it was a kind of rhythmic notation imprinted on the soft ground and, as he read it, he connected it with the sound of its formation.[84]

Perhaps, but Canetti's genealogy of the crowd doesn't take into account the possibility that the dance also expressed a sense of kinship. The tracker who tracks his prey also makes tracks, and this sympathetic identification, this mark of vulnerability, is also a sign of power. It may be that the dionysiac crowd grows self-destructive precisely because it ignores this. Making the mistake of imagining it tracks trackless wastes, it ends up hunting itself to a sacrificial death.

In any case, the agoraphobe is haunted by the idea of an approach that does not lead to 'falling over each other'. As Arendt remarks,

What makes mass society so difficult to bear is not the number of people involved . . . but the fact that the world between them has lost its power to gather them together, to relate and to separate them. The weirdness of this situation resembles a spiritualistic séance where a number of people gathered around a table might suddenly, through some magic trick, see the table vanish from their midst, so that two persons sitting opposite each other were no longer separated but also would be entirely unrelated to each other by anything tangible.[85]

In this case, Westphal's agoraphobic patients, who saw 'shining circles floating before their eyes,' saw something real. They glimpsed the lost relation which the ersatz community of the séance could only conjure up in spirit form. They saw, as Munch did in representing people with ghosts for faces, what had happened to faces in the crowd.

In support of her view that the Greek concept of action was highly individualistic and influenced 'in the form of the agonal spirit, the passionate drive to show oneself in measuring up against others that underlines the concept of politics prevalent in the city-states', Arendt notes that the Greek word for 'every one' (*hekastos*) is derived from *hekas* ('far off').[86] But perhaps this etymology preserves a different insight – that as, in the crowd, one never meets, the crowd, however large it grows, always remains remote. It does not permit what Emmanuel Levinas calls an 'ethical relation' to emerge, one 'which is not a coincidence or a lost union, but signifies all the surplus or all the goodness of a lost sociality' in which there exists 'a distance which is also proximity'.[87] In such a relationship, Levinas argues, taking 'the responsibility for the Other, being-for-the-other . . . stop[s] the anonymous and senseless rumbling of being'.[88] Facing the other, ethical agoraphobia is overcome.

Levinas distinguishes between the face which is a mask or sign for something and the face which is a trace. The mask face is what Arendt's séance worshippers see when they see each other. The face that interests Levinas is different. Traces or tracks allude to whatever cannot be controlled. They are only partially wiped out and replaced: 'In doing that which I wanted to do, I have done so many things I did not want. The act has not been pure, for I have left some traces. In wiping out these traces, I have left others.'[89] Traces are never exhausted by what they signify, and the face points to an otherness that can never be represented. This may be an *agoraphobic* insight. The psychotherapist John Heaton has described a patient with a particular form of space fear. She reported: 'My eyes are two holes in the sky. They seem to point to a beyond,' and 'When I was a child I felt we were all in a shoebox and the stars were the holes in the lid.'[90] Heaton finds Levinas explicated here:

> The face resists possession . . . It breaks through the form that would grasp it by inviting me to a relation incommensurable with an exercised power . . . The grace of the face's radiance provokes the idea of infinity which is necessary for separation and the Other to break through.[91]

A poetics of agoraphobia turns a place-making anxiety to good account. It harbours a design on the other other place of the agora. It imagines this site chiasmatically. It is characterized by a surplus of trajectories repeatedly performed, an evolving but constitutionally partial network of crossings and contradictions. The motivation of these activities is not gathering for its own sake, but the cultivation of a sociable and erotic art of meeting. The provisional topology described by these actions gives gathering an ethical force and turns the vortical crowd into a posed democracy. But to elucidate the poetics of this, one thing more is needed. Levinas's looking beyond the look of the other remains both axial and individualistic. What is needed, at least for a poetics of public spaces, is a *multiple* point of view (one which, admittedly, Levinas has also advocated), free of nostalgia for the one. And something more: a way of *grouping* the multiple so that it does not become another million or faceless crowd.

Writing in 1949 about *Biffures*, a book by the French writer Michel Leiris, Levinas explained the meaning of the title. *Bifurs*

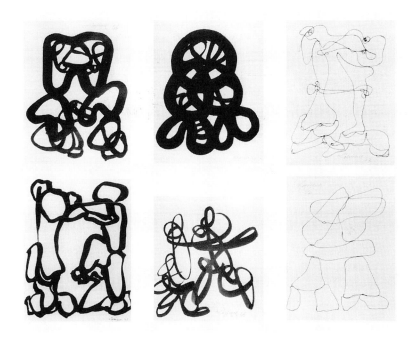

9–14 Charles Lapicque, pen-and-ink drawings: *Double tristesse*, 1946 (top left); *La rencontre*, 1946 (top middle); *Joyeuse rencontre*, 1947 (top right); *Rencontre*, 1947 (bottom left); *La conviction*, 1946 (bottom middle); *L'accolade*, 1947 (bottom right).

means 'bifurcations' or 'forks in the road'. *Biffures* means 'crossings out' or 'deletions'. Taken together, they suggest that 'it is not so much a question of exploring the new paths opened, or of holding to the corrected meaning, as of seizing thought at the privileged moment at which it turns into something other than itself.'[92] Levinas compared this literary technique to certain pen-and-ink drawings by Charles Lapicque: 'Destroying perspective in its function as the order of walking and of approach', it

> is not space that houses things, but things, by their deletion, that delineate space. The space of each object sheds its volume.

> From behind the rigid line there emerges the line as ambiguity.
> Lines rid themselves of their role as skeletons to become the
> infinity of possible paths of propinquity.[93]

In the field of perspectival drawing, Lapicque conceives of his lines as
tracks. He meets Lefebvre's objection, as his representational practice
conforms to the spaces he represents. But if, as I guess, Levinas had in
mind Lapicque's 1946–7 series *Figures entrelacées* (illus. 9–14), then
Lapicque's practice also contradicts Levinas's description of them. No
space nostalgia, or longing for the infinite informs the *Figures entrelacées*.
They are, as their name implies, chiasmatic figures in which human
presences are traced out rather than signified or represented. Lapicque
described them in terms that anticipated the tenets of Tachisme. They
sprang, he wrote, from interior, almost physical rhythms, from random
blots or traces [*de taches ou de traits*] that his hand traced aimlessly to
begin with. But this was not a preliminary to producing an abstract
design. The distinctiveness of Lapicque's random practice lay, he
insisted, in the fact that at a certain moment he perceived in his drawings people [*personnages*], in particular, two people entwined.[94]

Lapicque's drawings conjure up the other as an affective trace:
they reconfigure the other as a labyrinth formed of all the paths it has
taken. They recognize that this involves taking responsibility for the
other, being enlaced with the other's destiny. The result is not a mirror
symmetry – Lapicque's designs bear no resemblance to Rorschach
blots – but a doubled history, or meeting place. The Gemini figure is
not ambiguous. A desire of meeting shapes it, grouping the possible
paths of propinquity. But it does not signify anything. It is not a plan of
action or a hand-drawn map. The arrangement it makes cannot be
prefigured or repeated. It could not take place at a railway station.

THE CITY SQUARE

The space of meeting is a place of potential approaches. It is not
swallowed up and exhausted in actual meetings. It is not the trace
of a history of bumping into other people, but the spatialization of

approaches. This is an advantage city squares have over novels. In novels, it is always disappointing to find how easily characters meet. They seem to have no difficulty in finding each other. Within a page or two, on the slightest pretext, they are in conversation (or bed) together, plotting their fictional future, and the former history of possible meetings is wiped out. I would like to read a novel about the prehistory of such novels, in which the question of meeting is posed. It would see through the illusion of being life-sized to each other. It would give the distance between people a name. Such a book would document the duration of such intervals. Its characters would live at different *scales*, depending on their nearness to the emotional epicentre.

Perhaps the enterprise is unnecessary: city squares produce these effects spontaneously. Yet for this very reason, town planners, architects and landscape architects ignore them. The spaces they represent in architects' drawing practices lack duration. There is no calibration of nearness or farness. It is astonishing that the many-scaled perspective of the multiple is wholly absent. As a result, architects' meeting places are non-meeting places, spaces from which distance has been evacuated and where, in consequence, the adventure of the ethical relation cannot happen. They wipe out the history of approaches and its concomitant, the mortal pathways of loss. They create, in the guise of an immediate presencing, an absolute absence. The sociological rhetoric of functionality results from ignoring the allegorical discourse of the agora. Inverting the genealogy of public space, which is the interlaced, and contradictory, outflow of furrowing tracks, lines signifying passages are drawn into a blank page. The result is an estranging silence awaiting its traffic.

Above all, this indifference applies to *grouping*. It is true that digitally modelled animated walk-throughs can show spaces from every imaginable point of view. But an ensemble of prefixed relations viewed from a multiplicity of angles does not constitute a poetics of grouping. In the walk-through, no perspective is privileged over another, and yet the totality of relations is imagined perspectivally. An ultimate equivalence of parts is assumed, in which effects of distance remain illusory. Grouping, by contrast, embodies a *posed* spatial knowledge. Grouping is the significant gathering or *composition* of parts. It arrests differences of scale, transforming distances into a neighbourhood. Grouping is an art of making arrangements whose logic, as in Lapicque's drawings, consists in finding people there. In this way, a spatial disposition supplies an environmental hint to make an arrangement to meet.

Mention of Michel Leiris brings me to his book *Brisées*, and his observations there on the life and art of Alberto Giacometti. Among them, one finds this fragment:

> The sudden memory of a forest or of a clearing, depending on whether a random grouping of figures turns out to be denser or more diffuse. Instead of being destroyed like so many others, the figures had accumulated as though they had been made just for this grouping – in which they will have come into their final transformation.[95]

This, in essence, is the art of grouping: to create an arrangement uniquely for this occasion, the performance of a space of encounter like no other. And, as Leiris' allusion to the forest or clearing suggests, such an art simultaneously recovers the prehistory of the agora, whose origins, as etymology attests, lie in a double movement, back and forth between the city square and the wilderness.

Perhaps Samuel Beckett came closest to writing a prehistory of meeting. But as the plastic thinker of agoraphobia's spaces who contested Modernist urbanism on its own ground, it is Giacometti who best expresses the other other space of the city square. It is a curious historical oddity that the visual epiphany leading Giacometti to a new understanding of scale should have occurred on the Boulevard Saint-Michel – the same street in which Rilke, years earlier, feeling 'the twinge of an incipient fear', had latched on to his agoraphobic double and pursued him to the end. Here, in 1937, Giacometti felt the desire to represent a girlfriend 'as I had once seen her some distance away on the street'.[96] To represent this visual experience, he had to make her smaller than life-size. This was not all. Seeing her at a distance on the Boulevard Saint-Michel, Giacometti also 'saw all the black above her, the buildings'.[97] He found that,

> in order to convey the appearance of the whole and not lose myself in details, I had to choose an even greater distance. But even then, when I put in details, they seemed to contradict the whole . . . So I moved further and further back, until at last everything disappeared.[98]

Reinhold Hohl has questioned the view that these puzzling experiences represented an existential crisis – in which case, Henri Cartier-Bresson's 1961 photograph records a skilful performance, an agoraphobic semblance rather than a genuine panic (illus. 15). When Sartre and de Beauvoir took up Giacometti, they naturally stressed those aspects of his art that mirrored their own philosophical stance. In adopting some of their terms, he imitated them. 'For a long time [in 1941], when he was walking down the street, he had to test the solidity of the house walls with his hand to resist the abyss [*resister au gouffre*] that had opened up next to him,' de Beauvoir wrote.[99] In 1946, *le gouffre* also entered Giacometti's vocabulary briefly. But in a way, his spells of dizziness (Hohl has attributed them to a stomach ulcer[100]) were symptoms of an over-joining rather than an estrangement. It was not an abyss that he perceived. Quite the opposite. It was the illusion of self-sameness that had deserted him. As he observed, 'Lifesize does not exist. It is a meaningless concept. Lifesize is at most your own size – but you don't see yourself.'[101] The other side of the void, in which 'there was no longer any rapport between things', was the insight that things were related through their distances, and at their own scales.[102]

In short, Giacometti's interest in modelling groups in public spaces was neither pathological nor the result of an existential crisis. His was not an agoraphobic poetics, but a poetics of agoraphobia. The strongest proof of this is the persistence of his interest in making *compositions* with several figures – the 'hidden thread', as Hohl has called it, running through his whole stylistic development.[103] From the

15 Henri Cartier-Bresson, *Alberto Giacometti in rue d'Alesia, Paris*, 1961.

earliest days, when Giacometti's painter-father encouraged his son to notice the compositional potential of chance groupings of people in the streets of Bergell, it was a vision of the possible paths of propinquity that inspired him, not a metropolitan estrangement. As he wrote,

> Every moment of the day people come together and drift apart, and approach each other again to try to make contact anew. They unceasingly form and reform living compositions of incredible complexity. What I want to express in everything I do, is *the totality of this life*.[104]

Giacometti discovered that, to depict the totality, he had to distance himself from the scene. Wholeness, he found, was an effect of distance. Then, more radically still, he had to dissolve the viewpoint, casting groups that had no front or back, but that nevertheless seemed to cultivate a space between themselves that was different from the space occupied by the visitor to the gallery. I agree with Hohl. Compositions such as *The City Square* of 1948 (illus. 16) or *City Square (Three Figures, One Head)*, *The Forest (Seven Figures, One Head)* (illus. 17) or *The Glade (Nine Figures)* – all from 1950 – are not metaphors for 'the loneliness of man'.[105] Growing from the perception that others in the distance always look tall, however small they may appear – struck by this in Padua when he was only nineteen, Giacometti spoke of 'a fissure in reality'[106] – the sculptor wanted to capture the reality of meeting. His figures are co-extensive with the pedestal – now, instead of isolating them, it joins them. It is the pedestal that secures their separateness and difference from each other. The pedestal is the manifold of potential meeting-ways projected between them. It extends an invitation to statues to climb down from *their* pedestals and begin to walk.

In the distance, people did not succumb to the tyranny of the vanishing point: they turned into gods. If the distance could secure 'total seeing, absolute comprehension', then, Giacometti argued, a 'tiny figure, no matter what size it is, will take on the appearance of a god'.[107] De Beauvoir wrote that Giacometti considered the face 'an indivisible whole, a mood, an expression . . . he wanted to sculpt a face

16 Alberto Giacometti, *The City Square*, 1948, bronze.

in a concrete situation, in its existence for others, from a distance,' and she considered that this allied him with the interests of phenomenologists like Maurice Merleau-Ponty.[108] But the profounder philosophical affiliation is to 'the face' of Levinas. By cultivating the absolute distance where the other disappeared, Giacometti strove to evoke what Levinas called 'the "beyond" from which the face comes'.[109]

The face understood in this way is a 'visitation' – Levinas did not hesitate to call it a divinity[110] – and its trace transcends phenomenology's interest in true appearances. According to Levinas, the distinguishing mark of the face of the other is its 'elevation' or 'height'.[111] In the context of Giacometti's statues, hovering on the edge of sight, the full implication of Levinas's remark that 'the Other is higher than I am' becomes clear.[112] It means to glimpse in the fissure of being the totality of the divine.

One wonders how Giacometti's compositions would survive transfer from their own representational space to the space of the city square. In his groups with several figures, Hohl thinks, Giacometti 'unconsciously followed the natural law of grouping'.[113] What was this? As no point of view was privileged over another, it could hardly be aesthetically based. Hohl understands it metaphorically, as the accidental grasping of a situation whose 'organic-rhythmic determinants' capture the 'totality of life'.[114] This is why an arrangement of forest trees could be as suggestive as a group of people converging across a town square. Yet this is pretty vague. Leiris's description, quoted earlier, is more precise. A successful grouping is chiasmatic, like the agora. It is poised between growing more dense or diffusing. In this moment of accidentally achieved balance, a maximum ambiguity obtains. The space between figures is flirtatiously charged. A surplus of possible paths of propinquity opens up.

17 Alberto Giacometti, *The Forest (Seven Figures, One Head)*, 1950, bronze.

Towards the end of his life, Giacometti did indeed entertain the idea of creating 'a double of reality in real space, a sculpture in a city square peopled by living men and women'.[115] In 1959, he was invited to submit a project for a monumental sculptural group for the plaza of the Chase Manhattan Bank skyscraper in New York:

> He began to work out a composition he had in mind for decades, a representation of the 'totality of life' with larger-than-life figures in a style somewhere between traditional three-dimensional sculpture and mythical hieroglyph: standing women, walking men, and a huge head on a pedestal.[116]

At the time of his death six years later, nothing had been definitively resolved. Perhaps, as Hohl speculates, his final proposal was the siting of a single monumental figure 7 or 8 metres high. Perhaps not: in 1950, one of the skyscraper's architects had urged the artist to scale up an existing statue (*Three Men Walking*) to 18 metres in height. The artist refused – on an earlier occasion, he had, after all, noted that 'the smaller the figure was, the larger the square would seem'.[117] A skyscraper was large enough by itself – there was no point in trying to cut it down to size.

Perhaps, in the end, Giacometti was bound by his own insight that lifesize does not exist.[118] This was not only a sculptural concept: as the whittling down of the original idea for the Chase Manhattan Bank commission, and its eventual non-appearance, suggest, it was also an architectural indictment. An urban space turned out to be unable to support a net of relationships defined not in terms of externally regarded objects, but, as Merleau-Ponty put it, radiating 'out from me as the zero point, the centre',[119] a net which Giacometti understood as the subject of grouping.

About his painting Giacometti once wrote:

> I have often put just as many colours on my palette as my colleagues when starting in to work; I've tried to paint like them. But as I was working I had to eliminate one colour after another, no – one colour after the other dropped out, and what remained? Grey! Grey! Grey! My experience is that the colour that I feel, that I see, that I want to reproduce . . . means life itself to me; and that I totally destroy it when I deliberately put another colour instead. A red that I put violently into the picture damages it simply because it forces a grey out, a grey that belongs there, at exactly that spot.[120]

Giacometti's remark brings us to a final point. A poetics of agoraphobia cannot be wholly defined sculpturally, architecturally or even choreographically. The movement inhibition is *proprioceptive*. It originates in a *self*-awareness. The agoraphobe feels that seeing is no longer connected to moving. To let the eye range across the clarified volumes and surfaces of the rationalized city's immense spaces is to be seized with panic: here there is nowhere to go. In the moment this is sensed, the ground beneath one's feet no longer represents a position, a posed point of arrival or departure. The spot melts away to a pin-prick and a vanishing point. The result is vertigo and, lest the last slip of ground give way, petrification.

It follows that a therapeutic place-making not only involves an art of grouping. It also needs to engage the eyes. The agoraphobic gaze slides over smooth surfaces and experiences the same sensation as an inexperienced skater venturing out onto the ice. Better-placed shiny surfaces and volumes cannot cure this. Colours, textures and tones will also have to be negotiated. And, even more importantly, the distance itself will need to find its colour.

Focusing on this unfocusable shade makes it possible to return for a final time to the experience of Freud. It also, I think, indicates the difficulty of what is being proposed. A poetics of agoraphobia is not an aesthetic stance. It is the astonished and painful recognition of modernity's blind spot. The pressure not to notice what modern life destroys in the name of a progressive design on the future is immense. To conform to its vanishing-point perspective and its cult of light is easier. Agoraphobia is not only a fear of the clearing, when the act of clearing entails the advent of tracklessness. If we recall Giambattista Vico's poetic etymology, in which the Latin word *lucus* ('a place or clearing'), the Greek word *leukos* ('white') and another Latin word, *lux* ('light'), are said to share a common root, agoraphobia is also a fear of the light, when the light is identified with a blinding whiteness.[121]

As I've mentioned, Westphal described more than one agoraphobic patient who 'complained of seeing shining circles floating before their eyes'.[122] Commenting on what appears to be a similar sensation, Michael Balint considered it to be a physiological fact throwing light on primitive stages of psychic development. 'When one shuts one's eyes,' Balint wrote in 1955, 'one experiences something roughly hemispherical, surrounding one safely, the colour of which is grey if the intensity of light impinging on the eyelids is slight, or pink if the intensity is considerable.'[123] Noting that it is impossible to say whether this eye-grey or eye-pink is outside or inside us, nearer or farther away from a given object, Balint interpreted it as 'a clear instance of the friendly expanses, their harmony as yet undisturbed by any object, or, in other words: although there are no objects in it, it is not "horrid empty space", it is friendly'.[124]

Balint found this interpretation confirmed by the claim that the 'dream-screen' ('doubtless a counterpart in the dreaming state of the eye-grey when awake') is of the same hue, adding that 'most dreams are grey in grey'[125] – a phrase that strikingly recalls the description of Giacometti's 'grey-in-grey' *Grey Figure* (1957). It is tempting to recall further that the visual breakthrough Giacometti experienced in 1946, when he became able to 'perceive the distance which makes people appear real', occurred after watching a newsreel: '. . . instead of seeing a person on the screen, I saw – influenced by the drawings I was doing at the time – unfocused black spots that moved.'[126]

The most suggestive meditation on greyness occurs, though, in *The Interpretation of Dreams*. Having kept primly to the Ringstrasse earlier, one can be forgiven for detouring, at least briefly, into the free-associative pathways of Freud's labyrinth. In April 1885, Freud had assisted in an operation to relieve his father's unilateral glaucoma. Cocaine had been used in the operation as an anaesthetic – the ambitious Freud always regretted that, although he had glimpsed the drug's medical potential a few years earlier, credit for the discovery had gone to his colleague, Carl Koller (who had assisted in the operation on Jacob Freud). Nearly thirteen years later, these events re-emerged in the course of Freud's analysis of the 'Botanical Monograph' dream. One link in his associative chain of reasoning was: 'If ever I got glaucoma, I had thought, I should travel to Berlin and get myself operated on, incognito, in my friend's house.'[127]

Most Freudian accounts of this episode interpret it Oedipally:

> it would appear that Freud endeavoured to atone, perhaps according to the law of talion [an eye for an eye], for his partici-pation in his father's surgery. Behind this most probably lie the intense aggressive and negative feelings against his father, deriving from infantile sources and representing one half of the Oedipus complex. In his fantasy, Freud draws upon himself the punishment for his evil thoughts and wishes.[128]

But why? Unlike Ulysses plunging the burning stake into the Cyclops' single eye, our hero *saved* the sight of the one who stood in the way of his ambition. Why should Freud have felt guilty about removing the pressure inside one of his father's eyeballs? If, as the etymology of the first element in Oedipus' name suggests, swelling, sexual intimacy and knowledge through experience are derived from a single semantic cluster, Freud performed an act of ocular initiation. He *pricked* his father's eye to let in the light. The son was father to the man, initiating him into the virility of full-sightedness. The question is: Why was diminished or cloudy vision (Freud himself suffered from shortsightedness) desirable? What was aggressively removed, when the risk of blindness was prevented?

What was *regained* is easily answered – it was the integrated ego of the destructive character, *homo imperiosus* –

> recognis[ing] the necessary demands of duty as socially imposed (thus accepting the necessity to sublimate desires, postpone gratifications, and suppress counter qualities in his 'nature') ... subordinat[ing] emotions to socially educated reason in incorporating experience, rating emotional self-control in response to anything or anybody much more important than reactions of sensitivity or empathy[129]

– and his black-and-white way of seeing *qua* knowing the world:

> We can explore the retinas of our own eyes by looking at a piece of white paper; if we look at a black man we shall perhaps find out something about our own unconscious – not that the white man's image of the black man tells us anything about his own inner self, though it indicates that part of him which he has not been able to accept: it reveals his secret self, not as he is, but rather as he fears he may be. The negro, then, [and, we might add, the Jew] is the white man's fear of himself.[130]

Against this bleakly agoraphobic background, seeing the world in terms of *various shades of grey* might be a step towards historical, social and personal reintegration. And this, despite his submission to the necessary demands of socially imposed duty, Freud tried to do. On 2 November 1896, shortly after his father's death, Freud wrote to Fliess, about a 'nice dream I had the night after the funeral': 'I was in a place where I read a sign: You are requested to close the eyes.' He recognized the place as his local barbershop. The sign, he thought, had a double meaning: to do one's duty to the dead, and 'the actual duty itself'. Freud thought that the dream stemmed from survivor-guilt.[131]

In the *Interpretation of Dreams*, the dream is recalled differently –

During the night before my father's funeral I had a dream of a printed notice, placard or poster – rather like the notices forbidding one to smoke in railway waiting-rooms – on which appeared either 'You are requested to close the eyes' or 'You are requested to close an eye'.[132]

And Freud extracts a different double meaning from it – the words could refer to closing the corpse's eyes, or they could refer to his family's fear that they would be disgraced by the modesty of the funeral. But that is all. Instead of proceeding with the analysis begun in his earlier letter to Fliess, Freud leaves it at that, merely citing the ambiguous dream signpost as an example of the way dreams combine opposite meanings, or represent them as the same thing.

Another associative train of thought might begin here, though – with the usually ignored reference to the railway waiting room and the prohibition to smoke there. Freud was a heavy smoker. In his healthy times, he smoked about twenty cigars a day. The sight of him in his medical rooms wreathed in a cloud of smoke was a familiar one. Ludwig Binswanger recalled him 'smoking a cigar, his hand resting on the arm of his chair or on the desk'.[133] His son described the appearance of the waiting room, 'still thick with smoke', after Freud's Wednesday soirées: '. . . it seemed to me a wonder that human beings had been able to live in it for hours, let alone to speak in it without choking.'[134] His nephew remembered, 'When I was seventeen years old he offered me a cigarette; when I refused he said: "My boy, smoking is one of the most wonderful delights in this world".'[135]

The ambitious *homo imperiosus* of the unconscious, who had taken it upon himself to conquer and map its territory, had another, passive side. He liked to veil his boldness in smoke. He liked to bandage his barest pronouncements in mystery. It should be remembered that the glaucoma association arose in the course of a daydream after the dream: it occurred, one supposes, when Freud was reclining on a couch (his own analysand), idly studying the arabesques of cigar smoke winding above his head. To observe their trails forming will-o'-the-wisp shapes was to indulge in a kind of imaginal dreaming, and to do so in the key of grey. Smoking was a different way of seeing; it lent duration to time. Placing a veil of procrastination between the smoker and his responsibilities, it allowed him to inhabit a realm where opposite impulses co-existed. Unlike his ancient Greek namesake, Italo Svevo's Zeno could avoid the movement-inhibiting paradoxes that occur when life is governed by conscious either-or decisions – by smoking.[136] Smoke is like the honey that even Stalin cannot rush: it is the dimension of distance, and its volumes cannot be ghettoized or driven away.

No wonder that the smoking prohibition caused Freud particular anxiety. Getting onto the train and pulling away, he could light up, puffing on his cigar in time to the puffs of steam from the railway engine. A pressure to emit smoke was relieved. Perhaps it was phallic. Pointing out that 'very few men enjoy smoking in the darkness', a psychoanalyst, G. H. Green, writing in 1934, supposed that the 'visions, almost exclusively of women and girls' that people pipe-dream are masturbatory fantasies: 'If we may write the equation, smoke = semen, we are able to see the connection between huge clouds of smoke and fantasies of potency.'[137] No doubt. But to see through a veil of clouds was not to lose sight of reality, only to introduce the filter of distance. It was to lay over the scene a screen of winding tracks. The wind rushing in through the railway window was driven backwards by the iron progress of wheels on predetermined rails. In the railway compartment, though, it became tangled in the hair of smoke, producing the strangest eddies and plumes: so might reasoning, by way of the cigar's surplus of trails, smoke out the fertile shapes of unconscious life.

This, then, is my suggestion: if colours were the other of white, then grey was the *other* other of white, and the dominant hue of the agoraphobe's other other space, the agora where people other than ghosts met. In grey, Freud could feel at home; his fear of missing the train could be assuaged; the Jew's ghostly presence in Austro-Hungarian life and culture could be transformed into the mask of authority. At the same time, the piercing anti-Semitic stare was blunted. Freud located the beginnings of his phobia at the age of three. It was then that, travelling with his mother, he had seen, in the railroad station of Breslau, the first gas jets. They 'reminded me of souls burning in Hell'.[138] I suppose they caused in him a panic associated with a sense of exposure. He had a prophetic glimpse of what Ernst Bloch, writing in 1935 with the Nazi ascendancy in mind, later saw clearly: 'There is a night full of new horror stories – a night that is made only more intense by the overabundance of light bulbs, and the lack of other, more thoughtful forms of illumination.'[139]

Could smoke, historically co-opted to the fate of European Jewry, be recovered, its vision saved? The architect Daniel Libeskind has said that the 'blindingly intense light' of the first void in the Berlin Jewish Museum was

> inspired by the tale of a woman. Confined in a railway wagon, on her way to Auschwitz, she saw a light through the grating. That was all she could see. Maybe it was no more than lamps in a tunnel, but she believed it to be clouds, stars, sunshine. The desire to see that light once more got her through.[140]

In relating this story, Libeskind alludes to the revived responsibility of architecture. The promise of Modernism, to free humankind from dependence on nature, plunged it into a greater darkness. Swallowed up in Thomas Alva Edison's inventions, the void at the heart of the Enlightenment became palpable. Aspiring to be a 'second nature', modern buildings cultivated a blindness towards the more thoughtful light emanating from the night.

To give architectural expression to the light coming through the grating is to document the volume of the track. Truth, as the Italian philosopher Gianni Vattimo remarked, consists not in reflecting a given fact, but in responding to a destiny.[141] So with *Die Leere*, the void – although, with Lefebvre's spatial theoreticians in mind, the German word can also refer to a blank sheet of paper. The void, the space of Berlin, has to be voided, and this means avoiding another building. *Die*

Leere is not only a geometry of walls at an angle to 'Architecture', but 'a line which runs across Berlin. And,' Libeskind explains, 'the line is a white line of light which connects the dream to a tectonic and constructive Berlin of the future.'[142] It is not, though, an electrically powered floodlight, blinding, linear: its line (its descent) is shown in the Jewish Museum (which Libeskind called unofficially 'Between the Lines'[143]) to be fragmented, tortuous, vulnerable to disappearance.

The colour of disappearance is the colour of appearance. It is the colour of the 'appearance of the whole', when far-off faces are set into the black above and the buildings either side, like stars. It is the silver-grey of Libeskind's zinc-clad void, but it is also the hue of Freud's nightmare: glaucoma, the illness of seeing the world through a steely grey-blue veil, as if the environment were permanently smoke-bound, and the dawn (unless it is dusk) a long time coming. Its hollow green pallor draws attention to the absence of what Ernst Bloch calls 'the old, familiar this-worldliness of human nature and its encompassing arc of reason'.[144]

But the pressure it represents cannot be relieved by a simple operation. Glaucoma, like Freud's dream sign, can go either way. To see his end, Oedipus had first to exile himself from seeing. Many years later, grasping Hermes' hand, he learned to see again and became his own guide on the track. His death and apotheosis none but Theseus witnessed: 'Only the king we saw with upraised hand / Shading his eyes as from some awful sight, / That no man might endure to look upon.'[145] Reading between the lines of Sophocles' play, the King of Athens saw something like a streak of light. It could have been lamps in a tunnel, clouds, stars or sunshine.

GROUND ZERO

Agoraphobia is rather like Hester Prynne's badge: mention your interest in the subject, and there's scarcely anyone you bump into who doesn't confess to knowing someone who wears the secret letter 'A' sewn to their breasts.

According to one woman, agoraphobia runs in the family. Her grandmother is recalled cowering under tables or concealing herself in the clothes closet. The same witness states that on an ocean voyage, cooped up between decks, these panics were mysteriously suspended. Another describes a friend who adored walking in the country, but grew afraid when tall factory chimneys came into view. Yet another describes the horse rider whose vertigo commences when her foot touches the ground. One admits to a dread of smoothness, particularly in handrails. Another fears not being followed. Others are petrified because they *are* followed. They suppose that someone is looking at their legs and experience difficulty talking, first chattering, then stuttering to a halt. One woman thinks that she would be cured if she undressed and walked up and down the aisles of a cinema. A man accuses space of vertigo, observing how houses and pavements rotate round him when he stands perfectly still. This person experiences relief at the zoo, when looking at the sea lions: '. . . suddenly one of them comes to the surface, jumps into the air, and dives again, following a different direction.'[146]

This variety of symptoms presents the temptation to treat agoraphobia as R. D. Laing and others once treated schizophrenia. The alienation characterizing it is a symptom of a generalized social estrangement, whose cause lies in the discontents which the fragmentation of social life under late capitalism produces. If the pathological symptoms of the agoraphobe are discounted, this is the same argument feminist psychologists put forward when they contend that agoraphobia is a symptomatic reaction to the social, economic and political construction of women under patriarchy. The drawback, though, is that this approach seems to attribute to agoraphobia sufferers an insight they don't have. It risks discounting the suffering, the actual, chronically debilitating unease. If the *cure* for agoraphobia is a posed knowledge of relations, then the 'squatting man', as Canetti has described the agoraphobe, is not emancipated: he 'has made himself a prison in his cowering. Those who dare can enter, but he who is himself the prison will not be freed.'[147]

The psychoanalyst Edmund Bergler considered the writer to

be 'a neurotic with a self-devised cure',[148] adding: 'The typical writer, being himself a neurotic and therefore incapable of love, is no more competent to describe love than a blindman is to describe colours.'[149] But this is an eccentric hypothesis. Besides, as we found, insight into the *other* of colours depends on blinding of a kind. Agoraphobia is not a visionary insight into the general rottenness characterizing relations under capitalism. It is not the breath of fresh air that blows away the phantasmagoric smokescreens our ideology of self throws up between ourselves. It demeans the suffering of those who endure it, *whatever the condition may be*, to pretend otherwise.

In this book, I have tried to steer clear of these metaphorical approaches. The historical meanings of the agora – as assembly and place of assembly – define its scope. *Agora* turns out to be a term that resembles Freud's dream sign in combining opposite meanings, but common to all of these is a distinctively *environmental* unease or anxiety. On this reading, agoraphobia stems from the prospect of places being opened up that are not places. The crisis occurs as a confrontation with make-believe spaces. The opening they promise is infinitely estranging. The enlarged access they offer produces a concomitant *anomie*. A sense of vertigo is accompanied by a fear of asphyxiation: maximum mobility accompanied by maximum petrification – agora-claustro-phobia. The double-bind sensation arises from a sudden awareness of a lost relation. Characteristics of sociable space that had been taken for granted become conspicuous by their absence. Qualities of orientation, proximity and grouping, and their behavioural counterparts, gathering, lingering and the general gymnastic of a rhetorically conducted social existence, are missing.

The agoraphobe is one who feels this disorientation or *depayse-ment* viscerally, as a loss of standing. The ground physically slides from underneath her feet. At the kerb's edge, she hesitates like an apprentice skater on the brink of the ice. Her anxiety springs not from the new immensity of the clearings, or even from the terrifying traffic they now harbour. It arises from the clearing away of tracks. What appears as a removal of obstacles to progress inters the ground's historical fingerprint. The new mobility is billiard ball-like, not bipedal. Wheels are its medium, not feet. Pathways are subordinated to the direction of the road. Older evidences of leaning and tilting are, as far as possible, neutralized: drains minimize the inconvenience of tears.

In this kinetic, relational story, architecture tends to lose its central place. In the popular imagination, no account of dread-inducing spaces is possible without a discussion of the gigantic urban schemes of Hitler's design puppet, Albert Speer. But absolute size, as both Sitte and Giacometti recognized, is not critical. Besides, as defenders of Speer emphasize, the dimensions of his proposed constructions were 'astonishingly modest' when compared with New York's World Trade Center, the Houston Astrodome or the central axis of Brasilia.[150] Speer was as sympathetic to Sitte's critique of *Industriekultur* as he was receptive to Wagner's principles of town planning.[151] His monumentalism was conservative and traditional in comparison with the megalomaniac landscape-into-art proposals of the *Geist* and *Volk* school led by Bruno Taut.[152]

The significant genealogy is a textural one. It is the *smoothness* of Speer's architectural dreams that appals. But the history of the relinquishment of ornament is far older than Adolf Loos' 'naked' façades.[153] Commenting on Canetti's identification of smoothness with power, Werner Hoffmann observes:

> It was not the principles of clarity and utility that triumphed in the architecture of right angles and mirroring facades in the middle of our century, but, as Canetti was perhaps the first to see, the steel-and-glass formulae of anonymous power. Smoothness and 'the prestige of the power it conceals', can already be found in the characteristics of the architectural language 'around 1800' – not only in that of built and imagined prisons but also in the purist utopias of communality in which private and public life are regulated in every aspect.[154]

Hoffmann had in mind the architectural fantasies of Ledoux and Boullée, and it is Boullée's description of a design for a cemetery that supplies the ideal conditions, as it were, for the incubation of modern agoraphobia:

> A gloomy labyrinth of passageways where the dead rest in niches surrounds a massive, cavelike dome, through the vertex of which a shaft of daylight penetrates. From outside only the upper part of the sphere is visible: a mighty cupola. Fearful, one shrinks back from this terrible dome . . . The image of nothingness should offer the eye no point at which it can rest: neither wood nor meadow, neither valley nor river, and certainly not the life-giving gift of the sun.[155]

Hoffmann comments:

> In the mausoleums we see the beginnings of that pathos of denial which is being practised today in a far, far subtler manner, when windows that can be opened are done away with in office blocks, the outside world is coloured with tinted glass, and air conditioning fends off 'the life-giving gift of sun'.[156]

Towers form in response to agoraphobia. Horizontal exposure produces upright enclosure. The tallness is not height, but a phobic reaction to the ground disappearing from under our feet. It is a gathering-together in the absence of a place to meet. Now, tragically, the justness of Hoffmann's genealogy is proved: since 11 September, the greatest of towers turn out to have been a vertical cemetery.

When the ideology of smooth construction is discovered, the neglected *techne* of composition reassumes significance. The human other of the skater is the limper. 'The deeper implication of laming', James Hillman has written, 'is the verticality of the spirit.' The lame man, the one-legged man, finds that

> the left-right rhythm that steadies one with the mutual self-corrections of thesis and antithesis is off-balance, and with it, man's relation to the earth as walker who paces the dimensions of reality, taking its measure with his footsteps and his tempo.[157]

The new artist is the one who absorbs off-balance into his composition. The first musician of agoraphobia, Gustav Mahler, seems to have absorbed off-balance into his gait as well:

> I remember [him] walking down the Ringstrasse in Vienna, his hat in his hand . . . I often observed the convulsive movement of his right leg, an involuntary twitching, expressed in one to three arhythmical steps in walking or in a kind of stamping of his foot in stopping.[158]

This mention of the composer encourages me to offer one last speculation. At the beginning of this book, I mentioned one by Theodor Reik – how I came across the reference to Sigmund Freud's agoraphobia *while looking for something else*, and I *smoothed over* the little leap from one track to another. Agoraphobia, it seems, can be a characteristic of speaking and writing. Smoothing over discontinuities implies a dread of gaps opening up in the chain of logic, a fear perhaps of thinking and acting freely. This dread arises because those gaps are imagined as abysses or voids. But they are not: they are simply where the ground is rough, over-tracked, ambiguously delineated, humid or mist-streaked. It is a mistake to step over them without taking notice of what is there.

Westphal reported that an important element in the agora-phobe's armoury was his walking-stick. Most later psychological writers have commented that victims of agoraphobia are able to allay their panic when accompanied in the street by someone they trust. The walking-stick seems to play the same role in the absence of a human other. It is a tracking device when the agoraphobe (like the blinded Oedipus) is forced to become his own guide. It implies blindness. It also accompanies lameness. If a man were a monopod, as he is conceptually in a Cartesian description of the human's place in the environment, the walking stick is the prosthetic device he needs to mobilize himself. Its role is not confined to tapping the ground or lightly punctuating it with imprints of the ferrule. If Erik Satie could go about 'with a lighted clay pipe stuck in his pocket, its stem reaching up to his ear',[159] why not admit that a walking-stick can also be a pipe. A walking-stick may not leave a visible smoke-trail, but it can still conduct invisible figures.

The passage in Reik I had been searching for related to the history of the conductor's baton. Reik describes there how the ancient Greeks had two kinds of conducting. The leader of the chorus indicated the beat 'by stamping his foot, which was iron-soled'.[160] The progress of the musical composition could also be indicated 'by arm, hand, and finger motions corresponding to the rise and fall of the melody'.[161] In post-Classical music-making, cheironomia (as the latter system was called) came to predominate over foot-stamping. But not invariably: conductors in eighteenth-century France were known as *batteurs de mesure* and used a baton to mark time 'very audibly' – which brings me to Reik's anecdote about the famous French composer Jean-Baptiste Lully. Lully was conducting a *Te Deum* for the recovery from illness of Louis XIV when, 'in thumping the time on the floor with his long heavy baton, Lully struck his foot. He died from the consequences of the infection that resulted from his mistake.'[162]

But what, exactly, was his mistake? In a trivial sense, Lully miscalculated where he was putting his stick. But the profounder error was to mark time as if the spot didn't count for anything. The beat had been detached from rhythmical walking. It had ceased to track the dance physically, to notate and groove its progress in the ground. Lully fell over himself because of this. Accepting the smoothness of space, he found that he had nowhere to stand, that the ground he nominally inhabited was poisoned. The agoraphobe's baton *qua* walking-stick is a device for composing mobility into a figure of sociability. The *agoraios* might lean on it. The juggler might adapt it to balance a spinning plate. The street-urchin could grab it to unhat the man in the street. Imagine the harmony that could be brought to traffic if tram conductors harnessed its powers. The arabesques it describes (permanently grooved into the floor or ephemerally traced in the air) are the outlines of the lost relation, the other, who is never an immobile volume, but the face the distance wears. The labyrinth of all the paths it takes is the meeting place.

REFERENCES

INTRODUCTION: SIGNPOSTS

1 Theodor Reik, *The Search Within: The Inner Experiences of a Psychoanalyst* (New York, 1956), p. 260.
2 *Ibid.*, p. 261.
3 *Ibid.*, p. 262.
4 Søren Kierkegaard, *The Sickness unto Death*, trans. A. Hannay (London, 1989), p. 66.

1 TURNING OUT

1 Franz Kafka, 'Third Octavo Notebook', in *Wedding Preparations in the Country and Other Posthumous Writings*, trans. E. Kaiser and E. Wilkins (London, 1954), p. 73.
2 Dr Ireland, 'German Psychological Retrospect', *Journal of Mental Science* (1873), p. 457.
3 Carl E. Schorske, *Fin-de-Siècle Vienna, Politics and Culture* (London, 1980), p. 62.
4 Camillo Sitte, *The Birth of Modern City Planning*, trans. and commentary G. R. Collins and C. Crasemann Collins (New York, 1986), p. 183.
5 Dr Ireland, 'German Psychological Retrospect', p. 457.
6 *Ibid.*, p. 457.
7 Marshall Berman, *All That Is Solid Melts Into Air* (London, 1983), p. 159.
8 *Ibid.*, p. 159 note.
9 Robert Musil, *The Man Without Qualities*, trans. E. Wilkins and E. Kaiser (London, 1979), vol. 1, p. 3.
10 *Ibid.*, vol. 1, p. 7.
11 Edmund Bergler, 'Psychoanalysis of a Case of Agoraphobia', in *Selected Papers of Edmund Bergler, M.D., 1931–1961* (New York, 1969), p. 672.

12 Musil, *The Man Without Qualities*, vol. 1, p. 6.

13 Wilhelm Worringer, *Abstraction and Empathy: A Contribution to the Psychology of Style*, trans. M. Bullock (New York, 1953), pp. 15–16.

14 Musil, *The Man Without Qualities*, vol. 1, p. 7.

15 Georg Simmel, *Simmel on Culture: Selected Writings*, ed. D. Frisby and M. Featherstone (London, 1997), p. 184.

16 Sigmund Freud, *The Complete Psychological Works of Sigmund Freud*, ed. and trans. J. Strachey (London, 1953–75), vol. 1, p. 139.

17 *Ibid.*, vol. XVI, pp. 270–71.

18 *Ibid.*, vol. XVI, pp. 393, 407.

19 Schorske, *Fin-de-Siècle Vienna*, p. 64.

20 Freud, *The Complete Psychological Works*, vol. X, p. 115.

21 Siegfried Bernfeld and Suzanne Cassirer, 'Freud's First Year in Practice, 1886–1887', in H. M. Ruitenbeek, ed., *Freud as We Knew Him* (Detroit, 1973), pp. 252–65.

22 *Ibid.*, p. 261.

23 Anny Katan, 'The Role of "Displacement" in Agoraphobia', *International Journal of Psycho-Analysis*, 32 (1951), p. 46.

24 Ignacio Matte Blanco, 'Some Reflections on Psycho-Dynamics', *International Journal of Psycho-Analysis*, XXI (1940), p. 253.

25 Anthony Vidler, 'Psychopathologies of Modern Space: Metropolitan Fear from Agoraphobia to Estrangement', in M. S. Roth, ed., *Rediscovering History, Culture, Politics, and the Psyche* (Stanford, 1994), p. 28.

26 Le Corbusier, *The City of Tomorrow and Its Planning*, trans. F. Etchells (Cambridge, MA, 1971), p. 3.

27 *Ibid.*, p. 3.

28 *Ibid.*, pp. 3–4.

29 *Ibid.*, p. 11.

30 Maureen C. McHugh, 'A Feminist Approach to Agoraphobia: Challenging Traditional Views of Women at Home', in J. C. Chrisler, C. Golden and P. D. Rozee, eds, *Lectures on the Psychology of Women* (New York, c. 1996), pp. 353–4.

31 Esther da Costa Meyer, 'La Donna è Mobile: Agoraphobia, Women, and Urban Space', in D. Agrest, P. Conway and L. K. Weisman, eds, *The Sex of Architecture* (New York, 1996), pp. 152–3.

32 McHugh, 'A Feminist Approach', p. 340.

33 S. Russo, 'Chronophobia: A Prison Neurosis', *Mental Hygiene*, 27 (1943), pp. 581–91.

34 A. Bernard, and C. Jung, 'Contribution à l'étude de la cremnophobie', *Revue neurologique*, 36 (1929), pp. 435–50.

35 I. P. Glauber, 'On the Meaning of Agoraphilia', *Journal of the American Psychoanalytic Association*, 3 (1955), pp. 701–9.

36 S. N. Volkov, 'The Question of Agoraphobia Connected with Disorders of the Functions of the Vestibular Apparatus', *Nevropatologieia Psiekhiatrieia Ie Psiekhogiegieena*, 10 (1936), pp. 1750–55.

37 R. Ulrich *et al.*, 'Multiple Treatments for Agoraphobia through Habituation Training (Flooding) and Peripheral Limitation of Excitement', *Zeitschrift für Klinische Psychologie*, 4/3 (1975), pp. 209–33.

38 J. Mendel and D. Klein, 'Anxiety Attacks with Subsequent Agoraphobia', *Comprehensive Psychiatry*, 10/3 (1969), pp. 190–95.

39 J. Heiser and D. Defrancisco, 'The Treatment of Pathological Panic States with Propranolol', *American Journal of Psychiatry*, 133 (December 1973), pp. 1389–4.

40 D. Johnston and D. Gath, 'Arousal Levels and Attribution Effects in Diazepam-assisted Flooding', *British Journal of Psychiatry*, 123 (October 1973), pp. 463–6.

41 P. Tyrer, 'Towards Rational Therapy with Monoamine Oxidase Inhibitors', *British Journal of Psychiatry*, 128 (April 1976), pp. 354–60.

42 M. T. Haslam, 'The Relationship between the Effect of Lactate Infusion on Anxiety States and Their Amelioration by Carbon Dioxide Inhalation', *British Journal of Psychiatry*, 124 (July 1974), pp. 88–90.

43 Francis Bacon, *The New Organon and Related Writings*, ed. F. H. Anderson (Indianapolis, 1960), p. 56.

44 Rosalind Deutsche, 'Agoraphobia', in *Evictions: Art and Spatial Politics* (Cambridge, MA, 1996), p. 325.

45 John Llewelyn, *Emmanuel Levinas: The Genealogy of Ethics* (London, 1995), p. 204.

46 Schorske, *Fin-de-Siècle Vienna*, p. 64.

47 *Ibid.*

48 Henry George Liddell and Robert A. Scott, *Greek-English Lexicon* (Oxford, 1966), p. 13.

49 Richard Sennett, *The Conscience of the Eye* (London, 1990), p. xiii.

50 Vidler, 'Psychopathologies of Modern Space', p. 15.

51 *Ibid.*, p. 16.

52 *Ibid.*, p. 17.

53 Emanuel Miller, 'The Analysis of Agora-Claustrophobia, a Passive Anamnesis', *International Journal of Psycho-Analysis* (1930), pp. 253–67.

54 Michael Balint, 'Friendly Expanses – Horrid Empty Spaces', *International Journal of Psycho-Analysis*, XXXVI/4–5 (1955), pp. 227–8.

55 R. D. Laing, *The Divided Self: An Existential Study in Sanity and Madness* (London, 1965), p. 44.

56 *Ibid.*, p. 45.

57 *Ibid.*, p. 46.

58 *Ibid.*, p. 53.

59 *Ibid.*

60 *Ibid.*, p. 56.

61 J. D. Safran and L. S. Greenberg, 'Affect and the Unconscious: A Cognitive Perspective', in R. Stern, ed., *Theories of the Unconscious and Theories of the Self* (Hillside, NJ, 1987), p. 208.

62 Morris Eagle, 'The Psychoanalytic and the Cognitive Unconscious' in R. Stern, *Theories of the Unconscious and Theories of the Self* (Hillside, NJ, 1987), pp. 167–8.

63 Karl Popper, *The Open Society and Its Enemies* (Princeton, 1966), vol. 1, p. 174.

64 Simmel, *Simmel on Culture*, p. 175.

65 Vidler, 'Psychopathologies of Modern Space', p. 20.

66 Donald Levine, *The Flight from Ambiguity* (Chicago, 1985), p. 114.

67 Robert A. Nye, *The Origins of Crowd Psychology: Gustave LeBon and the Crisis of Mass Democracy in the Third Republic* (London, 1???), p. 68.

68 *Ibid.*, p. 68.

69 *Ibid.*

70 Deutsche, 'Agoraphobia', p. 319.

71 *Ibid.*, p. 273.

72 Le Corbusier, *The City of Tomorrow*, p. 131.

73 *Ibid.*, p. 164.

74 James Holston, *The Modernist City: An Anthropological Critique of Brasilia* (Chicago, 1989), p. 105.

75 *Ibid.*

76 *Ibid.*

77 *Ibid.*, p. 106.

78 Walter Benjamin, *One Way Street and Other Writings*, trans. E. Jephcott and K. Shorter (London, 1985), pp. 158–9.

79 Vidler, 'Psychopathologies of Modern Space', p. 26.

80 McHugh, 'A Feminist Approach', p. 354.

81 Benjamin, *One Way Street*, p. 294.

82 *Ibid.*, p. 294.

83 *Ibid.*, p. 301.

84 Bernfeld and Cassirer, 'Freud's First Year in Practice', p. 261.

85 Paul Goodman, *Kafka's Prayer* (New York, 1947), p. 13.

86 Rudiger Safranski, *Schopenhauer and the Wild Years of Philosophy*, trans. E. Osers (Cambridge, MA, 1990), p. 40.

87 *Ibid.*, p.16.

88 *Ibid.*

89 *Ibid.*

90 *Ibid.*, p. 52.

91 *Ibid.*, p. 82.

92 *Ibid.*, p.40.

93 *Ibid.*, p. 50.

94 *Ibid.*, p. 51.

95 *Ibid.*

96 Le Corbusier, *City of Tomorrow*, pp. 186–7.

97 *Ibid.*, p. 16.

98 *Ibid.*, p. 4.

99 *Ibid.*, p. 4, n. 1.

100 Sitte, *The Birth of Modern City Planning*, p. 68.

101 Vladimir Jankélévitch, *Correspondance: Une vie en toutes lettres* (Paris, 1995), p. 302.

102 Francis Macnab, *Footprints: Psychological and Psychoanalytic Explorations* (Melbourne, 1996), p. 4.

103 Max Brod, *The Biography of Franz Kafka*, trans. G. H. Roberts (London, 1947), p. 81.

104 Macnab, *Footprints*, p. 5.

105 Bente Torjusen, *Words and Images of Edvard Munch* (London, 1986), p. 38.

106 Schorske, *Fin-de-Siècle Vienna*, p. 85.

107 *Ibid.*, p. 9.

108 *Ibid.*

109 *Ibid.*, p. 19.

110 *Ibid.*, p. 97.

111 *Ibid.*, p. 85.

112 Dr Ireland, 'German Psychological Retrospect', p. 457.

113 Rainer Maria Rilke, *The Notebooks of Malte Laurids Brigge*, trans. S. Mitchell (New York, 1983), p. 61.

114 *Ibid.*, p. 62.

115 *Ibid.*, p. 63.

116 *Ibid.*

117 *Ibid.*, p. 64.

118 *Ibid.*, p. 65.

119 *Ibid.*

120 *Ibid.*, p. 66.

121 *Ibid.*

122 *Ibid.*, p. 67.

123 Callum Coats, *Living Energies* (Bath, 1995), p. 57.

124 Flora Thompson, *Lark Rise to Candleford* (London, 1948), pp. 240–41.

125 Peter Gay, *My German Question: Growing Up in Nazi Berlin* (New Haven, 1998), p. 38.

126 *Ibid.*

127 *Ibid.*

128 *Ibid.*, p. 39.

129 *Ibid.*, p. 40.

130 *Ibid.*, p. 133.

131 *Ibid.*, p. 134.

132 Martin Freud, *Glory Reflected* (London, 1957), p. 106.

133 *Ibid.*, p. 106.

134 Bergler, 'Psychoanalysis of a Case of Agoraphobia', p. 672.

135 Thomas Szasz, *Karl Kraus and the Soul Doctors: A Pioneer Critic and His Criticism of Psychiatry and Psychoanalysis* (Baton Rouge, 1976), p. 7.

136 Safranski, *Schopenhauer and the Wild Years of Philosophy*, pp. 111–12.

137 *Ibid.*, p. 127.

138 *Ibid.*, p. 137.

139 Goodman, *Kafka's Prayer*, p. 73.

140 Theodor Adorno, *Minima Moralia: Reflections from Damaged Life*, trans. E. F. N. Jeffcott (London, 1974), p. 153.

141 Simmel, *Simmel on Culture*, p. 149.

142 *Ibid.*, p. 223.

143 Georg Simmel, *Georg Simmel: On Women, Sexuality, and Love*, trans. G. Oakes (New Haven, 1984), p. 151.

144 Simmel, *Georg Simmel*, p. 150.

145 *Ibid.*, p. 151.

146 Brod, *The Biography of Franz Kafka*, p. 81.

147 Simmel, *Georg Simmel*, p. 155.

148 Roland Barthes, *Frammenti di un discorso amoroso* (Turin, 1979), p. 17.

149 Catherine Clement, *Syncope: The Philosophy of Rapture*, trans. S. O'Driscoll and D. M. Mahoney (Minneapolis, 1994), p. 288, translator's note 9.

150 Jonathan D. Spence, *The Memory Palace of Matteo Ricci* (London, 1988), p. 236.

151 *Ibid.*, p. 237.

152 Rainer Maria Rilke, *Letters 1910–1926*, trans. J. B. Greene and M. D. H. Norton (New York, 1947), p. 152.

153 *Ibid.*

154 Edward Casey, *The Fate of Place: A Philosophical History* (Berkeley, 1998), p. 271.

155 Rainer Maria Rilke, *Selected Poetry*, trans. S. Mitchell (London, 1982), p. 179.

156 *Ibid.*, p. 180.

157 Margaret Cohen, *Profane Illumination: Walter Benjamin and the Paris of Surrealist Revolution* (Berkeley, 1993), pp.187–8.

158 Sitte, *The Birth of Modern City Planning*, p. 236.

159 Pierre Jaccard, *Le Sens de la direction e l'orientation lointaine chez l'homme* (Paris, 1932), p. 163.

160 *Ibid.*, p. 164.

161 *Ibid.*, p. 305.

162 *Ibid.*, p. 102.

163 Gay, *My German Question*, p. 46.

164 *Ibid.*

165 Dr Ireland, 'German Psychological Retrospect', p. 457.

166 Guy de Maupassant, *Selected Short Stories*, trans. R. Colet (London, 1981), p. 366.

167 *Ibid.*

168 Adorno, *Minima Moralia*, p. 156.

169 *Ibid.*

170 *Ibid.*, p. 157.

171 Alberto Savinio, *Maupassant e 'L'altro'* (Milan, 1995), pp. 62ff.

172 Arnold Kellett, trans., *The Dark Side of Guy de Maupassant* (London, 1989), p. 135.

173 Savinio, *Maupassant e 'L'altro'*, p. 85.

174 Musil, *The Man Without Qualities*, vol. 1, p. 59.

175 T. Ribot, *Diseases of Memory: An Essay in the Positive Psychology* (London, 1882), p. 72.

176 Torjusen, *Words and Images of Edvard Munch*, p. 131.

177 *Ibid.*

178 *Ibid.*

179 Freud, *Glory Reflected*, p. 38.

180 *Ibid.*, p. 110.

181 Freud, *The Complete Psychological Works of Sigmund Freud*, vol. 1, p. 181.

182 Vidler, 'Psychopathologies of Modern Space', p. 26.

183 Milton L. Miller, 'On Street Fear', *International Journal of Psycho-Analysis* (1953), p. 237.

184 Kathleen A. Brehony, 'Women and Agoraphobia: A Case for the Etiological Significance of the Feminine Sex-Role Stereotype', in V. Franks and E. D. Rothblum, eds, *The Stereotyping of Women, Its Effects on Mental Health* (New York, 1983), p. 113.

185 Philip Evans and John Liggett, 'Loss and Bereavement as Factors in Agoraphobia: Implications for Therapy', *British Journal of Medical Psychology*, 44 (1971), p. 153.

186 Miller, 'The Analysis of Agora-Claustrophobia', p. 255.

187 McHugh, 'A Feminist Approach', pp. 340, 346.

188 Georg Simmel, *The Conflict in Modern Culture and Other Essays*, trans. and intro. K. P. Etzkorn (New York, 1968), p. 79.

189 Konstantin Stanislavsky, *Stanislavsky on the Art of the Stage*, trans. D. Magarshack (London, 1988), p. 225.

190 *Ibid.*

191 Benjamin, *One Way Street*, p. 267.

192 Sharon M. Carnicke, *Stanislavsky in Focus* (Amsterdam, 1998), p. 181.

193 Naomi Greene, '"All The Great Myths Are Dark": Artaud and Fascism', in G. A. Plunka, ed., *Antonin Artaud and the Modern Theater* (London and Toronto, 1994), pp. 112–13.

194 William M. S. Baker, 'From Ritual to Theater and Its Double', in Plunka, ed., *Antonin Artaud and Modern Theater*, p. 118.

195 Tadeusz Kantor, *A Journey Through Other Spaces: Essays and Manifestos, 1944–1990*, trans. M. Kobialka (Berkeley, 1993), p. 101.

196 C. P. Oberndorf, 'Folie à Deux', *International Journal of Psycho-Analysis*, XV (1934), p. 14.

197 *Ibid.*

198 Anthony Wilden, *Man and Woman, War and Peace* (London, 1987), pp. 22ff.

199 Harald Salfellner, *Franz Kafka and Prague* (Prague, 1998), p. 76.

200 *Ibid.*

201 Margarete Buber-Neumann, *Milena*, trans. R. Manheim (New York, 1988), p. 57.

202 *Ibid.*, p. 29.

203 *Ibid.*, p. 39.

204 *Ibid.*, p. 89.

205 *Ibid.*, p. 2.

206 *Ibid.*

207 *Ibid.*, p. 61.

208 Simmel, *Georg Simmel*, p. 155.

209 Buber-Neumann, *Milena*, p. 61.

210 Sitte, *The Birth of Modern City Planning*, p. 226.

211 Cohen, *Profane Illumination*, p. 174.

212 *Ibid.*

213 *Ibid.*, p. 231.

214 *Ibid.*, p. 236.

2 DRIVING

1 Thomas Szasz, *Karl Kraus and the Soul Doctors: A Pioneer Critic and His Criticism of Psychiatry and Psychoanalysis* (Baton Rouge, 1976), p. 109.

2 Martin Freud, *Glory Reflected* (London, 1957), p. 27.

3 Theodor Reik, *The Search Within: The Inner Experiences of a Psychoanalyst* (New York, 1956), p. 261.

4 Sigmund Freud, *The Complete Psychological Works of Sigmund Freud*, ed. and trans. J. Strachey (London, 1953–75), vol. XIII, p. 222.

5 Margaret Cohen, *Profane Illumination: Walter Benjamin and the Paris of Surrealist Revolution* (Berkeley, 1993), p. 249.

6 Carl E. Schorske, *Fin-de-Siècle Vienna, Politics and Culture* (London, 1980), p. 31.

7 *Ibid.*, p. 32.

8 Camillo Sitte, *The Birth of Modern City Planning*, trans. and commentary G. R. Collins and C. Crasemann Collins (New York, 1986), p. 36.

9 Freud, *Glory Reflected*, p. 34.

10 *Ibid.*, p. 35.

11 *Ibid.*, p. 27.

12 Samuel Rosenberg, *Why Freud Fainted* (New York, 1978), p. 101.

13 *Ibid.*

14 *Ibid.*, p. 144.

15 *Ibid.*

16 *Ibid.*, p. 146.

17 Morris Eagle, 'The Psychoanalytic and the Cognitive Unconscious' in R. Stern, ed., *Theories of the Unconscious*, pp. 155–90.

18 Reik, *The Search Within*, p. 175, n. 7.

19 J. D. Safran and L. S. Greenberg, 'Affect and the Unconscious: A Cognitive Perspective', in Stern, ed., *Theories of the Unconscious and Theories of the Self*, p. 208.

20 Richard Sennett, *The Conscience of the Eye* (London, 1990), p. xii.

21 Sigmund Freud, *The Interpretation of Dreams*, trans. J. Strachey (New York, 1960), p. 581.

22 Freud, *The Complete Psychological Works*, vol. VXI, p. 394.

23 *Ibid.*, vol. XVI, pp. 398–9.

24 *Ibid.*, vol. XVI, p. 399.

25 *Ibid.*, vol. XVI, p. 400.

26 *Ibid.*

27 *Ibid.*, vol. XX, p. 80.

28 *Ibid.*, vol. XX, p. 81.

29 *Ibid.*, vol. XX, pp. 108–9.

30 *Ibid.*, vol. XX, p. 109.

31 *Ibid.*, vol. XX, p. 127.

32 *Ibid.*

33 *Ibid.*

34 *Ibid.*, vol. XX, pp. 127–8.

35 *Ibid.*, vol. XX, p. 144.

36 Peter L. Rudnytsky, *Freud and Oedipus* (New York, 1987), p. 66.

37 Freud, *The Complete Psychological Works*, vol. XX, p. 84.

38 Ernest Jones, 'Freud's Early Travels', in H. M. Ruitenbeek, ed., *Freud as We Knew Him* (Detroit, 1973), p. 281.

39 *Ibid.*

40 *Ibid.*

41 Eduard von Hartmann, *Philosophy of the Unconscious*, trans. W. C. Coupland (London, 1884), vol. I, p. 317.

42 Eric H. Erikson, 'Freud's "Origins of Psycho-Analysis"', *International Journal of Psycho-Analysis*, XXXVI (1955), p. 11.

43 *Ibid.*

44 *Ibid.*

45 Siegfried Bernfeld and Suzanne Cassirer, 'Freud's First Year in Practice, 1886–1887', in Ruitenbeek, ed., *Freud as We Knew Him*, p. 195.

46 Maureen C. McHugh, 'A Feminist Approach to Agoraphobia: Challenging Traditional Views of Women at Home', in J. C. Chrisler, C. Golden and P. D. Rozee, eds, *Lectures on the Psychology of Women* (New York, 1996), p. 342.

47 Esther da Costa Meyer, 'La Donna è Mobile: Agoraphobia, Women, and Urban Space', in D. Agrest, P. Conway and L. K. Weisman, *The Sex of Architecture* (New York, 1996), p. 149.

48 Carl E. Schorske, *Fin-de-Siècle Vienna, Politics and Culture* (London, 1980), p. 85.

49 Freud, *Glory Reflected*, p. 53.

50 *Ibid.*, p. 85.

51 Boleslaw Prus, *The Sins of Childhood & Other Stories*, trans. B. Johnson (Evanston, IL, 1996), p. 213.

52 *Ibid.*, p. 220.

53 Freud, *Glory Reflected*, p. 86.

54 *Ibid.*, pp. 70–71.

55 Hanns Sachs, 'Freud: Master and Friend', in Ruitenbeek, ed., *Freud as We Knew Him*, p. 210.

56 *Ibid.*

57 *Ibid.*, p. 203.

58 Rosenberg, *Why Freud Fainted*, p. 77.

59 Freud, *The Interpretation of Dreams*, p. 366, n. 1.

60 Jean-Claude Margolin, 'Bachelard and the Refusal of Metaphor', in M. McAllester, ed., *The Philosophy and Poetics of Gaston Bachelard* (Washington, DC, 1989), p. 104.

61 Anna Freud-Bernays, 'My Brother Sigmund', in Ruitenbeek, ed., *Freud as We Knew Him*, p. 143.

62 Roy A. Grinker, 'Reminiscences of a Personal Contact with Freud', in Ruitenbeek, ed., *Freud as We Knew Him*, p. 182.

63 Henri F. Ellenberger, *Beyond the Unconscious*, trans. F. Dubor and M. S. Micale (Princeton, 1993), p. 98.

64 *Ibid.*

65 Freud, *The Interpretation of Dreams*, p. 541.

66 *Ibid.*, p. 577.

67 *Ibid.*, p. 576.

68 *Ibid.*, p. 530.

69 *Ibid.*, p. 574.

70 Freud, *The Interpretation of Dreams*, p. 595.

71 Walter Benjamin, *One Way Street and Other Writings*, trans. E. Jephcott and K. Shorter (London, 1985), p. 298.

72 Freud, *The Complete Psychological Works*, vol. XX, p. 127.

73 Hélène Deutsch, 'The Genesis of Agoraphobia', *International Journal of Psycho-Analysis*, X (1929), p. 57.

74 *Ibid.*, p. 69.

75 Edmund Bergler, 'Psychoanalysis of a Case of Agoraphobia', in *Selected Papers of Edmund Bergler, M.D., 1931–1961* (New York, 1969), pp. 683–4.

76 *Ibid.*, p. 684

77 Abraham A. Brill, 'Reflections, Reminiscences of Sigmund Freud' in Ruitenbeek, ed., *Freud as We Knew Him*, p. 162.

78 Freud, *The Interpretation of Dreams*, p. 197.

79 Meyer, 'La Donna è Mobile', p. 153.

80 Jean-Francois Lyotard, *Political Writings*, trans. B. Readings and K. Paul (Minneapolis, 1993), pp. 141–2.

81 Ludwig Binswanger, 'My First Three Visits with Freud in Vienna', in Ruitenbeek, ed., *Freud as We Knew Him*, p. 368.

82 Jennifer Rutherford, *The Gauche Intruder: Freud, Lacan and the White Australian Fantasy* (Melbourne, 2000), p. 32.

83 *Ibid.*, p. 36.

84 Szasz, *Karl Kraus and the Soul Doctors*, p. 109.

85 Rudolf Arnheim, *Visual Thinking* (Berkeley, 1969), p. 284.

86 *Ibid.*, p. 284.

87 Immanuel Kant, *Anthropology from a Pragmatic Point of View*, trans. M. J. Gregor (The Hague, 1974), p. 174.

88 *Ibid.*, p. 88.

89 *Ibid.*, p. 78.

90 *Ibid.*, p. 79.

91 *Ibid.*, p. 78.

92 Anthony Vidler, 'Psychopathologies of Modern Space: Metropolitan Fear from Agoraphobia to Estrangement', in M. S. Roth, ed., *Rediscovering History, Culture, Politics, and the Psyche* (Stanford, 1994), pp. 26–7.

93 Hannah S. Decker, *Freud, Dora, and Vienna 1900* (New York, 1991), p. 6.

94 'Freud's Love Letters: Intimations of Psychoanalytic Theory', in M. H. Sherman, ed., *Psychoanalysis and Old Vienna: Freud, Reik, Schnitzler, Kraus* (New York, 1978), p. 172.

95 Decker, *Freud, Dora, and Vienna 1900*, p. 200.

96 *Ibid.*

97 Hermann Broch, *The Spell*, trans. H. F. Broch de Rothermann (London, 1988), pp. 73–4.

98 Lyotard, *Political Writings*, p. 159.

99 Freud, *The Complete Psychological Works*, vol. XVI, p. 398.

100 Szasz, *Karl Kraus and the Soul Doctors*, p. 156.

101 J. Moussaieff Masson, ed. and trans., *The Complete Letters of Sigmund Freud to Wilhelm Fliess* (Cambridge, MA, 1985), p. 272.

102 Robert Eisner, *The Road to Daulis: Psychoanalysis, Psychology, and Classical Mythology* (Syracuse, NY, 1987), p. 10.

103 *Ibid.*, p. 11.
104 *Ibid.*, p. 21.
105 *Ibid.*
106 *Ibid.*
107 *Ibid.*, p. 31.
108 *Ibid.*, p. 13.
109 Rudnytsky, *Freud and Oedipus*, p. 56.
110 *Ibid.*, p. 65.
111 Y. S. Feldman, 'And Rebecca Loved Jacob', in P. Rudnytsky and E. H. Spitz, eds, *Freud and Forbidden Knowledge* (New York, 1994), p. 22.
112 *Ibid.*, p. 22, n. 7.
113 Eagle, 'The Psychoanalytic and the Cognitive Unconscious', p. 175, n. 7.
114 *Ibid.*, p. 175.

3 ALIGHTING

1 Raimo Anttila, *Greek and Indo-European Etymology in Action* (Amsterdam, 2000), p. 206.
2 Camillo Sitte, *The Birth of Modern City Planning*, trans. and commentary G. R. Collins and C. Crasemann Collins (New York, 1986), p. 143; see also pp. 243–4.
3 James Holston, *The Modernist City: An Anthropological Critique of Brasilia* (Chicago, 1989), p. 133.
4 *Ibid.*, p. 135.
5 *Ibid.*, p. 127.
6 Sitte, *The Birth of Modern City Planning*, p. 183.
7 Jacob Burckhardt, *History of Greek Culture*, trans. P. Hilty (New York, 1963), p. 10.
8 Sitte, *The Birth of Modern City Planning*, p. 146.
9 *Ibid.*, p. 150.
10 Henry George Liddell and Robert A. Scott, *Greek-English Lexicon* (Oxford, 1966), p. 13.
11 Robert Flacelière, *Daily Life in Greece at the Time of Pericles*, trans. P. Green (London, 1965), pp. 4–5.
12 Plato, *Gorgias*, trans. W. Hamilton (London, 1980), 447, p. 19.
13 Plato, *The Laws*, trans. T. J. Saunders (London, 1970), 917, p. 455.
14 Liddell and Scott, *Greek-English Lexicon*, p. 13.
15 *Plato's Phaedrus*, trans. R. Hackforth (Cambridge, 1952), 230d, p. 25.
16 Christopher Lyle Johnstone, 'Greek Oratorical Settings and the Problem of the Pnyx: Rethinking the Athenian Political Process', in C. L. Johnstone, ed., *Theory, Text, Context: Issues in Greek Rhetoric and Oratory* (Albany, 1996), p. 110.
17 Roberto Schezen, *Adolf Loos: Architecture 1903–1932* (New York, 1996), p. 14.

18 *Ibid.*

19 Martin Heidegger, *Parmenides*, trans. A. Schuwer and R. Rojcewicz (Bloomington, 1992), p. 44.

20 David Hesla, *The Shape of Chaos* (Minneapolis, 1971), p. 13.

21 *Ibid.*

22 Henri Lefebvre, *The Production of Space*, trans. D. Nicholson-Smith (Oxford, 1993), p. 159.

23 *Ibid.*, p. 237.

24 *Ibid.*, p. 249.

25 *Ibid.*, p. 237.

26 Peter Zucker, *Town and Square: From the Agora to the Village Green* (Cambridge, MA, 1970), pp. 44–5.

27 *Ibid.*, p. 45.

28 *Ibid.*, p. xi.

29 Richard Sennett, *The Conscience of the Eye* (London, 1990).

30 Wilhelm Worringer, *Abstraction and Empathy: A Contribution to the Psychology of Style*, trans. M. Bullock (New York, 1953), pp. 128–9.

31 James Hillman and Wilhelm Heinrich Roscher, *Pan and the Nightmare* (New York, 1974), *passim.*

32 Sennett, *The Conscience of the Eye*, pp. xi–xii.

33 James Hillman, 'Pothos: The Nostalgia of the Puer Eternus', in *Loose Ends: Primary Papers in Archetypal Psychology* (Dallas, 1974), p. 53.

34 S. Forde, *The Ambition to Rule* (Ithaca, NY, 1989), pp. 16–17.

35 *Ibid.*, p. 23.

36 *Ibid.*, p. 24.

37 P. Vidal-Naquet, *The Black Hunter: Forms of Thought and Forms of Society in the Greek World*, trans. A. Szegedy-Maszak (Baltimore, 1986), p. 272.

38 *Ibid.*, p. 273.

39 *Ibid.*, p. 275.

40 *Ibid.*, p. 276.

41 *Ibid.*, p. 272.

42 Rudolf Arnheim, *Visual Thinking* (Berkeley, 1969), pp. 284–5.

43 Michel de Montaigne, *The Essayes*, trans. J. Florio (London, 1927), vol. 3, p. 284.

44 Dio Chrysostom, *Dio Chrysostom*, trans. J. W. Cohoon and H. L. Crosby (London, 1932), 5 vols, vol. 2, p. 169.

45 Vidal-Naquet, *The Black Hunter*, p. 164.

46 *Ibid.*, p. 173.

47 Plutarch, *The Rise and Fall of Athens*, trans. I. Scott-Kilvert (London, 1980), p. 25.

48 Seneca, *Three Tragedies*, trans. F. Ahl (Ithaca, NY, 1986), pp. 133–5.

49 Anthony Vidler, 'Psychopathologies of Modern Space: Metropolitan Fear from Agoraphobia to Estrangement', in M. S. Roth, ed., *Rediscovering History, Culture,*

Politics, and the Psyche (Stanford, 1994), p. 17.

50 Robert Graves, *The Greek Myths* (London, 1964), vol. 1, p. 339.

51 Samuel Beckett, *For To End Yet Again and Other Fizzles* (London, 1976), pp. 25–6.

52 Apollonius of Rhodes, *The Voyage of Argo*, trans. E. V. Rieu (London, 1971), pp. 135–6.

53 Plutarch, *The Rise and Fall of Athens*, trans. I. Scott-Kilvert (London, 1980), p. 29.

54 *Ibid.*, p. 30.

55 Marcus Terentius Varro, *Varro on the Latin Language*, trans. R. G. Kent (Cambridge, MA, 1938), vol. 1, pp. 137–9.

56 Dr Ireland, 'German Psychological Retrospect', *Journal of Mental Science* (1873), p. 457.

57 *Ibid.*

58 Edmund Bergler, 'Psychoanalysis of a Case of Agoraphobia', in *Selected Papers of Edmund Bergler, M.D., 1931–1961* (New York, 1969), pp. 673–4.

59 Paul Carter, *The Lie of the Land* (London, 1996), p. 361.

60 Marcus Terentius Varro, *Varro on the Latin Language*, vol. 1, p. 139.

61 *Ibid.*, vol. 1, p. 141.

62 Louise Holland, *Janus and the Bridge* (Rome, 1961), p. 36.

63 *Ibid.*, p. 36, note.

64 *Ibid.*, p. 11.

65 *Ibid.*, pp. 22–3.

66 *Ibid.*, p. 57.

67 *Ibid.*, p. 24.

68 *Ibid.*, p. 25.

69 *Ibid.*

70 Sigmund Freud, *The Interpretation of Dreams*, trans. J. Strachey (New York, 1960), p. 339.

71 For example, Hélène Deutsch, 'The Genesis of Agoraphobia', *International Journal of Psycho-Analysis*, X (1929), p. 52.

72 Anttila, *Greek and Indo-European Etymology in Action*, p. 10.

73 Thomas Szasz, *Karl Kraus and the Soul Doctors: A Pioneer Critic and His Criticism of Psychiatry and Psychoanalysis* (Baton Rouge, LA, 1976), p. 48.

74 *Ibid.*

75 Mark Amsler, *Etymology and Grammatical Discourse in Late Antiquity and the Early Middle Ages* (Amsterdam, 1988), p. 8.

76 *Ibid.*, pp. 8–9.

77 Anttila, *Greek and Indo-European Etymology in Action*, p. 140.

78 *Ibid.*, pp. 133ff.

79 *Ibid.*, passim.

80 *Ibid.*, p. 140.

81 Sigmund Freud, *An Autobiographical Study*, trans. J. Strachey (London, 1946),

p. 104.

82 Anttila, *Greek and Indo-European Etymology in Action*, p. 2.

83 *Ibid.*, p. 3.

84 *Ibid.*, p. 4.

85 *Ibid.*, pp. 142–3.

86 *Ibid.*, p. 143.

87 *Ibid.*, p. 145.

88 *Ibid.*, p. 70.

89 *Ibid.*

90 *Ibid.*, p. 71.

91 *Ibid.*, p. 49.

92 *Ibid.*, p. 50.

93 *Ibid.*, p. 52.

94 *Ibid.*

95 Mario Papini, *Arbor Humanae Linguae* (Bologna, 1984), pp. 123ff.

96 Anttila, *Greek and Indo-European Etymology in Action*, p. 202.

97 *Ibid.*, pp. 23, 189.

98 *Ibid.*, p. 172.

99 Elias Canetti, *Crowds and Power*, trans. C. Stewart (London, 1962), pp. 186–7.

100 Vidler, 'Psychopathologies of Modern Space, p. 13.

101 Alfred Russel Wallace, *My Life: A Record of Events and Opinions* (London, 1905), vol. 2, pp. 192–3.

102 Rev. Samuel Marsden, 'Report to Archdeacon Scott on the Aborigines of N.S.W. (2 December 1826)', in L. E. Threlkeld, *Australian Reminiscences and Papers*, ed. N. Gunson (Canberra, 1974), vol. 2, p. 347.

103 Vidler, 'Psychopathologies of Modern Space', p. 26.

104 Ernest Giles, *Australia Twice Traversed* (London, 1889), vol. 1, p. 315.

105 Putnam, James, 'Personal Impressions of Sigmund Freud and His Work' in H. M. Ruitenbeek, ed., *Freud as We Knew Him* (Detroit, 1973), p. 41.

106 Edward John Eyre, *Journals of Expeditions of Discovery* (London, 1845), vol. 1, p. 271.

107 Charles Sturt, *Narrative of an Expedition into Central Australia* (London, 1849), vol. ii, p. 29.

108 Alan E. J. Andrews, ed., *Hume and Hovell 1824* (Hobart, 1981), p. 204.

109 *Ibid.*, p. 205.

110 Eyre, *Journals of Expeditions of Discovery*, vol. 2, p. 40.

111 Andrews, ed., *Hume and Hovell 1824*, p. 217.

112 Eyre, *Journals of Expeditions of Discovery*, vol. 1, pp. 111–12.

113 Immanuel Kant, *Anthropology from a Pragmatic Point of View*, trans. M. J. Gregor (The Hague, 1974), p. 78.

114 Colin Davis, *Levinas: An Introduction* (Cambridge, 1996), p. 48.

115 Callum Coats, *Living Energies* (Bath, 1996), p. 57.
116 Walter Benjamin, *One Way Street and Other Writings*, trans. E. Jephcott and K. Shorter (London, 1985), p. 301.
117 Kurt Lewin, *Principles of Topological Psychology*, trans. F. and G. Heider (New York, 1936), p. 117.
118 *Ibid.*
119 Anttila, *Greek and Indo-European Etymology in Action*, p. 189.
120 *Ibid.*, p. 204.
121 *Ibid.*
122 *Ibid.*, p. 190.
123 *Ibid.*, p. 213.
124 Plato, *Cratylus*, 420a, p. 455.
125 Plato, *The Laws*, 778e–779a, p. 260.
126 *Ibid.*, 778c–778d, p. 260.
127 Vidal-Naquet, *The Black Hunter*, p. 122.
128 *Plato's Phaedrus*, 230d, p. 25.
129 John Llewelyn, *Emmanuel Levinas: The Genealogy of Ethics* (London, 1995), p. 205.
130 Freud, *The Interpretation of Dreams*, p. 48.
131 Vidal-Naquet, *The Black Hunter*, p. 107.
132 Catherine Osborne, *Eros Unveiled: Plato and the God of Love* (Oxford, 1994), pp. 94–5.
133 *Ibid.*, pp. 95–6.
134 *Plato's Phaedrus*, 229a, p. 23.
135 Llewelyn, *Emmanuel Levinas*, p. 205.
136 Anttila, *Greek and Indo-European Etymology in Action*, pp. 139ff.
137 Llewelyn, *Emmanuel Levinas*, p. 202.

4 MEETING

1 Elias Canetti, *Notes from Hampstead: The Writer's Notes, 1954–1971*, trans. J. Hargraves (New York, 1998), p. 86.
2 Siegfried Kracauer, *From Caligari to Hitler: A Psychological History of German Film* (Princeton, 1970), p. 121.
3 *Ibid.*, p. 157.
4 *Ibid.*, p. 159.
5 *Ibid.*, p. 195.
6 *Ibid.*, p. 121.
7 *Ibid.*, p. 159.
8 *Ibid.*, p. 184.
9 *Ibid.*, p. 194.
10 *Ibid.*, p. 159.

11 Emanuel Miller, 'The Analysis of Agora-Claustrophobia, A Passive Anamnesis', *International Journal of Psycho-Analysis* (1930), p. 258.

12 Siegfried Kracauer, *Theory of Film: The Redemption of Physical Reality* (New York, 1960), p. 59.

13 *Ibid.*, p. 62.

14 *Ibid.*, p. 72.

15 Wilhelm Worringer, *Abstraction and Empathy: A Contribution to the Psychology of Style*, trans. M. Bullock (New York, 1953), p. 129.

16 Karl Popper, *The Open Society and Its Enemies* (Princeton, 1966), vol. 1, p. 174.

17 Worringer, *Abstraction and Empathy*, p. 129.

18 Kracauer, *Theory of Film*, p. 294.

19 *Ibid.*, p. 299.

20 *Ibid.*, p. 300.

21 André Breton, *Nadja*, trans. R. Howard (New York, 1960), p. 39.

22 Adam Phillips, *On Flirtation* (London, 1994), p. 157.

23 Esther da Costa Meyer, 'La Donna è Mobile: Agoraphobia, Women, and Urban Space', in D. Agrest, P. Conway and L. K. Weisman, eds, *The Sex of Architecture* (New York, 1996), p. 151.

24 Meyer, 'La Donna è Mobile', p. 149.

25 Gilles Deleuze, *Cinema 1: The Movement Image*, trans. H. Tomlinson and B. Habberjam (London, 1986), p. 59.

26 Emmanuel Levinas, *Basic Philosophical Writings*, ed. A. T. Peperzak, S. Critchley and R. Bernasconi (Bloomington, 1996), pp. 156–7.

27 Emmanuel Levinas, *Ethics and Infinity: Conversations with Philippe Nemo,* trans. Richard A. Cohen (Pittsburgh, 1985), p. 27.

28 Kracauer, *Theory of Film*, p. 68.

29 Robert Musil, *Young Törless*, trans. E. Wilkins and E. Kaiser (London, 1987), p. 135.

30 Kracauer, *From Caligari to Hitler*, p. 121.

31 Alexander Etkind, *Eros of the Impossible: The History of Psychoanalysis in Russia*, trans. N. and M. Rubins (Boulder, 1997), p. 318.

32 *Ibid.*

33 *Ibid.*

34 *Ibid.*, p. 319.

35 *Ibid.*, p. 50.

36 *Ibid.*

37 Hannah Arendt, *The Human Condition* (Chicago, 1958), p. 52. The italics are mine.

38 Louis A. Sass, *Madness and Modernism: Insanity in the Light of Modern Art, Literature and Thought* (New York, 1992), pp. 43–4.

39 Camillo Sitte, *The Birth of Modern City Planning*, trans. and commentary G. R. Collins and C. Crasemann Collins (New York, 1986), p. 65.

40 Michael Balint, 'Friendly Expanses – Horrid Empty Spaces', *International Journal*

of Psycho-Analysis, xxxvi/4–5 (1955), p. 227.

41 *Ibid.*, p. 228.

42 Umberto Boccioni, 'Manifesto Tecnico dei Pittori Futuristi, 11 Aprile 1910', in *Archivi di Novecento, vol 1, Umberto Boccioni* (Biella, 1982), p. 83.

43 Cornelis van de Ven, *Space in Architecture* (Assen, 1980), p. 150.

44 *Ibid.*

45 *Ibid.*

46 Roger Shattuck, *The Banquet Years: The Origins of the Avant Garde in France, 1885 to World War 1* (New York, 1968), p. 157.

47 Kracauer, *From Caligari to Hitler*, p. 194.

48 Zeno Birolli, *Umberto Boccioni, Racconto Critico* (Turin, 1983), p. 158.

49 *Ibid.*, p. 55.

50 Rosalind Deutsche, 'Agoraphobia', in *Evictions: Art and Spatial Politics* (Cambridge, MA, 1996), p. 324.

51 *Ibid.*, p. 326.

52 Meyer, 'La Donna è Mobile', p. 151.

53 *Ibid.*, p. 152.

54 Colin St John Wilson, 'The Natural Imagination', in *Architectural Reflections: Studies in the Philosophy and Practice of Architecture* (Oxford, 1992), p. 5.

55 *Ibid.*, pp. 5–6.

56 Henri Lefebvre, *The Production of Space*, trans. D. Nicholson-Smith (Oxford, 1993), p. 298.

57 Walter Benjamin, *The Arcades Project*, trans. H. Eiland and K. McLaughlin (Cambridge, MA, 1999), p. 473.

58 Walter Benjamin, *One Way Street and Other Writings*, trans. E. Jephcott and K. Shorter (London, 1985), pp. 298–9.

59 Anthony Vidler, 'Psychopathologies of Modern Space: Metropolitan Fear from Agoraphobia to Estrangement', in M. S. Roth, ed., *Rediscovering History, Culture, Politics, and the Psyche* (Stanford, 1994), p. 27.

60 *Ibid.*, p. 28.

61 Margaret Cohen, *Profane Illumination: Walter Benjamin and the Paris of Surrealist Revolution* (Berkeley, 1993), p. 191.

62 Adrian Rifkin, *Street Noises: Parisian Pleasure, 1900–1940* (Manchester, 1993), p. 7.

63 *Ibid.*, p. 206.

64 *Ibid.*, p. 204.

65 Plutarch, *L'Arte di Ascoltare* (Milan, 1995), p. 73.

66 Vidler, 'Psychopathologies of Modern Space', p. 20.

67 Georg Simmel, *Georg Simmel: On Women, Sexuality, and Love*, trans. G. Oakes (New Haven, 1984), p. 151.

68 Arendt, *The Human Condition*, p. 197.

69 *Ibid.*

70 Peter Zucker, *Town and Square: From the Agora to the Village Green* (Cambridge, MA, 1970), p. 30.

71 *Ibid.*, p. 31.

72 *Ibid.*, p. 37.

73 *Ibid.*, pp. 44–5.

74 William Cobbett, *Rural Rides* (London, 1985), p. 365.

75 Sitte, *The Birth of Modern City Planning*, pp. 159–60.

76 Kathleen Stewart, *A Space on the Side of the Road* (Princeton, 1996), p. 32.

77 *Ibid.*, pp. 33–4.

78 *Ibid.*, p. 34.

79 *Ibid.*, p. 32.

80 *Ibid.*

81 *Ibid.*

82 James Paull, 'Ambivalent Ground: Place, Post-Colonialism and Australian Writing', PhD proposal (University of New South Wales, 2001), p. 13.

83 Edward Casey, *The Fate of Place: A Philosophical History* (Berkeley, 1998), pp. 243–4.

84 Elias Canetti, *Crowds and Power*, trans. C. Stewart (London, 1962), p. 31.

85 Arendt, *The Human Condition*, pp. 52–3.

86 *Ibid.*, p. 38.

87 Levinas, *Ethics and Infinity: Conversations with Philippe Nemo*, p. 11.

88 *Ibid.*, p. 52.

89 Levinas, *Basic Philosophical Writings*, p. 4.

90 John Heaton, 'The Other and Psychotherapy', in R. Bernasconi and D. Wood, eds, *Re-reading Levinas* (Bloomington, 1991), p. 8.

91 Heaton, 'The Other and Psychotherapy', p. 9.

92 Emmanuel Levinas, 'The Transcendence of Words: On Michel Leiris's Biffures', in *Outside the Subject* (London, 1990), p. 145.

93 *Ibid.*, p. 146.

94 Charles Lapicque, *Les Dessins de Lapicque au Musée national d'art moderne* (Paris, 1978), p. 18.

95 Michael Leiris, *Brisees: Broken Branches*, trans. L. Davis (San Francisco, 1989), p. 138.

96 Reinhold Hohl, *Alberto Giacometti* (London, 1972), p. 274.

97 *Ibid.*, p. 234.

98 Dieter Honisch, 'Scale in Giacometti's Sculpture', in A. Schneider, ed., *Alberto Giacometti: Sculpture, Paintings, Drawings* (Munich, 1994), p. 65.

99 Hohl, *Alberto Giacometti*, p. 207.

100 *Ibid.*, p. 304, n. 63.

101 *Ibid.*, p. 133.

102 *Ibid.*, p. 277.

103 *Ibid.*, p. 31.

104 *Ibid.*

105 *Ibid.*, p. 140.

106 *Ibid.*, p. 245.

107 *Ibid.*, p. 276.

108 *Ibid.*, p. 275.

109 Levinas, *Basic Philosophical Writings*, p. 59.

110 Levinas, *Ethics and Infinity*, p. 92.

111 *Ibid.*, p. 88.

112 *Ibid.*, p. 88.

113 Hohl, *Alberto Giacometti*, p. 140.

114 *Ibid.*

115 *Ibid.*, p. 143.

116 *Ibid.*, p. 282.

117 *Ibid.*

118 *Ibid.*, p. 133.

119 *Ibid.*, p. 227.

120 *Ibid.*, p. 282.

121 Giambattista Vico, *La Scienza Nuova* (Milan, 1977), p. 402.

122 Dr Ireland, 'German Psychological Retrospect', p. 457.

123 Balint, 'Friendly Expanses', p. 231.

124 *Ibid.*, pp. 231–2.

125 *Ibid.*, p. 232.

126 Hohl, *Alberto Giacometti*, p. 277.

127 Freud, *The Interpretation of Dreams*, p. 170.

128 Alexander Grinstein, *Sigmund Freud's Dreams* (New York, 1980), p. 53.

129 H. John Field, *Toward a Programme of Imperial Life: The British Empire at the Turn of the Century* (Westport, CT, 1982), p. 233.

130 Octave Mannoni, *Prospero and Caliban: The Psychology of Colonization*, trans. P. Powesland (London, 1956), p. 200.

131 J. Moussaieff Masson, ed. and trans., *The Complete Letters of Sigmund Freud to Wilhelm Fliess* (Cambridge, MA, 1985), p. 131.

132 Freud, *The Interpretation of Dreams*, p. 318.

133 Ludwig Binswanger, 'My First Three Visits with Freud in Vienna', in Ruitenbeck, ed., *Freud as We Knew Him*, p. 362.

134 Martin Freud, *Glory Reflected* (London, 1957), p. 110.

135 Harry Freud, 'My Uncle Sigmund', in Ruitenbeck, ed., *Freud as We Knew Him*, p. 312.

136 Richard Klein, *Cigarettes Are Sublime* (Durham, NC, 1993), p. 98.

137 G. H. Green, 'Some Notes on Smoking', *International Journal of Psycho-Analysis*, IV (1923), p. 325.

138 Eric H. Erikson, 'Freud's "Origins of Psycho-Analysis"', *International Journal of*

Psycho-Analysis, (1955), p. 11.

139 Ernst Bloch, 'Technology and Ghostly Apparitions', in *Literary Essays* (Stanford, 1998), p. 320.

140 Leo Gullbring, 'Daniel Libeskind's Jewish Museum in Berlin,' *Frame 7* (1999), p. 26.

141 Gianni Vattimo, *The Adventure of Difference: Philosophy after Nietzsche and Heidegger*, trans. G. Blamires (London, 1993), pp. 54ff.

142 Daniel Libeskind, *Jewish Museum Berlin* (Berlin, 1999), p. 30.

143 Daniel Libeskind, with Don L. Bates, 'A Conversation between the Lines', *El Croquis*, no. 80 (1996), p. 86.

144 Bloch, 'Technology and Ghostly Apparitions', p. 320.

145 Sophocles, 'Oedipus at Colonus', in *Sophocles*, trans. F. Storr (London, 1946), vol. 1, p. 293.

146 Ignacio Matte Blanco, 'Some Reflections on Psycho-Dynamics', *International Journal of Psycho-Analysis*, XXI (1940), p. 279.

147 Werner Hofmann, 'All Smooth', in *Essays in Honour of Elias Canetti*, trans. M. Hulse (London, 1987), p. 7.

148 Bergler, 'Psychoanalysis of Writers and of Literary Productivity', p. 396.

149 *Ibid.*, p. 401.

150 Leon Krier, 'Une architecture du desir', in L. Krier, ed., *Albert Speer: Architecture, 1932–1942* (Brussels, 1985), p. 19.

151 *Ibid.*, p. 15.

152 Iain B. Whyte, *Bruno Taut and the Architecture of Activism* (Cambridge, 1982), pp. 76ff.

153 Peter Haiko, 'The "Obscene" in Viennese Architecture of the Early Twentieth Century', in P. Werkner, ed., *Egon Schiele: Art, Sexuality, and Viennese Modernism* (Palo Alto, 1994), p. 93.

154 Hofmann, 'All Smooth', p. 9.

155 *Ibid.*, pp. 9–10.

156 *Ibid.*, p. 10.

157 James Hillman, 'Pothos: The Nostalgia of the Puer Eternus', in *Loose Ends: Primary Papers in Archetypal Psychology* (Dallas, 1974), p. 103.

158 Theodor Reik, *The Search Within: The Inner Experiences of a Psychoanalyst* (New York, 1956), pp. 251–2.

159 Roger Shattuck, *The Banquet Years: The Origins of the Avant Garde in France, 1885 to World War I* (New York, 1968), p. 133.

160 Reik, *The Search Within*, p. 511.

161 *Ibid.*

162 *Ibid.*, p. 512.

Adorno, Theodor, *Minima Moralia: Reflections from Damaged Life*, trans. E. F. N. Jeffcott (London, 1974)

Amsler, Mark, *Etymology and Grammatical Discourse in Late Antiquity and the Early Middle Ages* (Amsterdam, 1988)

Andrews, Alan E. J., ed., *Hume and Hovell 1824* (Hobart, 1981)

Anttila, Raimo, *Greek and Indo-European Etymology in Action* (Amsterdam, 2000)

Apollonius of Rhodes, *The Voyage of Argo*, trans. E. V. Rieu (London, 1971)

Arendt, Hannah, *The Human Condition* (Chicago, 1958)

Arnheim, Rudolf, *Visual Thinking* (Berkeley, 1969)

Bacon, Francis, *The New Organon and Related Writings*, ed. F. H. Anderson (Indianapolis, 1960)

Baker, William M. S., 'From Ritual to Theater and Its Double', in G. A. Plunka, ed., *Antonin Artaud and Modern Theater* (London and Toronto, 1994)

Balint, Michael, 'Friendly Expanses – Horrid Empty Spaces', *International Journal of Psycho-Analysis*, XXXVI/4–5 (1955), pp. 225–41

Barthes, Roland, *Frammenti di un discorso amoroso* (Turin, 1979)

Beckett, Samuel, *For To End Yet Again and Other Fizzles* (London, 1976)

Benjamin, Walter, *One Way Street and Other Writings*, trans. E. Jephcott and K. Shorter (London, 1985)

—, *The Arcades Project*, trans. H. Eiland and K. McLaughlin (Cambridge, MA, 1999)

Bergler, Edmund, 'Psychoanalysis of a Case of Agoraphobia', in *Selected Papers of Edmund Bergler, M.D., 1931–1961* (New York, 1969), pp. 672–86

—, 'Psychoanalysis of Writers and of Literary Productivity', in *Selected Papers of Edmund Bergler, M.D., 1931-1961*, pp. 368–402

Berman, Marshall, *All That Is Solid Melts Into Air* (London, 1983)

Bernard, A., and C. Jung, 'Contribution à l'étude de la cremnophobie', *Revue neurologique*, 36 (1929), pp. 435–50

Bernasconi, Robert, and David Wood, eds, *The Provocation of Levinas: Rethinking the Other* (London, 1988)

Bernasconi, Robert, and Simon Critchley, *Re-reading Levinas* (Bloomington, 1991)

Bernfeld, S., 'An Unknown Autobiographical Fragment by Freud', *American Imago*, 4/1 (1946), pp. 3–19

Bernfeld, Siegfried, and Suzanne Cassirer, 'Freud's First Year in Practice, 1886–1887', in H. M. Ruitenbeek, ed., *Freud as We Knew Him* (Detroit, 1973), pp. 252–65

Binswanger, Ludwig, 'My First Three Visits with Freud in Vienna', in *Freud as We Knew Him*, pp. 360–68

Birolli, Zeno, *Umberto Boccioni, Racconto Critico* (Turin, 1983)

Blanco, Ignacio Matte, 'Some Reflections on Psycho-Dynamics', *International Journal of Psycho-Analysis*, XXI (1940), pp. 253–79

Bloch, Ernst, 'Technology and Ghostly Apparitions', in *Literary Essays* (Stanford, 1998)

Boccioni, Umberto, 'Manifesto Tecnico dei Pittori Futuristi, 11 Aprile 1910', in *Archivi di Novecento, vol 1, Umberto Boccioni* (Biella, 1982)

Bowers, Kenneth S., and Donald Meichenbaum, eds, *The Unconscious Reconsidered* (New York, 1984)

Brehony, Kathleen A., 'Women and Agoraphobia: A Case for the Etiological Significance of the Feminine Sex-Role Stereotype', in V. Franks and E. D. Rothblum, *The Stereotyping of Women, Its Effects on Mental Health* (New York, 1983), pp. 112–28

Breton, André, *Nadja*, trans. R. Howard (New York, 1960)

Brill, Abraham A., 'Reflections, Reminiscences of Sigmund Freud' in *Freud as We Knew Him*, pp. 154–69

Broch, Hermann, *The Spell*, trans. H. F. Broch de Rothermann (London, 1988)

Brod, Max, *The Biography of Franz Kafka*, trans. G. H. Roberts (London, 1947)

Buber-Neumann, Margarete, *Milena*, trans. R. Manheim (New York, 1988)

Burckhardt, Jacob, *History of Greek Culture*, trans. P. Hilty (New York, 1963)

Canetti, Elias, *Crowds and Power*, trans. C. Stewart (London, 1962)

—, *The Secret Heart of the Clock: Notes, Aphorisms, Fragments, 1973–1985*, trans. J. Agee (New York, 1989)

—, *Notes from Hampstead: The Writer's Notes 1954–1971*, trans. J. Hargraves (New York, 1998)

Capps, Lisa, and Elinor Ochs, *Constructing Panic: The Discourse of Agoraphobia* (Cambridge, MA, 1995)

Carnicke, Sharon M., *Stanislavsky in Focus* (Amsterdam, 1998)

Carter, Paul, *The Lie of the Land* (London, 1996)

Casey, Edward, *The Fate of Place: A Philosophical History* (Berkeley, 1998)

Clement, Catherine, *Syncope: The Philosophy of Rapture*, trans. S. O'Driscoll and D. M. Mahoney (Minneapolis, 1994)

Coats, Callum, *Living Energies* (Bath, 1995)

Cobbett, William, *Rural Rides* (London, 1985)

Cohen, Margaret, *Profane Illumination: Walter Benjamin and the Paris of Surrealist Revolution* (Berkeley, 1993)

Davis, Colin, *Levinas: An Introduction*, (Cambridge, 1996)

Decker, Hannah S., *Freud, Dora, and Vienna 1900* (New York, 1991)

Deleuze, Gilles, *Cinema 1: The Movement Image*, trans. H. Tomlinson and B. Habberjam (London, 1986)

Denti, Giovanni, *Adolf Loos, Architettura è Citta* (Florence, 1992)

Deutsch, Hélène, 'The Genesis of Agoraphobia', *International Journal of Psycho-Analysis*, X (1929), pp. 51–70

Deutsche, Rosalind, 'Agoraphobia', in *Evictions: Art and Spatial Politics* (Cambridge, MA, 1996), pp. 269–327

Dio Chrysostom, *Dio Chrysostom*, trans. J. W. Cohoon and H. L. Crosby (London, 1932), 5 vols.

Eagle, Morris, 'The Psychoanalytic and the Cognitive Unconscious' in R. Stern, ed., *Theories of the Unconscious and Theories of the Self* (Hillside, NJ, 1987), pp. 155–90

Eisner, Robert, *The Road to Daulis: Psychoanalysis, Psychology, and Classical Mythology* (Syracuse, NY, 1987)

Ellenberger, Henri F., *Beyond the Unconscious*, trans. F. Dubor and M. S. Micale (Princeton, 1993)

Erikson, Eric H., 'Freud's "Origins of Psycho-Analysis"', *International Journal of Psycho-Analysis*, XXXVI (1955), pp. 1–15

Etkind, Alexander, *Eros of the Impossible: The History of Psychoanalysis in Russia*, trans. N. and M. Rubins (Boulder, 1997)

Evans, Philip, and John Liggett, 'Loss and Bereavement as Factors in Agoraphobia: Implications for Therapy' *British Journal of Medical Psychology*, XLIV (1971), pp. 149–54

Eyre, Edward John, *Journals of Expeditions of Discovery*, 2 vols (London, 1845)

Feldman, Y. S., 'And Rebecca Loved Jacob', in P. Rudnytsky and E. H. Spitz, eds, *Freud and Forbidden Knowledge* (New York, 1994)

Flacelière, Robert, *Daily Life in Greece at the Time of Pericles*, trans. P. Green (London, 1965)

Field, H. John, *Toward a Programme of Imperial Life: The British Empire at the Turn of the Century* (Westport, CT, 1982)

Forde, S., *The Ambition to Rule* (Ithaca, NY, 1989)

Forge, Andrew, *Soutine* (London, 1965)

Frampton, Kenneth, 'Adolf Loos: The Architect as Master Builder', in Roberto Schezen, *Adolf Loos, Architecture 1903–1932* (New York, 1996) pp. 14–21

Freud, Anna, 'The Relation of Beating-Phantasies to a Day-Dream', *International Journal of Psycho-Analysis*, IV (1923), pp. 89–102

Freud, Harry, 'My Uncle Sigmund', in H. M. Ruitenbeek, ed., *Freud as We Knew Him* (Detroit, 1973), pp. 312–13

Freud, Martin, *Glory Reflected* (London, 1957)

Freud, Sigmund, *The Complete Psychological Works of Sigmund Freud*, ed. and trans. J. Strachey, 24 vols (London, 1953–75)

—, *The Interpretation of Dreams*, trans. J. Strachey (New York, 1960)

—, *An Autobiographical Study*, trans. J. Strachey (London, 1946)

Freud-Bernays, Anna, 'My Brother Sigmund', in H. M. Ruitenbeek, ed., *Freud as We Knew Him* (Detroit, 1973), pp. 140–47

Gay, Peter, *My German Question: Growing Up in Nazi Berlin* (New Haven, 1998)

Gelder, M. G., 'Specific and Non-specific Factors in Behaviour Therapy', *British Journal of Psychiatry*, CXXIII (October 1973), pp. 445–62

Giles, Ernest, *Australia Twice Traversed*, 2 vols (London, 1889)

Glauber, I. P., 'On the Meaning of Agoraphilia', *Journal of the American Psychoanalytic Association*, III (1955), pp. 701–9

Goodman, Paul, *Kafka's Prayer* (New York, 1947)

Gravagnuolo, Benedetto, *Adolf Loos: Theory and Works*, trans. C. H. Evans (Milan, 1982)

Graves, Robert, *The Greek Myths*, 2 vols (London, 1964)

Green, G. H., 'Some Notes on Smoking', *International Journal of Psycho-Analysis*, IV (1923), pp. 323–5

Greene, Naomi, '"All The Great Myths Are Dark": Artaud and Fascism', in G. A. Plunka, ed., *Antonin Artaud and the Modern Theater* (London and Toronto, 1994)

Grinker, Roy A., 'Reminiscences of a Personal Contact with Freud', in H. M. Ruitenbeek, ed., *Freud as We Knew Him* (Detroit, 1973), pp. 180–85

Grinstein, Alexander, *Sigmund Freud's Dreams* (New York, 1980)

Haiko, Peter, 'The "Obscene" in Viennese Architecture of the Early Twentieth Century', in P. Werkner, ed., *Egon Schiele: Art, Sexuality, and Viennese Modernism* (Palo Alto, 1994), pp. 89–100

Hallam, Richard, 'Agoraphobia: Deconstructing a Clinical Syndrome', *Bulletin of The British Psychological Society*, 36 (1983), pp. 337–40

Gullbring, Leo, 'Daniel Libeskind's Jewish Museum in Berlin,' *Frame* 7 (1999)

Harrison, Jane, *Themis* (London, 1963)

Hartmann, Eduard von, *Philosophy of the Unconscious*, trans. W. C. Coupland, 3 vols (London, 1884)

Haslam, M. T., 'The Relationship between the Effect of Lactate Infusion on Anxiety States and Their Amelioration by Carbon Dioxide Inhalation', *British Journal of Psychiatry*, 124 (July 1974), pp. 88–90

Heaton, John, 'The Other and Psychotherapy', in R. Bernasconi, Robert and David Wood, eds, *The Provocation of Levinas: Rethinking the Other* (London, 1988), pp. 5–14

Heidegger, Martin, *Being and Time*, trans. J. Macquarrie and E. Robinson (Oxford, 1980)

—, *Parmenides*, trans. A. Schuwer and R. Rojcewicz (Bloomington, 1992)

Heiser, J., and D. Defrancisco, 'The Treatment of Pathological Panic States with

Propranolol', *American Journal of Psychiatry*, 133 (December 1973), pp. 1389–4

Hesla, David, *The Shape of Chaos* (Minneapolis, 1971)

Hillier, Bill, *Space Is the Machine* (Cambridge, 1996)

Hillman James, 'Pothos: The Nostalgia of the Puer Eternus', in *Loose Ends: Primary Papers in Archetypal Psychology* (Dallas, 1974)

Hillman, James, and Wilhelm Heinrich Roscher, *Pan and the Nightmare* (New York, 1974)

Hofmann, Werner, 'All Smooth', in *Essays in Honour of Elias Canetti*, trans. M. Hulse (London, 1987)

Hohl, Reinhold, *Alberto Giacometti* (London, 1972)

Holland, Louise, *Janus and the Bridge* (Rome, 1961)

Hollier, Denis, *Absent Without Leave: French Literature under Threat of War*, trans. C. Porter (Cambridge, MA, 1997)

Holston, James, *The Modernist City: An Anthropological Critique of Brasilia* (Chicago, 1989)

Honisch, Dieter, 'Scale in Giacometti's Sculpture', in Angela Schneider, ed., *Alberto Giacometti: Sculpture, Paintings, Drawings* (Munich, 1994), pp. 65–9

Ireland, Dr, 'German Psychological Retrospect', *Journal of Mental Science* (1873), pp. 456–8.

Jaccard, Pierre, *Le Sens de la direction et l'orientation lointaine chez l'homme* (Paris, 1932)

Jankélévitch, Vladimir, *Correspondance: Une vie en toutes lettres* (Paris, 1995)

Jean, Raymond, *Paul Eluard par lui-même* (Paris, 1968)

John, Michael, *Politics and the Law in Late Nineteenth-Century Germany* (Oxford, 1989)

Johnston, D., and D. Gath, 'Arousal Levels and Attribution Effects in Diazepam-assisted Flooding', *British Journal of Psychiatry*, 123 (October 1973), pp. 463–6

Johnstone, Christopher Lyle, 'Greek Oratorical Settings and the Problem of the Pnyx: Rethinking the Athenian Political Process', in C. L. Johnstone, ed., *Theory, Text, Context: Issues in Greek Rhetoric and Oratory* (Albany, 1996), pp. 97–128

Jones, Ernest, *The Life and Work of Sigmund Freud* (New York, 3 vols 1953–1981)

—, 'Freud's Early Travels', in H. M. Ruitenbeek, ed., *Freud as We Knew Him* (Detroit, 1973), pp. 275–82

Kafka, Franz, 'Third Octavo Notebook', in E. Kaiser and E. Wilkins, eds, *Wedding Preparations in the Country and Other Posthumous Writings* (London, 1954)

Kant, Immanuel, *Anthropology from a Pragmatic Point of View*, trans. M. J. Gregor (The Hague, 1974)

Kantor, Tadeusz, *A Journey Through Other Spaces: Essays and Manifestos, 1944–1990*, trans. M. Kobialka (Berkeley, 1993)

Katan, Anny, 'The Role of "Displacement" in Agoraphobia', *International Journal of Psycho-Analysis*, 32 (1951), pp. 41–50

Kellett, Arnold, trans., *The Dark Side of Guy de Maupassant* (London, 1989)

Kerenyi, Karl, *Dionysos: Archetypal Image of Indestructible Life*, trans. R. Mannheim (Princeton, 1976)

Kierkegaard, Søren, *The Sickness unto Death*, trans. A. Hannay (London, 1989)

Kihlstrom, John F., 'Conscious, Subconscious, Unconscious: A Cognitive Perspective', in Kenneth S. Bowers and Donald Meichenbaum, eds, *The Unconscious Reconsidered* (New York, 1984)

Klein, Richard, *Cigarettes Are Sublime* (Durham, NC, 1993)

Kracauer, Siegfried, *From Caligari to Hitler: A Psychological History of German Film* (Princeton, 1970)

—, *Theory of Film: The Redemption of Physical Reality* (New York, 1960)

Krier, Leon, 'Une architecture du desir', in L. Krier, ed., *Albert Speer: Architecture, 1932–1942* (Brussels, 1985)

Kullman, Karl, '(Dis)Oriented Visions: Toward a Current Poetics of Landscape Architecture', Master's thesis, University of Western Australia, 2000

Laing, R. D., *The Divided Self: An Existential Study in Sanity and Madness* (London, 1965)

Lapicque, Charles, *Les Dessins de Lapicque au Musée National d'Art Moderne* (Paris, 1978)

Le Corbusier, *The City of Tomorrow and Its Planning*, trans. F. Etchells (Cambridge, MA, 1971)

Lefebvre, Henri, *The Production of Space*, trans. D. Nicholson-Smith (Oxford, 1993)

Leiris, Michael, *Brisees: Broken Branches*, trans. L. Davis (San Francisco, 1989)

Leslie, Esther, *Walter Benjamin: Overpowering Conformism* (Stirling, VA, 2000)

Levinas, Emmanuel, *Entre Nous: On Thinking-of-the-Other*, trans. M. B. Smith and B. Harshaw (London, 1998)

—, *Basic Philosophical Writings*, ed. A. T. Peperzak, S. Critchley and R. Bernasconi (Bloomington, 1996)

—, *Ethics and Infinity: Conversations with Philippe Nemo*, trans. Richard A. Cohen (Pittsburgh, 1985)

—, 'The Transcendence of Words: On Michel Leiris's Biffures', in *Outside the Subject* (London, 1990)

Levine, Donald, *The Flight from Ambiguity* (Chicago, 1985)

Lewin, Kurt, *Principles of Topological Psychology*, trans. F. and G. Heider (New York, 1936)

Libeskind, Daniel, *Jewish Museum Berlin* (Berlin, 1999)

Libeskind, Daniel, with Don L. Bates, 'A Conversation between the Lines', *El Croquis*, no. 80 (1996)

Liddell, Henry George, and Robert A. Scott, *Greek-English Lexicon* (Oxford, 1966)

Llewelyn, John, *Emmanuel Levinas: The Genealogy of Ethics* (London, 1995)

Lyotard, Jean-Francois, *Political Writings*, trans. B. Readings and K. Paul (Minneapolis, 1993)

McAllester Jones, Mary, *Gaston Bachelard, Subversive Humanist* (Madison, 1991)

McHugh, Maureen C., 'A Feminist Approach to Agoraphobia: Challenging Traditional Views of Women at Home', in J. C. Chrisler, C. Golden and P. D. Rozee, eds, *Lectures on the Psychology of Women* (New York, 1996), pp. 339–57

Macnab, Francis, *Footprints: Psychological and Psychoanalytic Explorations* (Melbourne, 1996)

Mannoni, Octave, *Prospero and Caliban: The Psychology of Colonization*, trans. P. Powesland (London, 1956)

Margolin, Jean-Claude, 'Bachelard and the Refusal of Metaphor', in M. McAllester, ed., *The Philosophy and Poetics of Gaston Bachelard* (Washington, DC, 1989)

Marsden, Rev. Samuel, 'Report to Archdeacon Scott on the Aborigines of N.S.W. (2 December 1826)', in L. E. Threlkeld, *Australian Reminiscences and Papers*, ed. N. Gunson, 2 vols (Canberra, 1974)

Matthews, J. H., *Surrealism and Film* (Ann Arbor, 1971)

Maupassant, Guy de, *Selected Short Stories*, trans. R. Colet (London, 1981)

Mendel, J, and D. Klein, 'Anxiety Attacks with Subsequent Agoraphobia', *Comprehensive Psychiatry*, 10/3 (1969), pp. 190–95

Meyer, Esther da Costa, 'La Donna e Mobile: Agoraphobia, Women, and Urban Space', in D. Agrest, P. Conway and L. K. Weisman, eds, *The Sex of Architecture* (New York, 1996), pp. 141–56

Miller, Emanuel, 'The Analysis of Agora-Claustrophobia: A Passive Anamnesis', *Internatioanl Journal of Psycho-Analysis* (1930), pp. 253–67

Miller, Milton L., 'On Street Fear', *International Journal of Psycho-Analysis* (1953[?]), pp. 232–40

Montaigne, Michel de, *The Essayes*, trans. J. Florio, 3 vols (London, 1927)

Moussaieff Masson, J., ed. and trans., *The Complete Letters of Sigmund Freud to Wilhelm Fliess* (Cambridge, MA, 1985)

Musil, Robert, *The Man Without Qualities*, trans. E. Wilkins and E. Kaiser, 2 vols (London, 1979)

—, *Young Törless*, trans. E. Wilkins and E. Kaiser (London, 1987)

Nye, Robert A., *The Origins of Crowd Psychology: Gustave LeBon and the Crisis of Mass Democracy in the Third Republic* (London, 1975)

Oatley, K., and D. Hodgson, 'Influence of Husbands on the Outcome of their Agoraphobic Wives' Therapy', *British Journal of Psychiatry*, 150 (1987), pp. 380–86

Oberndorf, C. P., 'Folie à deux', *International Journal of Psycho-Analysis*, XV (1934), pp. 14–24

Osborne, Catherine, *Eros Unveiled: Plato and the God of Love* (Oxford, 1994)

Panofsky, Erwin, *Studies in Iconology* (New York, 1962)

Papini, Mario, *Arbor Humanae Linguae* (Bologna, 1984)

Paull, James, 'Ambivalent Ground: Place, Post-Colonialism and Australian Writing', PhD thesis in progress, University of New South Wales, 2001

Perry, Campbell, and Jean-Roch Laurence, 'Mental Processing Outside of Awareness: The Contributions of Freud and Janet', in Kenneth S. Bowers and Donald Meichenbaum, eds, *The Unconscious Reconsidered* (New York, 1984)

Phillips, Adam, *On Flirtation* (London, 1994)

Plato, *Gorgias*, trans. W. Hamilton (London, 1980)

Plato's Phaedrus, trans. R. Hackforth (Cambridge, 1952)

—, *The Laws*, trans. T. J. Saunders (London, 1970)

—, *Cratylus*, trans. B. Jowett, in *The Collected Dialogues of Plato*, ed. E. Hamilton and
    H. Cairns (New York, 1963)

Plutarch, *The Rise and Fall of Athens*, trans. I. Scott-Kilvert (London, 1980)

—, *L'Arte di Ascoltare* (Milan, 1995)

Popper, Karl, *The Open Society and Its Enemies* (Princeton, 1966), 2 vols

Pozzato, Bruno, *Umberto Boccioni* (Biella, 1982)

Prus, Boleslaw, *The Sins of Childhood & Other Stories*, trans. B. Johnson (Evanston, 1996)

Putnam, James, 'Personal Impressions of Sigmund Freud and His Work' in H. M.
    Ruitenbeek, ed., *Freud as We Knew Him* (Detroit, 1973), pp. 28–49

Reik, Theodor, *The Search Within: The Inner Experiences of a Psychoanalyst* (New York,
    1956)

—, *The Secret Self: Psychoanalytic Experiences in Life and Literature* (Westport, CT, 1956)

Ribot, T., *Diseases of Memory: An Essay in the Positive Psychology* (London, 1882)

Rifkin, Adrian, *Street Noises: Parisian Pleasure, 1900–1940* (Manchester, 1993)

Rilke, Rainer Maria, *Selected Poetry*, trans. S. Mitchell (London, 1982)

—, *The Notebooks of Malte Laurids Brigge*, trans. S. Mitchell (New York, 1983)

—, *Letters 1910–1926*, trans. J. B. Greene and M. D. H. Norton (New York, 1947)

Rosenberg, Samuel, *Why Freud Fainted* (New York, 1978)

Rudnytsky, Peter L., *Freud and Oedipus* (New York, 1987)

Ruitenbeck, H. M., ed., *Freud As We Knew Him* (Detroit, 1973)

Russo, S, 'Chronophobia: A Prison Neurosis', *Mental Hygiene*, 27 (1943), pp. 581–91

Rutherford, Jennifer, *The Gauche Intruder: Freud, Lacan and the White Australian Fantasy*
    (Melbourne, 2000)

Rycroft, Charles, 'Some Observations on a Case of Vertigo', *International Journal of
    Psycho-Analysis* (1953), pp. 241–7

Sachs, Hanns, 'Freud: Master and Friend', in H. M. Ruitenbeek, ed., *Freud as We Knew
    Him* (Detroit, 1973)

Safran, J. D., and L. S. Greenberg, 'Affect and the Unconscious: A Cognitive
    Perspective', in R. Stern, ed., *Theories of the Unconscious and Theories of the Self*
    (Hillsdale, NJ, 1987), pp. 191–212

Safranski, Rudiger, *Schopenhauer and the Wild Years of Philosophy*, trans. E. Osers
    (Cambridge, MA, 1990)

Salfellner, Harald, *Franz Kafka and Prague* (Prague, 1998)

Santner, Eric L., *My Own Private Germany: Daniel Paul Schreber's Secret History of
    Modernity* (Princeton, 1996)

Sass, Louis A., *Madness and Modernism: Insanity in the Light of Modern Art, Literature and
    Thought* (New York, 1992)

Savinio, Alberto, *Maupassant e "L'altro"* (Milan, 1995)

Schezen, Roberto, *Adolf Loos: Architecture 1903–1932* (New York, 1996)

Schneider, Angela, 'As If from Afar: Constants in the Work of Alberto Giacometti', in *Alberto Giacometti: Sculpture, Paintings, Drawings* (Munich, 1994), pp. 71–5

Schorske, Carl E., *Fin-de-Siècle Vienna: Politics and Culture* (London, 1980)

Segal, Charles, *Dionysiac Poetics and Euripides' Bacchae* (Princeton, 1997)

Seneca, *Three Tragedies*, trans. F. Ahl (Ithaca, NY, 1986)

Sennett, Richard, *The Conscience of the Eye* (London, 1990)

Shattuck, Roger, *The Banquet Years: The Origins of the Avant Garde in France, 1885 to World War I* (New York, 1968)

Sherman, M. H., ed., *Psychoanalysis and Old Vienna: Freud, Reik, Schnitzler, Kraus* (New York, 1978)

Simmel, Georg, *Georg Simmel: On Women, Sexuality, and Love*, trans. G. Oakes (New Haven, 1984)

—, *The Conflict in Modern Culture and Other Essays*, trans. and intro. K. P. Etzkorn (New York, 1968)

—, *Simmel on Culture: Selected Writings*, ed. D. Frisby and M. Featherstone (London, 1997)

Sitte, Camillo, *The Birth of Modern City Planning*, trans. and commentary G. R. Collins and C. Crasemann Collins (New York, 1986)

Sophocles, 'Oedipus at Colonus', in F. Storr, trans., *Sophocles*, 2 vols (London, 1946)

Spence, Jonathan D., *The Memory Palace of Matteo Ricci* (London, 1988)

Spielrein, S., 'L'Automobile – Symbole de la puissance mâle', *International Journal of Psycho-Analysis*, IV (1923), p. 128

Stanislavsky, Konstantin, *Stanislavsky on the Art of the Stage*, trans. D. Magarshack (London, 1988)

Stern, Raphael, ed., *Theories of the Unconscious and Theories of the Self* (Hillsdale, NJ, 1987)

Stewart, Kathleen, *A Space on the Side of the Road* (Princeton, 1996)

Sturt, Charles, *Narrative of an Expedition into Central Australia*, 2 vols (London, 1849)

Szasz, Thomas, *Karl Kraus and the Soul Doctors: A Pioneer Critic and His Criticism of Psychiatry and Psychoanalysis* (Baton Rouge, LA, 1976)

Taylor, Robert R., *The Word in Stone: The Role of Architecture in the National Socialist Ideology* (Berkeley, 1974)

Thompson, Bruce, *Schnitzler's Vienna: Image of a Society* (London, 1990)

Thompson, Flora, *Lark Rise to Candleford* (London, 1948)

Torjusen, Bente, *Words and Images of Edvard Munch* (London, 1986)

Tyrer, P., 'Towards Rational Therapy with Monoamine Oxidase Inhibitors', *British Journal of Psychiatry*, 128 (April 1976), pp. 354–60

Ulrich, R., *et al.*, 'Multiple Treatments for Agoraphobia through Habituation Training (Flooding) and Peripheral Limitation of Excitement', *Zeitschrift für Klinische Psychologie*, 4/3 (1975), pp. 209–33

Van de Ven, Cornelis, *Space in Architecture* (Assen, The Netherlands, 1980)

Varro, Marcus Terentius, *Varro on the Latin Language*, trans. R. G. Kent, 2 vols (Cambridge, MA, 1938)

Vattimo, Gianni, *The Adventure of Difference: Philosophy after Nietzsche and Heidegger*, trans. G. Blamires (London, 1993)

Vico, Giambattista, *La Scienza Nuova* (Milan, 1977)

Vidal-Naquet, P., *The Black Hunter: Forms of Thought and Forms of Society in the Greek World*, trans. A. Szegedy-Maszak (Baltimore, 1986)

Vidler, Anthony, 'Psychopathologies of Modern Space: Metropolitan Fear from Agoraphobia to Estrangement', in M. S. Roth, ed., *Rediscovering History, Culture, Politics, and the Psyche* (Stanford, 1994), pp. 11–29

Volkov, S. N., 'The Question of Agoraphobia Connected with Disorders of the Functions of the Vestibular Apparatus', *Nevropatologieia Psiekhiatrieia Ie Psiekhogiegieena*, 10 (1936), pp. 1750–55

Wallace, Alfred Russel, *My Life: A Record of Events and Opinions*, 2 vols (London, 1905)

Whyte, Iain B., *Bruno Taut and the Architecture of Activism* (Cambridge, 1982)

Wilden, Anthony, *Man and Woman, War and Peace* (London, 1987)

Wilson, Colin St John, 'The Natural Imagination', in *Architectural Reflections: Studies in the Philosophy and Practice of Architecture* (Oxford, 1992)

Worringer, Wilhelm, *Abstraction and Empathy: A Contribution to the Psychology of Style*, trans. M. Bullock (New York, 1953)

Zanuso, Billa, *The Young Freud* (Oxford, 1986)

Zucker, Peter, *Town and Square: From the Agora to the Village Green* (Cambridge, MA, 1970)

1 'Freed from Architecture: Reflecting on Art, the most modern man walked the streets. Suddenly he stopped abruptly: he had found what he had looked for in vain for such a long time.' A caricature from *Illustrirtes Wiener Extrablatt*, January 1911. Photo: Österreichische Nationalbibliothek, Vienna

2 'Heartrending Farewells of the father of a family about to cross the street in front of the Gare de L'Est', a 1911 cartoon by Capy as reproduced by Le Corbusier in *The City of Tomorrow*, 1926

3 Werner Heldt, *Aufmarsch der Nullen (Meeting)*, 1933–4, charcoal drawing. Photo: Berlinische Galerie, Landesmuseum für Moderne Kunst, Photographie und Architektur/Udo Hesse

4 Edvard Munch, *Evening on Karl Johan Street*, 1896, hand-coloured lithograph. Nelson Blitz Junior Collection, New York. Photo: Bente Torjusen, courtesy of Nelson Blitz Junior

5 J. Buhlmann's 'ideal restoration' of the Athenian agora (marketplace), reproduced in Camillo Sitte's *Der Städte-Bau nach Seinen Kunstlerischen Grundsätzen* of 1889.

6 A still from Paul Wegener and Carl Boese's 'street film', *Der Golem, wie er in die Welt kam* (1920). Source: Stiftung Deutsche Kinemathek – Filmmuseum Berlin

7 Chaim Soutine, *Village Square, Céret, c.* 1921, oil on canvas. The Henry and Rose Pearlman Foundation, Inc./Photo: Bruce M. White

8 Boccioni, Umberto, *La Città che sale*, 1910, oil on canvas. The Museum of Modern Art (Mrs. Simon Guggenheim Fund, 1951), New York. Photo: © The Museum of Modern Art, New York/Scala, Florence

9, 10, 11, 12, 13, 14 Charles Lapicque pen-and-ink drawings: *Double tristesse*, 1946 (top left); *La rencontre*, 1946 (top middle); *Joyeuse rencontre*, 1947 (top right); *Rencontre*, 1947 (bottom left); *La conviction*, 1946 (bottom middle); *L'accolade*, 1947 (bottom right). Musée nationale d'Art Moderne, Paris

15 Henri Cartier-Bresson, *Alberto Giacometti in rue d'Alésia, Paris*, 1961, photograph.
    Photo: © Henry Cartier-Bresson/Magnum Photos
16 Alberto Giacometti, *The City Square*, 1948, bronze. The Museum of Modern Art,
    New York/Photo: © The Museum of Modern Art, New York/Scala, Florence
17 Alberto Giacometti, *The Forest (Seven Figures, One Head)*, 1950, bronze. Wilhelm-
    Lehmbruck-Museum, Duisburg/Photo Credit: Max Baumann